Cape Town after Apartheid

Cape Town after Apartheid

Crime and Governance in the Divided City

Tony Roshan Samara

 University of Minnesota Press
Minneapolis
London

A version of chapter 2 was previously published as "Youth, Crime, and Urban Renewal in the Western Cape," *Journal of Southern African Studies* 31, no. 1 (March 2005): 209–27. Portions of chapters 3 and 4 were previously published as "Policing Development: Urban Renewal as Neoliberal Security Strategy," *Urban Studies* 47, no. 1 (January 2010): 197–214.

Cartography by Steve McClure, George Mason University

Published by the University of Minnesota Press
111 Third Avenue South, Suite 290
Minneapolis, MN 55401-2520
http://www.upress.umn.edu

QM LIBRARY
(MILE END)

Library of Congress Cataloging-in-Publication Data
Samara, Tony Roshan.
Cape Town after apartheid : crime and governance in the divided city /
Tony Roshan Samara.
   p.; cm.
   Includes bibliographical references and index.
   ISBN 978-0-8166-7000-0 (hc : alk. paper) — ISBN 978-0-8166-7001-7 (pb : alk. paper)
   1. Crime—South Africa—Cape Town. 2. Crime prevention—South Africa—Cape Town. 3. Violence—South Africa—Cape Town. 4. Gangs—South Africa—Cape Town. 5. Police—South Africa—Cape Town. I. Title.
   HV7150.5.Z8C427 2011
   364.96873'55—dc22

                                                                    2010032604

Printed in the United States of America on acid-free paper

The University of Minnesota is an equal-opportunity educator and employer.

17 16 15 14 13 12 11   10 9 8 7 6 5 4 3 2 1

Contents

Acknowledgments

The following work received support from many people over the years, and if not for some of them it likely never would have been completed. Avery Gordon, my mentor at the University of California at Santa Barbara, was instrumental in helping me to formulate the project in its early stages, and, although it has changed much since then, I still see her influence clearly in this final version. Indeed, what I have learned from Avery has become a part of my own intellectual and political vision, and I feel very fortunate to have studied with her.

Anyone who has done this type of work understands that it is impossible to do it well without help. Over the course of the fieldwork, help came in many forms. It may have been a small kindness or favor, or come from someone I met once by chance and then never again. Other times, it was long-term help that was essential to the project, or it was given by people with whom I eventually became close friends. I would especially like to thank all of the people I interviewed for the project or who took the time to sit with me and talk about their experiences or areas of expertise. I am particularly grateful in this regard to Valda Lucas and Renée Rossouw; they are part of a generally unappreciated and undervalued group of youth workers in Cape Town who are largely responsible for what little youth development is happening there.

Thanks to Shaheen Ariefdien, Nazli Abrahams, and Erna Curry, the indispensable ones, year after year. Each has been central to the intellectual and political development of this work and to helping me navigate the social and spatial terrain of the city. Their friendship is perhaps the most important thing that I take with me as I leave this project behind.

I also thank Oko Camngca, Marlon Burgess, Shannon Wentz, and Steve McClure for stepping in at key moments to help out: Oko for assisting with interviews, Marlon and Shannon for their work on the digital images, and Steve for expert mapmaking. My time in Cape Town could not have been what it was without my home in Woodstock on Roodebloem Road and my home away from home on Aandblom Street.

I am also indebted to the reviewers of the manuscript, John Hagedorn, Clifford Shearing, and especially Martin Murray. Their feedback was invaluable and led to substantial improvements in the final manuscript. My editor at Minnesota, Jason Weidemann, and his assistant, Danielle Kasprzak, have been great to work with and were instrumental in bringing out the best possible version of the book. I am grateful to them for their work.

Finally, no support has been stronger and more unwavering than that which my parents have provided over so many years. The determination and discipline it can take to complete a project of this scope are gifts they gave to me. This book is dedicated to them.

Abbreviations and Acronyms

ANC	African National Congress
Asgisa	Accelerated and Shared Growth Initiative for South Africa
CBD	Central Business District
CCTV	Closed circuit television system
CFRS	Cape Flats Renewal Strategy
CID	City Improvement District
Core	Community Outreach Forum
Cosatu	Congress of South African Trade Unions
CPF	Community Policing Forum
DA	Democratic Alliance
EXCO	Cape Town Municipal Executive Council
GEAR	Growth, Employment, and Redistribution
ICD	Independent Complaints Directorate
Idasa	Institute for Democracy in South Africa
IDP	Integrated Development Programme
ISS	Institute for Security Studies
MADAM	Multi-Agency Delivery Action Mechanism
MEC	Member of the Executive Committee
NCPS	National Crime Prevention Strategy
NGDS	National Growth and Development Strategy
NICRO	National Institute for Crime Prevention and the Reintegration of Offenders
NIS	National Intelligence Service
NNP	New National Party
Nodoc	National Operations Coordinating Mechanism
NP	National Party
NURP	National Urban Renewal Programme
PAGAD	People Against Gangsterism and Drugs
POCA	Prevention of Organized Crime Act
POPCRU	Police and Prison Civil Rights Union
RDP	Reconstruction and Development Programme
SACP	South African Communist Party

SANDF	South African National Defence Force
SAPS	South African Police Service
SAPU	South African Police Union
STEP	Street Terrorism and Enforcement Prevention Act
WCPDC	Western Cape Provincial Development Council

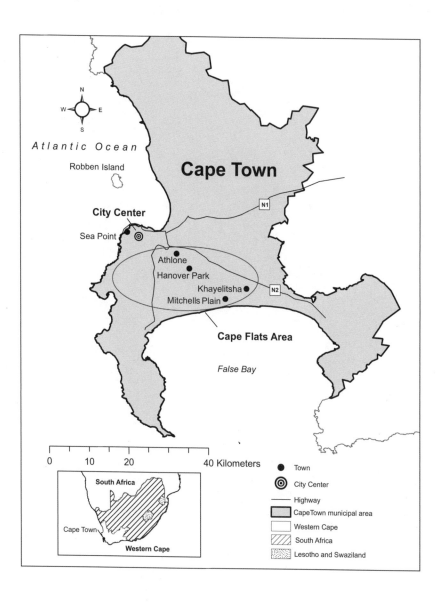

Urban Geopolitics, Neoliberalism, and the Governance of Security

In December 2006, newspapers in Cape Town reported that high school students in the Cape Flats communities of Hanover Park and Nyanga were caught in the middle of yet another brutal gang war linked to the drug trade. This particular outbreak of violence was so disruptive that high school matriculation rates plummeted, dropping to 33 percent at Hanover Park's Mount View High, down from 82 percent the year before. Principal Archie Benjamin told reporters from the *Cape Argus* that the dramatic decrease could be attributed to the ongoing gang wars. "Sometimes, learners had to stay away for about two weeks and, at times, those living in the war zones could not attend classes."[1] One student told the *Argus*, "It's been a tough year. There have been gunshots here and there, but we had no choice but to study." Just five months later, in May 2007, local media reported another "crime wave" linked to area schools that the Western Cape provincial government referred to as crime "hot spots."[2]

These latest outbreaks of violence on the Cape Flats, the vast working-class and poor townships that surround this internationally renowned city on the sea, generated a familiar set of responses. Amid calls for "zero tolerance" for drugs and school violence, government officials and school administrators dispatched hundreds of crime-fighting volunteers and police reservists to patrol the schools and make arrests when necessary. Provincial education officials pointed out that R4.19 million ($600,000) had already been spent on safety gates, burglar bars, barbed wire, mesh wire, alarm systems with armed response, and secure fencing, and that new laws would allow random searches and drug testing of students.[3] At the same time, officials promised more progressive social development initiatives, from conflict management and intervention training to provincial and national measures to specifically address gangsterism, drugs, and school safety.[4]

Not long after these incidents had drawn attention to crime and violence in township schools, reports of street people being harassed by police and, more often, by private security guards began to emerge from the affluent city center. Street children and homeless or destitute adults in the downtown have been routinely demonized by local press, downtown business interests, and city authorities for years as manifestations of urban blight and threats to urban revitalization, primarily because of the crimes they allegedly commit and the fear they induce in the more affluent classes with whom they share this contested space. Particularly disturbing were the deaths of three people living on the streets in July 2007 alone, one allegedly from exposure after police confiscated her blankets in the middle of winter.[5] Some of the street people in the city center and their advocates view the increase in harassment as linked to a growing intolerance for both adults and children living on the streets in the wake of a new "quality of life" bylaw approved by the city council in May 2007. This "nuisance" law includes, among other things, prohibitions on begging, washing clothes in public, and failing to move along when ordered to do so by a security officer, prohibitions which many feel were specifically crafted to criminalize behaviors associated with the urban poor. Although complaints of harassment are nothing new, the allegations of an increase and the passage of the bylaw seemed to be linked to a push for continued revitalization of the Central Business District, particularly as Cape Town prepared for the global media spotlight during the 2010 World Cup.

These two examples, as different as they are, begin to sketch the outlines of contemporary urban governance in Cape Town. First, they draw our attention to a perceived relationship between security and socioeconomic development and the role of this perception in shaping governance. Second, they provide a glimpse of the meaning of urban renewal in the imaginations of urban elites and the myriad ways in which young people—young men in particular—be they students, workers, gangsters, or street children, appear in this vision. Third, they illustrate how those who govern the city are responding to crime and the fear of crime. Finally, they highlight a central concern of the following chapters, that Cape Town, like many cities, is a city divided, both socially and spatially. Communities on the Cape Flats are home to the vast majority of Cape Town residents, and these communities stand in stark contrast to the affluent and predominantly white downtown and surrounding suburbs. Although South Africa's urban areas are often, and in many ways unfairly, linked to crime, the reality is that crime and its victims are highly localized. In Cape Town, the majority of the city's crime happens on the Cape Flats, far from the tourists and wealthier residents clustered in and around the city's core. Making sense of the similarities binding together these disparate urban spaces and the differences that separate them makes up the bulk of the following analysis as these themes are explored in greater detail.

The scope of the book, however, is not limited to an explication of the local dimensions of governance in Cape Town. Important as they may be for understanding the ongoing struggles in the city to escape the bonds of apartheid, the skirmishes of the Cape Flats' gang violence and the plight of Cape Town's homeless have a significance that extends far beyond the city itself. As we will see, the city today is governed through a complex network in which local and global forces clash and combine to reproduce the fractured urban spaces inherited from apartheid but which are also found in other cities with very different histories. Indeed, these stories underscore the extent to which Cape Town's two cities are linked to a wider urban world: one is a well-connected global brand that attracts tourists and investments from all corners of the globe, the other an underdeveloped urban periphery that has more in common with expanding ghettos across the global South than with the glittering Euro-themed downtown just kilometers away.

This book examines the relationship between these two distinct, yet deeply intertwined areas in a way that is attentive to the uniqueness of this city, while also drawing out those dynamics that characterize a significant trend in contemporary global urbanism, particularly for prominent cities of the global South, by focusing on the processes through which the divisions of the apartheid era are reproduced and managed under conditions of liberal democracy, and the role played by contemporary forces of neoliberalism in giving both form and substance to a new iteration of apartness. A close look at Cape Town reveals how this iteration is generated through a transnational network of neoliberal urban governance in which the local and extra-local combine to produce an approach to governance that is both grounded in the specificity of this city and, at the same time, is an expression of an increasingly generalized form observable in many cities. City authorities work closely with business elites and private security companies to implement urban security management strategies that would be familiar to residents of many aspiring world class cities. These strategies are employed for the purpose of "reclaiming" and "revitalizing" core urban spaces to anchor citywide development, including the under-developed townships, but in the process they instead contribute to the reproduction of inequalities that marked the apartheid city. While there are certainly similar efforts in other parts of the city, also driven to varying degrees by a similar market logic, the division between the central city and the townships is the fundamental sociospatial division of the city, and the one that fundamentally defines its political character. It is from here that a critical appraisal of the city's urban governance regime must proceed.

The city's approach to urban security is not only "rational" within the context of market-driven or neoliberal economic development, but in fact is essential to this approach. Neoliberal governance and its definition of development and related security requirements shape urban renewal in both the sprawling townships and the concentrated downtown–suburban core, though in quite distinct ways that link each of them to rich and poor areas, respectively, in other cities. Across both areas policing plays a central role. In the affluent downtown, the police, both public and private, are deployed as an integral part of a development process in which security, defined as the need to protect economically and socially valuable urban spaces, is a crucial first step. In the townships, on the other hand, security is defined as the policing of underdevelopment, sometimes explicitly but more often implicitly, in relation to the threat poor areas pose to the city center. Describing these two divergent forms of policing and their implications, explaining how and why they persist, and examining their relationship to each other is the central concern of the book.

The approach to crime and urban renewal in Cape Town is one example of a global phenomenon in which cities become key sites of economic growth, conflict, and political governance. Although Cape Town is unique in many respects, it is at the same time faced with, and forced to respond to, a set of challenges generated by inequality and conflict at the local scale that bedevil many cities, and a narrowing range of options as a consequence of changes at the national and global scales. Here, as elsewhere, development and urban renewal have been subsumed under and articulated through neoliberalism, which, although appearing in many guises, means for all cities under its sway renewed and reinvigorated tensions between the demands of "free markets" and those of populations.[6] Though they vary in intensity by time and place, these tensions have put the issue of urban security squarely on the agenda of urban elites, those private and public actors who collectively constitute the networks through which decisive formal and informal power is mobilized for the project of shaping of urban spaces. Terrorism, political unrest, and crime loom large in the imaginations of these elites as a central governance challenge for local, market-driven accumulation regimes with global reach, and security has, perhaps predictably, infused urban revitalization and renewal plans across the global urban landscape.

Within this context, the commitment by the postapartheid state to a relatively progressive approach to crime and socioeconomic development is steadily slipping away, even as crime assumes a central place within development discourse. Although the shift cannot be explained by reference to neoliberalism alone, crucial to the change is a powerful narrative of urban (and urban-driven) prosperity that frames threats to economically dynamic downtown or central city spaces as the primary obstacle to development more broadly. The logic underpinning this narrative is a by now familiar market logic in which development is understood primarily in terms of gross domestic product, foreign investment, tourism, dynamic financial services and property industries, and other income-generating activity by the private sector, often with the support of the state, and city leaders find themselves having to be more attentive than ever to their city's international image. Neoliberal urban governance is the result of bundling these related security and development agendas into a coherent governance ideology and related set of practices in which so-called free markets provide guiding principles and reference points for ordering urban life.

The situation in Cape Town mirrors that in other prominent cities in South Africa and beyond. In these cities, distinct interests have converged to produce a somewhat new urban reality in which pursuit of "world city" status establishes the basic constraints and possibilities for urban development.[7] Cities in many countries have been cut loose from receding social welfare states—where one existed at all—and have been left to make their own way, so to speak, in the global economy as part of a neoliberal growth strategy pioneered in North America in the 1970s, marked by a sharpening of intercity competition for resources. The response by many urban elites has been to adopt, by choice or necessity, some version of urban entrepreneurialism and to view cities themselves as income-generating entities.[8] A corollary to this political-economic shift in the relationship between society and the city is a renewed concern with safety and security that centers on crime, disorder, and "quality of life," defined in relation to a revitalized urban economy and associated urban cultures. First in the United States and Europe, but now in many cities with aspirations of New York–style revitalization, the ensuing social struggles can be described as the outgrowth of a renewed urban offensive against "decay" driven in part by the scramble to reclaim and secure "neglected" or "besieged" city spaces.[9]

These dynamics played out in Cape Town and South Africa over the decade following the negotiated end of National Party rule. In 1996, at the national level, the African National Congress (ANC) abandoned the social welfare–oriented Reconstruction and Development Programme (RDP) in favor of the neoliberal Growth, Employment and Redistribution (GEAR) plan. Simultaneously, the government declared a war on crime, citing not only the toll that crime takes on victims and communities, but also the obstacle it poses to the strategy of socioeconomic development through investment-led economic growth. The result is that approaches to crime reduction have come to rely disproportionately on aggressive law enforcement and the alleged deterrent and incapacitating role of an efficient criminal justice system, while development, at least in the townships, awaits the stable and secure environment that reduced crime is said to provide. Criminal justice reform of the apartheid-era system, although it is addressing many of the more extreme abuses of the pre-1994 period, is being recoded, referring more and more to a traditional approach of building up the capacity of the criminal justice system rather than fundamentally transforming both it *and* the state's overall approach to crime and socioeconomic development.

Governance in the city reflects the approach to security and development at the national level, and the basic tenets of this approach are embraced by key elements of the private sector, the major political parties, and the public. Urban entrepreneurialism in Cape Town, as we will see, revolves in crucial ways around the idea that the fight against crime is central to a development strategy that hinges on the city's ability to draw investment from around the world. The war on crime, in this sense, is a principle response by the state and by urban elites to the challenge of governance in the city. Its emergence, however, cannot be explained simply by reference to the dictates of neoliberalism or to the still considerable momentum of the recent past. Rather, as we will see, it is best understood as the outcome of a particular configuration of the relationship between security and development that, although it has deep historical roots in the apartheid and colonial eras, has gained new life in the uncertain and unstable postapartheid present. What we are in fact witnessing in urban South Africa is a relatively seamless, though far from uncontested, transition in governance from apartheid to neoliberalism.

The empirical focus here is on urban renewal, the emergence of a war on crime, and the criminalization of black youth in postapartheid Cape Town.[10] The significance of these related phenomena for understanding the larger project of urban governance in the city is explored from the perspective of socioeconomic development for youth, which in principle unifies the ANC, civil society, and even opposition parties. The youth demographic is a crucial one in South Africa, as in much of the global South, because of its size and because of the repeated, if highly unfair, associations made between poor youth and various forms of insecurity. Youth in South Africa, as a category, is an especially powerful symbol because of the role young people played in the antiapartheid struggle, and the sacrifices this required of them. Although the passage of time, the potency of counternarratives linking youth and criminality, and the coming of age of a postapartheid generation are eroding this power, youth development remains central to political discourse, albeit in ways that grow increasingly complex and even contradictory. Crime has come to dominate talk about order, prosperity, and security over the past decade, and youth as criminals and gangsters are steadily reoccupying the privileged place they held during the apartheid years, when they were conceived of as communists and terrorists. They are seen once again as threats rather than as victims and survivors of grinding, systemic poverty. In the context of urban governance, black youth have reemerged at the intersection of security and development in the contested terrain of the city.

Insecurity in the Global South: Toward an Urban Geopolitics

Although not a central preoccupation of this book, geopolitical shifts in governance and security at the global scale form an important backdrop to developments at the national and local scales, and these require a brief discussion if we are to fully understand why urban governance has taken the form it has in Cape Town.[11] What we are witnessing is the merging of specific security and development agendas under a pervasive logic of neoliberalism that is global in scope and varied in its many manifestations. Urban renewal in Cape Town is one case of this global phenomenon, whereby certain challenges linked to failed or underdeveloped states are coded, and responded to, primarily as threats to local, national, or transnational processes of wealth accumulation and economic growth and to the lifestyles associated with them; furthermore, these threats are increasingly included in discussions of threats to national and international security by policymakers, security specialists, and other dominant voices in the global public sphere. Examples range from piracy off the coast of Somalia to gang violence in urban slums, but what binds these issues together is the tendency to reduce complex and multidimensional socioeconomic challenges of global significance to very conventional security challenges.[12] Development reemerges in this formulation rather weakly, as an end product, or a relatively passive appendage of the robust process of making spaces (local, national, transnational) secure, and this dynamic has become central to post–Cold War geopolitics.

Dominant security discourse and practice during the Cold War were generally delinked from the developmental concerns of people and focused more on the geopolitical relationships between states. Early in the post–Cold War period there was a widespread optimism that a new relationship between security and development could be forged and, further, a hope that a radical reconceptualization of the concept of security itself was possible. The militarist and state-centric understanding of security that prevailed during the confrontation between the two superpowers neglected many of the most immediate and deep-seated sources of insecurity for the majority of the world's population. Most notable for its absence from this understanding was any real attention to the socioeconomic causes of insecurity, of poverty and inequality themselves as sources of insecurity, and the reality that for millions of people, their own governments were the greatest perpetrators of violence and human rights abuses. It was only in the 1990s that these and other issues not traditionally viewed as security issues were successfully pushed onto the international security agenda, primarily by intellectuals and activists from the Third World, feminists, and development-oriented nongovernmental organizations (NGOs) associated with the human security movement.[13] In 1994 the United Nations Human Development Report provided the first detailed and systemic approach to human security, and although change was occurring in more traditional venues as well, it was here that the challenge to the so-called realist school of geopolitics emerged onto the world stage.[14]

In addition to challenging prevailing conceptions of security at the highest levels of international politics, the UN report pushed the critique further by contradicting the received wisdom from realist circles that security is both separate from and must precede development, while the Zapatistas and the antiglobalization movements propelled the debate forward from below. Since September 2001, however, the United States has led the charge to reassert a more traditional approach to security; development remains on the global agenda to an extent that was absent during the Cold War but tightly bound to—and to some extent defined by—this older approach. In the year following the 9/11 attacks and preceding the World Summit on Sustainable Development held in Johannesburg in August 2002, political and economic elites from British prime minister Tony Blair to UN Secretary General Kofi Annan and World Bank head James Wolfensohn went so far as to draw attention to the relationships among poverty, terrorism, and global security, arguing that underdevelopment was in fact a security issue.[15] In March of that year, reformed neoliberal crusader Jeffery Sachs observed: "The extreme poverty of the bottom billion is shocking, morally intolerable and dangerous—a breeding ground of disease, terrorism and violence."[16]

Growing unease about the instability that underdevelopment generates suggests that the narrower definition of security has not passed quietly into history along with the Cold War. Rather, the global development agenda of the now post–Washington Consensus continues to be constrained by and articulated through the national security interests of powerful states and transnational interests of global capital. The "pragmatic" agenda of global governance that has resulted is what Canadian political scientist Robert Cox calls global poor relief and riot control, in which the production of security means attempts "to prevent the way in which societies have been evolving through globalisation from destabilising the central structures of globalisation."[17]

The merging of security and development agendas under conditions of globalization leads to a knitting together of international bodies—from the UN to aid organizations, military establishments, NGOs, private security companies, and multinational corporations—into transnational networks of global governance administered primarily from the global North.[18] According to Peter Wilkin, these governance networks are not geared toward the amelioration of social crisis, but rather are structures assembled for "containment and quarantine of the effects of global poverty, . . . for protecting states from the world's most impoverished people."[19] Despite the celebration with which many of today's proponents of globalization greeted the end of the Cold War, a decidedly pessimistic core exists at the center of new elite approaches to security and development. This pessimism is rooted in the fact that the problems of conflict, unrest, and instability cannot be solved within the current geopolitical framework of fundamental disparity and the structures and processes that sustain it.[20] Governance, at all levels, is evolving according to this reality, and nowhere is this more apparent, and perhaps more important, than in the city.

Fear in the City: The Centrality of Security to Neoliberal Urban Governance

The focus of this book is on how these governance dynamics operate at the urban scale. It is concerned with the relationship between security and development that gives neoliberal governance in many places its form, and especially with identifying and elaborating the meaning and role of security in the development process and its relationship to the reproduction of sociospatial inequalities in Cape Town. Scholars across a range of disciplines have documented the rise and dominance of an approach to governance, across a variety of scales, informed by key principles of contemporary neoliberalism, including, most notably, the preeminence of the "free market" in allocating goods and services, the retreat or reconfiguration of the state to accommodate the requirements of transnational market forces, and an emphasis on policies promoting and protecting free trade, foreign direct investment, and private property rights.[21] The following section discusses why the urban scale is of particular importance for understanding this project, the politics of urban security governance that are integral to defining it, and the specific role that policing, crime, and the criminal play in its execution; doing so will provide the necessary theoretical and conceptual framework for the subsequent discussion of Cape Town.

Neoliberal principles of economic reform originally came to prominence through their application at the national level in the global South. Although change was already afoot in the nations and cities of the global North as well, it was the structural adjustment programs of the World Bank and the International Monetary Fund in the 1980s and 1990s, and the intimately related prescriptions of the Washington Consensus, that first drew attention and notoriety to the ascent of neoliberalism as a global governance force.[22] The requirements for installing this new governance regime were substantial, and their implementation often necessitated significant restructuring of the state and the strict management of often intense political resistance to all or part of the project. Neoliberal restructuring thus was immediately politicized within the geopolitical contexts of the late Cold War and, eventually, post–Cold War globalization. Indeed, neoliberal economic restructuring was often linked quite explicitly by its advocates within the multilateral institutions, sympathetic think tanks, and government to political liberalization and democratization, even as some critics viewed it as an attempt at postcolonial resubordination of the South through an attack on nationalist and social welfare–oriented states.[23] Although free markets and political freedom in this ideological formulation are both essential, together driving societies forward toward the end of history, the subordination of politics to "objective" market principles—or perhaps more accurately the rise of market-driven geopolitics—is what truly defines what some call neoliberal democracy as a governance project.[24]

The legitimacy of this national-level reform project in the global South collapsed in the first decade of the new century under pressure from social movements, the leaders of many so-called emerging economies, and the growing evidence of its failure.[25] Neoliberalism, however, was already discovering or creating new circuits of power along which to travel—or expanding existing ones—and scales at which to operate; today it finds its most dynamic expression in the city. Much has been written about cities in the era of globalization, with areas of inquiry ranging from topics as varied as the command and control functions of wealthy and powerful global cities to the challenges facing aspiring "world cities" and the still unmapped sociopolitical terrain of the massive and ungovernable urban slums.[26] Although this literature is vast, it is held together by a sense that the urban scale has emerged as a central one for the study of a wide range of social phenomena that are global in scope. Neoliberalism, of course, is far from the only analytical frame through which to make sense of the city and its place in the world, but it has proven itself to be a powerful and durable one for both opponents and proponents. This is due in large part to the central role that cities play in the networks of global neoliberalism, but also because neoliberalism has had and continues to have such a profound impact on so many cities, large and small, and the communities within and across them.

There are five themes in the research on urban neoliberalism that are of particular relevance here and that provide reference points for the discussion of neoliberal governance and security in Cape Town. First, neoliberalism has no single or essential form or expression, but is shaped by the many localities and contingencies it encounters as it moves through spaces and across scales.[27] There are likely as many articulations of neoliberal urban governance as there are cities in which we find it, with many still to come. Second, as the preceding suggests, neoliberalism operates at different scales and across various spaces, often simultaneously.[28] The focus on urban neoliberalism here is in recognition of the urban scale as a particularly important one in this historical period, but this choice represents a temporary abstraction intended to highlight the urban features of neoliberalism, not to represent the city as an absolutely discrete scale or space relative to others in which neoliberalism operates in isolation. Third, neoliberalism is a process, not a state, with creative, adaptive abilities.[29] To the extent that we can capture it at all, we are always looking at dynamic phenomena constantly in flux. Assessments of how neoliberal governance operates will therefore need to be sensitive to how it adapts to obstacles and opportunities and how it changes over time. Fourth, the state remains vitally important to neoliberal projects, not only in a support role, but also as a primary conduit for disseminating neoliberal ideology, formulating and implementing policy, and, importantly, managing security.[30] Rather than fading into the background, the state, or components of the state, can become an essential node within transnational networks of governance that traverse and even remake social, political, legal, and territorial boundaries.[31] Finally, neoliberalism in cities has shown itself to be a powerful force in shaping the urban terrain.[32] As a form of governance it produces, fractures, and destroys cityscapes, either combining with or eliminating competing or parallel governance regimes; it would be difficult to ignore its role in the making of the contemporary city. Drawing from these themes, my intention is to track neoliberalism as it exists and operates within the urban space that is Cape Town, but also, in the process, to elicit the coherence of the concept and identify its relevance beyond specific times and places as a political project and, more pointedly, an exercise of power.

As an exercise of power, neoliberal governance is perhaps understood less than it should be in the growing urban concentrations of the global South, where inequality and governance challenges are greatest. Mike Davis has remarked that many of these cities have become dumping grounds for "surplus populations" left to fend for themselves in the aftermath of structural adjustment and excluded from work in formal urban economies.[33] Urban governance, whatever forms it may take in the future, will therefore have to address the relative permanency of today's slums and the "surplus people" who populate them, and the reality of an urban future dominated by the slum is already a cause of much concern within the institutions of global governance. Security vis-à-vis Third World slums in particular has recently emerged as a central and constitutive trope in narratives of urban geopolitics, particularly, as we saw earlier, after 2001. At the 2004 meeting of the World Urban Forum in Barcelona, for example, participants drew the link between "extremism" and urban slums, warning that the former could flourish if the growth of severe urban poverty is not checked. To be fair, UN Habitat, which convened the forum, took free-trade advocates to task, drawing attention to the failure of their policies to address the poverty from which this extremism emerges and identifying underdevelopment, not the poor themselves, as the real threat.[34] However, the discourse of the ungovernable and dangerous slum has already found its way into the plans of the states and other institutions responsible for actually framing and responding to the geopolitical security threats of the future, representing a troubling convergence of security and development narratives.[35]

Urban Governance, the Police, and Civilization

The governance of security has become central to urban politics. The relationship between neoliberalism and security in the Third World city, however, particularly the aspects of neoliberal governance that are directly concerned with the production of security, is not well documented, whereas there is a wealth of research on the neoliberal restructuring and regulation of the urban economy and the production of poverty and inequality. Studying neoliberalism from the point of view of security governance reveals that it has two thickly connected disciplinary rationales, one concerning adherence to the principles of the market economy, the other a logic of security for protecting this economy and the social organization that sustains it.[36] Security is certainly a concern in all cities, but the security challenge is qualitatively different in many cities of the global South than it is in the cities of the North. This concern is further heightened in cities such as Cape Town, which aspire to a certain global prominence and image, yet struggle with extreme inequality, a majority poor population, and high crime. Here security is more than simply one aspect of neoliberal restructuring among many—it is fundamental to, and shapes, the entire process. Security in this context constitutes a central task and orientation of governance across these cities, although it is pursued differently in different city spaces and among different populations, and security consciousness is apparent throughout their urban governance networks.

Securing the city can be divided into two general governance processes, corresponding roughly to the basic sociospatial divisions of many cities: first, the securing of affluent, generally core or central city spaces, the populations and activities for which they are intended, and the political economies concentrated within them; and second, securing the vast slums or townships, often on the urban periphery, that are home to the majority of the urban population. As we will see, the governance of these two areas is part of a coherent and rational governing ideology expressed through the language of development or, more specifically, urban renewal, but there are stark differences between them in the actual meaning and practice of security. The differences are rarely, if ever, mutually exclusive, and these distinct urban spaces are connected by much more than simply an overarching ideology of governance; there may be a range of fortifications of the borders between the two, but these remain porous nonetheless. As a consequence, approaches to the governance of security characteristic of the core can be found in the periphery, just as certain places and populations within the core are subject to types of governance more commonly found in the periphery. Some aspects of governance also traverse these borders; for example, the securing of transport lines that bring workers from the periphery into the core and, importantly, back out again is vital to the operations of the neoliberal city. Finally, there are many variations in how this basic division manifests; in some cities it may conform to a relatively straightforward spatial division, in others the particular form it takes may be more complex or blurred. However, though not universal by any means, this division is fundamental to the ordering of many prominent cities, certainly to Cape Town, and therefore guides the analysis here.

The first process is perhaps the more well-known aspect of neoliberal security governance, given the focus of much of the research on cities of the global North. Urban inequalities and uneven development drew increased attention as many urban economies began to revive in the late 1970s, giving rise to a new politics of security expressed as the need to protect not only urban revitalization as an economic process but also the cultural revival of cities and the newly arrived populations driving it. Researchers have pointed to urban neoliberalism in particular as linked to a "civilizing mission" aimed at reclaiming parts of the city and restoring the "natural order" by regulating certain people and communities, New York City being the most famous case and a source of inspiration to neoliberal urban boosters around the world.[37] Security governance in the cores of these cities developed as projects for supporting neoliberal restructuring and produced new state/market articulations that significantly changed the nature of governance.[38] Studies have pointed to a local state retreating, advancing, or being otherwise reconfigured, as private actors move to the center of security governance, resulting in a neoliberalization of the local state and the emergence of private governance structures that act like states.[39] As state and market institutions, actors, organizations, and processes become integrated, the result is security networks or assemblages of varying scope, missions, and degrees of permanence that facilitate the decentralization of governance.[40] While government and business interests are generally the driving force of these efforts, they often also include NGOs and nonprofit organizations, citizens groups, and the media. Whatever the specific configuration, taken together, these hybrid structures constitute the disciplinary arm of neoliberal democracy in the urban core. Through these structures, rights guaranteed through constitutional democracy are in effect nullified in practice, as the urban poor become disenfranchised transients in quasi-privatized urban spaces, always in danger of being cast out.

The second process concerns the much larger project in cities of the global South: securing the urban periphery. Approaches to governance here are also contoured by the principles and demands of neoliberalism, but the governance challenges are qualitatively and quantitatively different due to the size of peripheral territories and populations. The governance of slums, townships, and other concentrations of the poor and marginalized across the urban South may differ in many respects, but there is substantial continuity that is captured in the rationalizing discourses of managing the threats they are thought to pose to privileged spaces and decreasing crime as a precursor to genuine development. Private sector actors, NGOs, and other groups are involved in governance here as well, but the state's role tends to be much more pronounced than in the urban core. In Cape Town, for example, the developmental state does not retreat as much as it is securitized, ostensibly as part of the urban renewal process. Despite the progressive developmental rhetoric in which it is couched, the governance of security in the periphery is reduced largely to a collection of repressive practices deployed by a punitive and in some ways very disorganized state that impacts wide swaths of the population without significantly improving living conditions or paving the way for development. Thus, while both areas are integrated into an overarching governance network, the configurations and expressions of that network vary according to the distinct sociospatial characteristics of core and periphery.

The governance of security can, of course, encompass a wide range of phenomena, but in this book the focus is on crime and policing, the binary frequently invoked by political, academic, private sector, and media figures to frame the challenge and solution to socioeconomic development in many cities. In the case of South Africa, it has become virtually common sense for many commentators inside and outside the country that without the prior establishment of security in the form of crime reduction, economic growth and development cannot happen.[41] Crime is both a real problem and a powerful symbol of danger that can sabotage the ability of aspiring world cities of the global South to ascend the global hierarchy of cities; but in the neoliberal city, the threat of crime is invoked as part of a larger narrative, which not only rationalizes the governance of security as described, but also contributes to the reproduction of the sociospatial inequalities that define the city. It would be virtually impossible to understand neoliberal urban governance in Cape Town without understanding how this deployment of crime operates within the city.

The set of responses to the crime challenge by powerful national, regional, and urban actors across the world has taken a number of clearly identifiable forms, not bound by geography, that can reasonably be called a transnational and globalizing approach to punitive urban governance, and there is a substantial literature documenting and analyzing this approach.[42] Central to the practices that collectively constitute the governance of security is policing. While the production of security involves a transnational network comprising many actors, much of the day-to-day work required to reproduce neoliberal urban spaces is carried out by public and private police, and understanding the nature and consequences of this work is crucial to understanding the making of modern urban spaces.[43] The police are often the most public face of the official authority in many high-crime cities and communities, and it is they who are tasked with clearing the way, so to speak, for neoliberal development by establishing a particular type of security. Typically, policing as a development issue has been understood in the context of political development at the national level and the reform of authoritarian, corrupt, and otherwise inadequate criminal justice institutions in transitioning societies. The debates here revolve around the question of the role that policing can play in helping or hindering democratic transition.[44] However, much of the recent work on gentrification, urban renewal and revitalization, and urban security has rescaled these debates, examining the role of policing in what we might call transitioning cities.[45]

As central agents of neoliberal development and security governance, organized around the management and suppression of insecurity, police are better understood in the context of their role in policing underdevelopment than in facilitating the transition to democracy. Across cities of the global South, their task in terms of governance is often to maintain an acceptable level of order in certain spaces while containing the volatility of others. Two trends in policing in particular are important for understanding how police attempt to achieve these related tasks: (1) a shift to the policing of space and (2) the rise of nonstate policing agents and structures.[46] The first has become more prominent as city leaders adjust to the reality of an urban future marked by sociospatial fragmentation and differentiated, uneven development. At the heart of this adjustment is the development of location-specific governance strategies that correspond to the sociospatial contours of the city, described earlier in the discussion of governance processes. These strategies, through their implementation, constitute the actual work of spatial production; in other words, through the differentiated policing of space, policing practice contributes to the production or reproduction of those spaces.

The second trend is a prime example of hybrid governance and the changing relationships between the state and private sector. The privatization of security, however, must be understood as significant for sociological reasons that lie beyond the rather limited scope of market rationality and cost-effectiveness, particularly when we are interested in governance under conditions of severe urban inequality.[47] The steady drift of governance toward private and public/private assemblages should be read as a dispersion of not only policing functions but also of police accountability, while at the same time security increasingly becomes a commodity rather than a public good or right, acquired (or not acquired) according to the same logic with which the market distributes all its products.[48] The result is improved security for those able to participate in the formal security market, as well as a more prominent role for actors and structures of private governance linked to property interests and further removed from even nominal democratic control. From this emerge exclusionary urban spaces that may be public in form but are policed by private security under the authority of private actors, and a form of quasi-privatized citizenship mediated by market access and the ability to participate in the culture and economy of commodity consumption.[49]

The Neoliberalization of Racial Governance

Tensions in South Africa surrounding crime, policing, and economic growth spiked once again in September 2009, when South African President Jacob Zuma voiced support for a controversial "shoot to kill" policy for police facing down the nation's hardened criminals. Meeting with police and national security officials, he explicitly referred to the threat crime posed to the 2010 World Cup and to the confidence of investors wanting to do business in the country to underscore the importance of the issue.[50] The controversy intensified when, just over a week later, a three-year-old boy, Atlegang Phalane, was shot and killed by police chasing a murder suspect in Midrand, near Johannesburg. Speaking in the wake of the killing, Deputy Police Minister Fikile Mbalula stood by the government's tough stance, stating that when it came to "hard-nut-to-crack, incorrigible criminals," police must just "shoot the bastards." Commenting on the tragic and inevitable consequences of such a policy, he added, "Where you are caught in combat with criminals, innocent people are going to die—not deliberately but in the exchange of fire. They are going to be caught on the wrong side, not deliberately, but unavoidably."[51]

The death of Atlegang Phalane shows just how combustible the combination of crime, violence, inequality, and neoliberalism can be in South Africa, and the devastating consequences of iron-fisted approaches to crime. It reveals the desperation that violent crime provokes and the lengths to which the state and significant portions of the public are willing to go to combat it. The controversy also introduces us to a central character in the political drama of the city: the criminal. This complex character and the fear he generates (for it is the real and imagined violent crimes of males that fuel this fear) are absolutely crucial to the project of neoliberal urban governance in Cape Town. It is the criminal—unpredictable, irrational, and violent—who personifies the dangers lurking in the territories beyond the edges of downtown and gives form to some of the deep-seated racial anxieties that still shape the city.[52] This association of danger with crime and the urban poor is, of course, not new, and South African history contains many episodes in which the migration of rural black Africans to urban areas was met with white fear and a range of social control mechanisms, ranging from the subtle to the brutal.[53]

The historical dimension is important because it would be a mistake to reduce the power of racially coded anxieties to the interests or needs of neoliberalism. Rather, what we see today is the fusing of a neoliberalism that is both local and transnational with a social infrastructure that has been maintained over the years explicitly through the governance of race. Racial governance, governance in which the production or reproduction of racial inequalities is the effect, has been an organizing force of South African history since the seventeenth century and of its urban history since the late nineteenth century. During the course of this history, racial governance has taken a variety of forms and been implemented through many different processes and practices, but the control of "dangerous" young men has been an unmistakable and recurring theme.[54] Thus, the approach here is to take the governance of security in Cape Town today as one important contemporary iteration of this theme, not a wholly new phenomenon. As a contemporary expression, it is important in its own right, but much of the following analysis is equally concerned with how racial governance has been translated from white rule and apartheid to multiracial democracy and neoliberalism.

The violence, uncertainty, and turmoil of the transition acted as a bridge across which security-driven governance traveled into the democratic era. It did not arrive into the post-1994 period unchanged, however; instead, as overt political violence declined, crime and the criminal emerged as powerful symbols of the reigning disorder, and these were quickly woven into both dominant and popular narratives at the local and national levels to frame the problems facing the new South Africa, and the solutions. Rationalizing a return to security consciousness and, in a sense, security culture required what is perhaps the most significant achievement of postapartheid racial governance: the reproduction of "common sensibilities" regarding the subjects in need of control, which soon focused the attention of the new governance regime on developing strategies to do so. Although in form the subject produced through these governing sensibilities differed from the heroic "lion" of the antiapartheid movement, in content he remained young, black, and living on the periphery, both literally and figuratively. In this way South Africa entered into the modern, civilized world of the liberal democracies in much the way Brazil had almost a decade earlier, caught in the pincers of criminal and police violence; Atlegang Phalane is only the most recent casualty of the resulting war.[55]

The criminal has become a ubiquitous presence across the urban worlds of the North and South, a figure simultaneously marginal and central in the drama of the city.[56] Still, Cape Town is different from other cities, including other South African cities, even as in broad outlines its story of crime, violence, and repression is a familiar one. Owing to its status as the historic home of the coloured, or so-called "mixed-race," population and the specific form of structural marginalization of coloured communities throughout centuries of white rule, the criminal here has been constructed in the image of the working-class coloured male, captured in the concept of the *skollie,* or gangster, thug in Afrikaans.[57] "Amoral, weak, criminal and untrustworthy"[58]—the *skollie* embodies the criminal through historical categories of race, gender, class, and age, in ways that mark most if not all young coloured men in Cape Town to some extent. The focus here is on the two specific contemporary expressions of the *skollie* that ground the governance of security in everyday lives and everyday spaces: the street child in the city's core and the gangster in the periphery. Both categories are underpinned by a history of racial formation in which the criminal shaped a range of governmental interventions into and against working-class coloured communities.

Although I make no distinction between coloured and black African street children here, the discussion of township gangs is specifically a discussion of coloured gangs. Contrary to popular perception, these are by no means the only gangs that operate in Cape Town. Local black African gangs also exist, though the general perception is that they are less entrenched than the coloured gangs and their influence tends to be more cyclical and more confined to the townships in which they operate.[60] There are also increasing numbers of foreign syndicates operating in Cape Town, from other regions on the continent and as far away as Russia, East Asia, and Latin America.[61] However, coloured gangs, because of their intimate relationship with the history and development of Cape Town, their relative size, and their central position in public debates and personal nightmares around crime and urban renewal in the city, are the focus of this study. Through their participation in the area's

economy, their pervasiveness in poor communities, and their mobilization of many young people, the gangs of the Cape Flats coloured communities figure prominently in existing urban renewal efforts and have
become a convenient and popular scapegoat on which to pin both the
crime crisis and the failure of meaningful socioeconomic development.
Coloured gangs also receive much greater attention from the media and
public than other gangs and crime syndicates, and the young *skollie* as
a menace to society is an important image in the war on crime on the
peninsula. Finally, unlike any other city in the country, the coloured
population is a majority here and will likely remain a plurality even if
this should change; the future of this city, one way or another, lies in the
outcome of the conflicts currently brewing across the Cape Flats.

Structure of the Research and the Book

Data on crime, youth, and policing in Cape Town today are drawn from
a variety of sources, including the efforts of many fine researchers and
journalists working inside South Africa. Data are also drawn from field
work conducted in the city between 2001 and 2006, and the research is
primarily about these years, although substantial background material
on the mid- to late 1990s in Cape Town is provided and some developments post-2006 are discussed. Interviews were conducted with youth
workers, gang members, representatives of civic organizations working
in the area of juvenile justice, researchers, community organizers from
anticrime groups, and advocates for the poor. I spent many hours with
youth workers active in some of the most high-crime, poverty-stricken
areas in the Cape Flats, where South Africa's gang problem is thought to
be most severe, participated in meetings between community groups and
police antigang and intelligence units, and made numerous visits to the
juvenile section of Pollsmoor prison. I also had access to the Social Justice
Resource Project at the University of Cape Town, thanks to support from
the Centre of Criminology (formerly the Institute for Criminology),
which houses an extensive collection of information and research on
crime in South Africa. Data for the chapter on street children came from
interviews with youth workers, city documents, news reports, and analysis of news coverage in local papers. Most of my attention went to people
from and active in the communities affected by crime and those on the
receiving end of criminal justice and security governance. Although the

voices of police and government officials are important, these are, I think, relatively overrepresented in research on crime and urban renewal generally. At the same time, this is not an ethnography, nor is it a study of these communities; instead, it is an attempt to make visible the social forces and sets of relationships that have shaped, and continue to shape, the city of Cape Town.

The book is divided into the following chapters:

Chapter 1 contains two sections addressing the processes of neoliberalization. The first outlines the implementation of neoliberalism at the national level after 1994, the growing political crisis facing the ANC and its partners in government, and the emergence of crime as a central governance challenge. The resulting war on crime became, in part, the security corollary to neoliberal economic reform as development strategy and took the form it did as the result of opportunities and constraints facing this transitioning society as it sought international legitimacy, financing, and expertise. The second section of the chapter addresses these issues with regard to Cape Town specifically and demonstrates how neoliberal urban renewal and the war on crime have come to underpin governance in the postapartheid city.

Chapter 2 is focused on street children in the affluent, disproportionately white city center and opens with a discussion of youth in the transition and the emergence of crime as a governmental category through which to represent marginalized young people of color. As the chapter reveals, urban renewal is central to this process, functioning as a dominant discourse and mechanism through which security governance is conceived and implemented. It does so by documenting and analyzing a racially coded moral panic concerning the city center between 2000 and 2003 that mobilized a "public" consensus around a project of downtown revitalization and economic recovery predicated on eradicating the threat posed by "out of control" street children. The project was defined by the deployment of a range of social control mechanisms—public, private, and hybrid—to clear and control members of marginalized populations, who were rendered de facto noncitizens in the process.

Chapters 3 through 5 take as their focus the part of the city in which most people live, the townships of the Cape Flats, and contrast neoliberal governance here with approaches in the city center. Chapter 3 introduces readers to the primary enemy in the war on crime, the gangs of the Cape Flats, before turning to a discussion of the Cape Flats Renewal Strategy, the CFRS, through which city authorities identified crime and gangsterism as the primary obstacles to development of the Flats and institutionalized security governance within what was ostensibly a socioeconomic development program. The chapter then offers a description of postapartheid policing, ostensibly to combat gangs but which in practice often contributes insecurity to township communities.

Chapter 4 delves further into the relationship between the security forces and township communities. It begins with a discussion of the impact that hard policing has had on the people the police are meant to protect, on crime rates, and on the ability of communities to trust police. Next, the chapter addresses the issue of social crime prevention, an approach to crime reduction in line with the progressive transformation of the criminal justice system. As the chapter shows, social crime prevention measures are not being implemented in any sustained fashion, and narrow definitions of security continue to exert influence over policing strategies. The chapter concludes with an in-depth discussion of community/police relations, placing emphasis on the barriers, from the point of view of many communities, to productive partnerships.

Finally, chapter 5 begins with a discussion of the continued underdevelopment of the Cape Flats, and the increased tendency of the state to view unrest generated by poverty and inequality as a security threat. The focus then shifts to youth development specifically and to the reproduction of "surplus" populations of young people that provide fodder for the gangs, the criminal justice system, and the public's outrage over crime. In the chapter, I discuss the very real benefits that gangs provide for many boys and young men and make the argument that the prison system serves only to normalize gangsterism and the violence to which so many are already exposed, thus contributing to the further destabilization of the township communities to which most prisoners eventually return.

It is my hope that this study of urban governance in Cape Town can contribute to the understanding of new mechanisms of social control under conditions of neoliberal democracy and unequal development, and point us toward possible interventions in their reproduction. The examination of crime, policing, and development in South Africa supports the original position of the ANC and of civil society organizations from around the globe that human security cannot be secured outside the context of political, social, and economic empowerment. Conversely, there is little evidence to suggest that security results from expansion of security networks and the fortification of preexisting social divisions. The persistence of a reactive and repressive governance network in the city and of an urban renewal strategy in which a yet-to-be transformed criminal justice system occupies a prominent place signal a troubling trend, but one that can be observed at many urban nodal points in the global system. What it suggests is that the basic geopolitical terrain of the post–World War II period has not undergone as fundamental a shift as is often believed. Instead, developments in Cape Town and elsewhere indicate that the global security network to which this terrain has given rise is in the process of evolving in response to the varied challenges posed to it under conditions of globalization, and that these challenges are becoming concentrated in the cities of the global South. Current approaches to urban governance seem to suggest that in terms of the global have-nots, those who govern cities are preparing for a long period of low-intensity conflict in which inequality and the insecurity it breeds represent the greatest challenge of the day.

Security and Development in Postapartheid South Africa

South Africa may have avoided a full-scale civil war as the apartheid system crumbled because of the commitment by the major parties to what was eventually a successful peace negotiation. The criminal violence of the post-1994 period, however, concentrated in the same communities already reeling from high levels of political violence, challenges the notion of a relatively peaceful transition. Indeed, as the writer Mike Nicol has commented, it could be argued that urban crime became a replacement for the civil war that never happened.[1] Nicol's observation, and the high crime rates that inform it, puts into question the extent to which security has become a reality for most South Africans and chronic underdevelopment a receding memory. Although formal apartheid itself began to fade almost immediately, this does not mean that South Africa entered a post-conflict phase in 1994; rather, the nation continues to exist somewhere between war and peace.

This chapter, divided into two sections, provides a brief overview of changes in governance in South Africa since 1994, as overtly political violence gave way to a "crime wave" and the new government turned its attention to the country's considerable economic challenges. In the first section, I highlight some key moments in the arrival of neoliberalism to the country and its relationship to the socioeconomic and political challenges facing the nation. The section also includes a brief discussion of security governance, tracing its evolution from the apartheid era into the early postapartheid years. The discussion centers on a key moment in the evolution of postapartheid governance: the emergence of a war against crime. Combined with the shift to neoliberalism, the state's approach to crime produced a distinct form of neoliberal governance with very clear South African characteristics but which nevertheless has much in common with variations found elsewhere; with respect to security specifically, the crucial bond between many forms of neoliberal governance is the repositioning of crime from being a consequence of underdevelopment to representing, instead, the primary obstacle to development. Over the course of the following chapters, we see how this shift is articulated in Cape Town.

The second section of the chapter introduces the city of Cape Town as seen through the lens of social and spatial inequality and examines the relationship between emerging forms of governance on national and local scales. Crime and development frame the challenges to South Africa's transition away from totalitarianism and the legacy of unequal development in many ways. Major elections revolve around promises to tackle both head-on, and no serious political figure or party can avoid staking out bold positions on these issues. Ebrahim Rasool, the former premier for the Western Cape for the African National Congress, speaking just prior to the 2004 elections that gave his party control of the province for the first time, made clear that the ANC considered job creation, poverty, and crime the most pressing of the region's problems.[2] The initial promise of a balanced approach to crime and development, however, has fallen victim to numerous countervailing pressures, with the result that "fighting crime" has emerged not only as the principle security strategy for the city but also as a central development strategy. Central to this shift is the repositioning of Cape Town's poor (and their communities), from victims and survivors of apartheid to problems, in this new aspiring world city.[3]

As will become clear, although the emerging relationships among crime, security, and development draw much of their vitality from the requirements of the market economy, the state played a central role in the early stages of the formation of postapartheid governance structures and processes. The consequences of real crime in the townships and the symbolic meanings of crime for economic transition and recovery were certainly decisive factors in those early days, but the state also had its own quite distinct interests in waging a war on crime. Given the extent to which antiapartheid resistance took the form of making townships ungovernable, a pressing concern of the new government was to reassert control over the urban peripheries and reestablish legitimacy through the invigoration of local governments.[4] Faced with a distinct, and still forming, set of political and economic constraints and opportunities, as well as actual state capacity, the state's efforts soon coalesced into a local variation of controlling and containing unrest in the peripheries on the one hand, and reclaiming and fortifying the downtown center on the other. In the early days of the transition, the state did a significant portion of the heavy lifting in the creation of Cape Town's postapartheid neoliberal governance regime.

Neoliberalism and the Postapartheid Future

GEAR and the Turn to Neoliberalism

The most significant moment in the postapartheid economic fortunes of South Africa arguably came in 1996, when the Reconstruction and Development Programme was abandoned in favor of the Growth, Employment, and Redistribution plan. To many the shift indicated that the ANC was committed to what Patrick Bond has called homegrown structural adjustment, a self-imposed program of economic austerity similar to what the World Bank and International Monetary Fund had been prescribing for underdeveloped nations in one form or another over the course of almost three decades.[5] Although the RDP did not stand in opposition to neoliberal economic reform, it did contain a strong social welfarist element that sought to balance market approaches with a commitment to state support for the public sector and social services. GEAR, on the other hand, depended almost exclusively on market mechanisms, particularly privatization, fiscal "discipline," and foreign direct investment, and had little appeal beyond an increasingly multiracial national elite and their foreign partners. Once this shift had been made, there was in reality very little the government could do in terms of development but wait for economic growth to begin. In the meantime, however, it had to contend with worsening inequality, growing unemployment, an impatient population, and, of course, the crisis of high crime.

A chorus of voices across South Africa claimed at the time that GEAR represented a prioritization of the international financial community over the needs of the vast majority of people, and the decidedly undemocratic manner in which GEAR was introduced suggests that key figures in government were well aware that abandoning the RDP would be highly unpopular.[6] In 2003, longtime ANC member and high-ranking official Ben Turok confirmed what some had already suspected, that not only were many within the higher ranks of the ANC left out of the decision making process but GEAR was in fact drawn up in conjunction with experts from the key institutions of transnational neoliberal governance. Turok relates that in June of 1996 twenty members of Parliament from the ANC were called into a meeting with Minister of Finance Trevor Manuel and told that a new economic plan had been adopted. Although allowed to ask some questions, no one was allowed to see the plan before it was introduced to Parliament. According to Turok, the principal author of the document was Richard Ketley, an official from the World Bank. Reaction to the new program was overwhelmingly negative, with the Congress of South African Trade Unions (Cosatu) referring to it as simply a form of structural adjustment that linked economic prosperity to the application of market principles and cutting "unnecessary" government spending.[7] In the end, the fact that GEAR was adopted in secret and included no consultation with ANC partners or even with many ANC officials drew more attention to perhaps the most unpopular move the new government made in the early years of the transition.

Although GEAR was sprung upon an unsuspecting South Africa rather suddenly, it represented the culmination of a process that had been in motion for some time, its neoliberal prescriptions the result of negotiations between certain figures from the liberation movement, representatives of elite Western financial and political communities, international capital, and the old regime that began in the 1980s.[8] The controversy it generated, however, foreshadowed a number of looming conflicts (1) within the tripartite alliance of the ANC, Cosatu, and the South African Communist Party (SACP), (2) within the ANC itself, and (3) between the state and civil society. The conflicts were exacerbated by the failure of GEAR to deliver on the promises its proponents were making; namely, that fiscal discipline would act as a magnet for foreign investment, which in turn would provide the necessary capital to finally undo decades of intentional underdevelopment. By the time Thabo Mbeki was reelected in 2004, GEAR was widely considered a failure by the ANC's alliance partners and civil society organizations, leaving most South Africans, economically speaking, as bad or worse than they had been before.[9] Macroeconomic order may have been restored, but for the majority of the population, basic issues of housing, health care, employment, gender equity, crime, and safety had been severely neglected.

Indeed, the two biggest issues for South African voters in the decade following apartheid, according to surveys, were crime and the economy, particularly jobs. In the country as a whole, unemployment increased steadily after 1996, making it perhaps the most pressing issue facing the government.[10] Surveys conducted annually by the Institute for Democracy in South Africa (Idasa) between 1994 and 2006 revealed that economic concerns were central and growing to the majority of the population.[11] The question the Idasa survey posed was: "What are the most important problems facing this country that the government ought to address?" Respondents were allowed to choose three issues. The most frequently cited issue was consistently jobs; although crime spiked as a concern between 1994 and 1998, it dropped steadily after this period and placed below all other categories by 2006 (see Figure 1). Furthermore, although a high concern with employment has been fairly consistent across racial groups—from about 52 percent for whites to 63 percent for black Africans—there was a significant difference with crime. The Idasa survey shows that almost 50 percent of whites cited crime as a priority, whereas only 32 percent of coloureds and 18 percent of black Africans did so, even as victimization surveys show that members of these populations are much more likely to be crime victims.

Despite the clear need to expand employment, after almost a decade of GEAR the nation had actually shed jobs, and the official unemployment rate in 2007 reflected a national crisis, reaching 25.5 percent, with other estimates ranging up to 45 percent.[12] The crisis is distributed unevenly by race and gender. According to census data, although the official unemployment

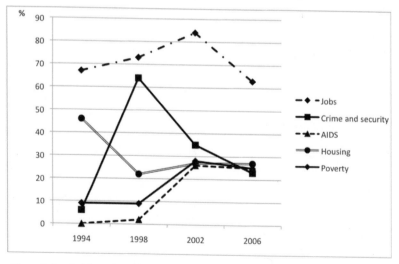

Figure 1. South African's public agenda over time. Source: Afrobarometer Briefings, Institute for Democracy in South Africa, Pretoria, 2006.

rate for men was 21 percent in 2007, down slightly from a high of 27 percent in 2003, the unemployment rate for women was 30 percent, down from a high of 36 percent in 2003. Racial disparities in employment are even more pronounced. In the Western Cape, for example, where unemployment is below the national average, the official unemployment rates in 2002 were 29 percent for black Africans, 19 percent for coloureds, 15 percent for Indians, and 4.2 percent for whites.[13] The pressure on the government comes not only from the employment issue itself, but from a crisis of confidence in the state's entire strategy for socioeconomic development.

Having come under sustained criticism for its macroeconomic policies, the ANC in 2006 responded with the Accelerated and Shared Growth Strategy for South Africa (Asgisa). Asgisa is an attempt to blunt the criticism that economic policies were benefiting capital at the expense of labor and the unemployed by introducing measures aimed primarily at infrastructure development, social welfare, and service delivery, made possible now that GEAR has succeeded in getting the macroeconomic house in order. Asgisa set off another round of debate about economic policy and social transformation at the national level, with criticism of the strategy from business, community, and labor sectors, as well as from academic researchers.[14] What Asgisa has not done, however, is fundamentally shift the perception that the ANC and its governing partners are failing to address poverty and inequality in any meaningful way. In fact, the ANC leadership, along with the major opposition parties with which it shares power, consistently defended GEAR and its legacy while inequality continued to rise, making it all the more necessary to shine the spotlight on other reasons for the failure of development to take hold.

Security and Development in South Africa: The State Targets Crime

Crisis and instability were endemic features of South Africa in the post–World War II period. The rise of the National Party in 1948 came amid the intense conflicts within white society generated by the war; and in the early years of its rule, the party faced a number of challenges on the road to consolidating power.[15] The official founding of the Republic of South Africa in 1961 also occurred in the context of national turmoil, as the massacres at Sharpeville and Langa the year before sparked waves of resistance to the apartheid system and led to the birth of the armed struggle by the various liberation movements.[16] Although the late 1960s and early 1970s were relatively calm, the uprisings of 1976 heralded yet another period of national unrest, which would last until the transfer of power in 1994. Indeed, one way to characterize the apartheid state is as perpetually lurching from crisis to crisis, its methods of governance defined by efforts to contain the tensions upon which the existence of the state, and the white society on whose behalf it ruled, depended. Since the elections that brought the ANC to power, the state has become more stable, as its authority now stems from the consent of most of the governed. The crises of the apartheid period, however, rather than disappearing, have taken new forms or have been redefined. The high levels of crime and inequality facing South African society are the better-known examples of continuing crisis; others include xenophobia, interracial and interethnic tensions, community unrest, and the impact of HIV/AIDS and other public health threats. For the great majority of South Africans, daily insecurity is in this sense an unfortunate tie that binds apartheid and postapartheid South Africa.

Management of this crisis of development has become the central preoccupation of national, provincial, and municipal governments, as well as of the major political parties. As long as underdevelopment remains a reality for the majority of South Africa's citizens, however, the state will be forced into an essentially defensive, reactive security posture, be it in response to organized political resistance or "disorganized" and well-organized criminal activity—seeking to contain crises to which, some would argue, its own policies directly contribute. Unable to provide the promised development that would undermine the criminal economy, the state has opted to declare war on the criminals. Unfortunately, this aggressive approach repeats a common and well-recognized miscalculation of states everywhere: that a reliance on force and the state's repressive machinery can produce national security. As in the past, the state's problematic approach to the twin challenges of security and development continues to lay the foundation for perpetual crisis.

Domestic social control in South Africa has traditionally been the domain of the criminal justice system and, most prominently, the state police. The use of this force in a social control/quasi-military capacity is a well-known feature of law enforcement in the colonial context, and apartheid represented just one variation on this theme.[17] In fact there is little evidence of any significant change in direction in South African policing in the preapartheid and apartheid periods, and the role of the police had always been to enforce racially based legal codes in what was a formalized policy of population control. Successive waves of urbanization, in particular, beginning at least as far back as the late nineteenth century, created substantial panic among whites about crime, disorder, and young black men. The state response, especially after the National Party had come to power in the midcentury, was to legislate the movement of black people and deploy the police to administer and uphold various laws whose ultimate function was to secure the borders between black and white South Africa, maintaining the socioracial purity of the latter in the process. When disorder began to take the form of resistance to National Party rule, the state again responded through the legal system, steadily criminalizing all forms of dissent. Here too, it was the police who were responsible for enforcement. The rise of the youth-led movement in the mid-1970s saw the pattern repeat. By this point the police had evolved from a quasi-military force and taken on military and paramilitary functions as an integral part of the counterinsurgency war against the antiapartheid movement.[18] What is clear in all of these instances is that the criminal justice system always operated at the juncture of white fear and black "danger." At its most overt, the function of the system was to police physical and racial boundaries, while less visibly it was central to the reproduction of those very boundaries. The police holding cells, courts, and prisons functioned as the schoolrooms in which the lessons of white supremacy and racial separation were taught, and resisted, daily.

Efforts began in the mid-1990s to change the form and function of the criminal justice system, with some important successes to date. Apartheid laws, of course, have been removed, and the role of the police has been radically reconceptualized in relation to the country's black and white communities. As we will see, in practice many of the most disturbing features of the criminal justice system remain, most notably the high proportion of black youth annually dragged through it and the high numbers of black men in prison. One important cause of both these phenomena is the continued emphasis on aggressive policing, arrests, and imprisonment as the principal measures to fight crime and secure the development process, while the stated commitment to social crime prevention remains largely rhetorical.[19] The fear of many national and local elites is that the country's reputation for high crime will frighten away the very investors upon whom market-based development depends. In ways small and large, securing the country for investment, for tourism, and for other forms of market-driven accumulation and growth has thus become central to neoliberal development strategies at the national and municipal levels. Consequently, the criminal justice system, and policing in particular, has been reinsinuated into the new nation's development process. The increasing reliance on police to combat crime, however, is in many ways generating, rather than ameliorating, social conflict. Incidents of police brutality and misconduct, for example, remain a serious problem, and many South Africans argue that law enforcement officers, in many cases, are indifferent or hostile in their interactions with people. Many feel that in their mandate to wage war on criminals, police continue to treat black communities as "enemy territory" and that policing practices still bear the stamp of militarism. This approach not only risks contributing to the further destabilization of communities, but can have a negative effect on the ability of residents and police to work together, as overly aggressive policing often casts too wide a net. Relations between police and communities also remain tense in many cases because of widespread corruption, ongoing mistrust, and the perceived ineffectiveness of the police force in addressing the crimes that most affect people in the townships and rural areas across the country and are further complicated by the use of police to enforce evictions, service cut-offs, and other unpopular measures that evoke the apartheid era. What these challenges illustrate is not only the unchanging nature of policing in South Africa, but also the particular dangers posed by urban development programs—shaped by a particular neoliberal rationality rather than racial apartheid—that rely on repressive forms of policing.

In 1996, the government unveiled its National Crime Prevention Strategy (NCPS), which articulated a set of priorities specifically intended to translate the sentiments of the "Ready to Govern" guidelines into programs and policies. "Ready to Govern," adopted at the ANC's national conference in May of 1992, spoke to major issues that the antiapartheid movement would face once the transition began, envisioned a democratic South Africa, and reflected a growing sensibility across the global South about the real threats to people's security. The ANC's position at the time is worth citing at length:

> For several decades the apartheid regime has relied on its formidable police, defence and intelligence structures to maintain the system of apartheid and minority rule and to suppress popular resistance to that system. As a result of its Total Strategy, the whole of the South African state and society became militarized.

National security was pursued primarily through military and paramilitary means. The effects of this approach to security are evident: high levels of violence and crime, economic decline, regional arms races, destabilization and perpetual insecurity throughout the sub-continent.

The South African security institutions themselves developed a racist, closed, secretive, undemocratic structure, lacking legitimacy in the eyes of the people. The process of democratization under way in our country will not be complete without addressing this problem.

Underdevelopment, poverty, lack of democratic participation and the abuse of human rights are regarded as grave threats to the security of people. Since they invariably give rise to conflict between individuals, communities and countries, they threaten the security of states as well.[20]

Although a dramatic departure from previous approaches to crime, the NCPS was far less ambitious than "Ready to Govern" even in its conceptualization. It emphasized a shift from focusing primarily on crime control, dealing with crimes after they happen, to crime prevention, relying on what it calls four pillars: (1) reforming the criminal justice system to make it an effective deterrent and improving access to the system for disempowered groups, (2) reducing crime through environmental design, (3) reasserting public values through education campaigns intended to involve communities in addressing the crime problem, and (4) addressing transnational organized crime. It also outlined seven priority crimes to address: firearms crimes, organized crime, white collar crime, gender/child violence, intergroup violence, vehicle theft and hijacking, and corruption in the criminal justice system.

The NCPS and the National Urban Renewal Programme (NURP), introduced three years later, were the two primary national initiatives intended to address the twin challenges of crime reduction and social development, and both map out relatively progressive visions of crime prevention that link crime reduction to development. The NCPS was in fact one of the original six pillars of the 1996 National Growth and Development Strategy (NGDS), which included crime prevention as part of an overall economic development strategy and made "links between crime and the economic development of the country and its people [that] had not been seen before in government policy."[21] The NGDS was

abandoned almost immediately, however, in the broader shift in government development strategy from RDP to GEAR, which occurred in the
same year the NGDS was announced and abandoned. The six social development pillars of the NGDS were, through GEAR, replaced by one overarching strategy: neoliberal economic reform.[22]

As crime dominated headlines from the mid-1990s on and public concern escalated, pressure on the ANC to act decisively grew from
many quarters, and near the end of the 1990s a shift could be observed
in the state's approach to crime. "Ready to Govern" explicitly states that
crime and security must be addressed through remedying underdevelopment, but as the decade wore on, crime became mentioned most often in
relation to its function as an *obstacle* to development. The often explicit
theory underlying the shift is that crime is so out of control that until it is
reduced below a certain threshold, the disorder it engenders will undermine efforts to achieve economic growth and implement genuine social
development; therefore, increasing the deterrent capacity of the criminal
justice system should take priority within the government's broader
development strategy.[23] The reduced rates of crime this would presumably
produce would create the necessary space in which nascent development
efforts could survive and flourish.

The NCPS survived the demise of the NGDS, but its implementation
has been uneven, with the crime control elements of the strategy drawing more resources than prevention, and certain crimes on the priority list
being emphasized more than others. An assessment of the NCPS after its
first year found that

> virtually no action has been taken on the two "social pillars" of the
> strategy, with all the available funding to date already devoted to the
> reform of the criminal justice system, and to border patrol. . . . [T]he
> original national priorities have not been tackled with equal
> vigor—crimes against women and children were subsumed under
> the national victim empowerment programme. This reflects the
> traditional ghettoisation of issues affecting women, children, and
> victims, and indicates a lack of interest in what are probably the most
> prevalent violent crimes in South Africa.[24]

The assessment found similar deficiencies in the areas of rehabilitation
of offenders and corruption in the criminal justice system. What these

developments suggested is that from the start, the ideals of "Ready to Govern" and other early documents were rapidly being overtaken by a more "pragmatic" state relationship to crime. The NCPS, once the centerpiece of the state's crime prevention policy, has today become a small component of the police, as the focus has shifted to shorter-term crime control.[25] Over the intervening years between the adoption of "Ready to Govern" and the present, the language of crime and development has been crowded out by words of war. When asked by an interviewer in 1999 if he had a watchword for his approach to crime, the late minister of safety and security Steve Tshwete, prefiguring deputy police minister Mbalula by a decade, replied, "War! We have to form a united front across the ranks because our common enemy is the criminal [element] out there."[26] Although there is certainly a danger in assessing policy on the basis of the blustery pronouncement of politicians, particularly in what was an election year, the shift to a form of "tough policing" is undeniable. Representatives of the state continue to acknowledge the socioeconomic roots of the crime problem, but increasingly the practice is closer to warlike rhetoric. Although many South Africans hoped that the end of the militarized apartheid state would translate into a peace dividend that could fuel social development, much of the spending on defense was simply transferred to the police in the early transition years.[27]

The criminal justice budget as a whole in South Africa has undergone stunning growth since the end of apartheid, increasing from R14 billion in 1995 to R71 billion in 2009.[28] A significant portion of this spending has gone to the South African Police Service (SAPS), which began a major expansion in the late 1990s that continued throughout the first decade of the new millennium. The police budget grew at a rate averaging more than 10 percent between 2000–01 and 2007, when it reached R28.7 billion, an increase directly reflected in the sharp increase in police personnel.[29] In 2002, the SAPS committed to increase the size of its force from 127,000 to 140,000 and reached this goal relatively quickly, by 2004. The new minister of safety and security, Charles Nqakula, promised that the police force would number more than 150,000 by 2005, but in retrospect this promise appears quite modest, as it reached 183,000 in 2009 and should climb to 200,000 by 2012.[30] In addition to these increases, the South African Police Service Amendment Act of 1998 enabled the creation of separate and independent municipal police forces, and by 2002 the major metropolitan areas of Durban, Johannesburg, Pretoria, and Cape Town had all established their own city police services as well, with full police powers save the authority to investigate crimes.[31]

These increases in public policing complemented an already large private security industry that was itself in the midst of a dramatic expansion. By 1999, the private sector was a R7 billion ($1 billion)/year industry, employing almost 500,000 people and outnumbering the public police more than 4 to 1.[32] Between 1997 and 2009 the number of private security guards in the country grew from 115,000 to 300,000, and more than 5,000 private security companies were registered, with 2,500 of these employing security guards.[33] Private police are generally used to protect commercial and industrial interests, as well as the homes of those South Africans who can afford them.[34] In the future, according to the SAPS, private police will take responsibility for visible policing, while the SAPS will focus more on priority crimes: drug trafficking, car theft, violent crime, and organized crime.[35] Expansion, integration, and deployment of the private/public policing apparatus is part of a broader shift in strategy and tactics that stem from an emerging political pragmatism within the national government and across political parties. Realizing that high crime rates could not be brought down substantially in the short or medium term, political elites, facing pressure to do just that, began to pursue and advocate for crime *control*, which, as we will see in the next chapter, is intimately linked to defending the core of the neoliberal city. For all intents and purposes, this amounts to a delinking of crime reduction and social development, the goal instead being to minimize the disruption caused by crime to certain areas and to certain processes.

Indications as to how the newly expanded SAPS would direct its resources came in 2000, when national police commissioner Jackie Selebi announced a three-year crime-combating strategy called Operation Crackdown. The strategy had three components: first, a spatial governance component in which authorities would focus on the 140 "hot spots" in which more than 50 percent of crime in South Africa is committed, according to police. These would be clustered into "crime combating zones" and targeted by law enforcement (and the military, when necessary). The second component centered around intelligence-driven policing of organized crime, with the intent of disrupting syndicates, closing down the flow of stolen goods and the markets for these goods, and arresting runners and leaders. Finally, Crackdown would roll out medium-term social crime prevention measures to address socioeconomic developmental deficits in the impacted areas.[36]

The first major operation under the new strategy was carried out in March 2000, in the Johannesburg neighborhoods of Hillbrow, Yeoville, and Berea. These are high-density residential urban areas with high crime and many immigrants from neighboring African countries. The following account and assessment of the operation is taken from a report by Eric Pelser, a researcher at the Institute for Security Studies in Pretoria.[37] Operation Crackdown relied essentially on a massive cordon and search and seizure, deploying more than 1,000 heavily armed police and military personnel over the period of almost a week. It borrowed from similar approaches in the United States during its War on Drugs in the 1980s and early 90s.[38] Officers put up 114 roadblocks, searched 22,568 vehicles, raided and searched 293 buildings, and searched 25,324 people. In the end, 14 people were arrested for serious crimes (violent crimes and drug dealing), 512 for less serious crimes (e.g., urinating in public, prostitution), and 7,068 for suspicion of being in the country illegally. Confiscated in the operation were 57 firearms, 284 stolen vehicles, and large quantities of drugs.

One week later a similar operation was carried out just to the north, in Pretoria. Although police officials pointed to the success of the operations in reducing crime in the targeted areas and challenging the alleged impunity of criminals operating in the neighborhoods, the operations were criticized for their massive sweep and harassment of suspected undocumented inhabitants (many of whom turned out not to be in the country illegally after all). The effects of crime reduction were also questioned because of the "hit and run" nature of the operations, which tended to simply displace crime temporarily. Because of the resources needed to mount such operations, and their temporary impact, their cost-effectiveness was questioned. The massive arrests also overwhelmed the already overburdened courts, prisons, and immigration department. Finally, there appeared to have been no social crime prevention projects approved for the areas.[39]

The importance of the new official crime-fighting strategy, which was a clear departure from, rather than an extension of, the NCPS, is in its use of overwhelming force as the leading edge of crime control and the apparent abandonment of any genuine social development component. High-profile operations on the scale of those in Johannesburg and Pretoria may not be the norm, but they do represent a model upon which smaller operations and general, day-to-day crime fighting increasingly were, and continue to be, based. Indeed, the ensuing years saw a rise in state intrusion into the everyday lives of millions of people through a dramatic deployment of the policing net across the country, consisting of cordon and search operations, roadblocks, search of persons and vehicles, and stop and searches.[40] Operation Crackdown also signaled a movement in the direction of normalizing paramilitary policing under conditions of formal democracy, and coincided with increased involvement of the military itself with policing functions. The government not only turned to the military for large-scale cordon and search operations, but has also deployed defense forces to carry out border patrolling and intelligence operations (leading some security analysts to wonder whether the early successes in demilitarizing South Africa were in danger of being reversed).[41] In the process, however, the scope of crime-fighting strategies narrowed, and criminal justice reform of the system inherited from apartheid began to be defined largely by building the capacity and efficiency of the criminal justice system, strengthening the networks that stretch from the police on the street through the courts and, finally, into the prisons.

Perhaps not unexpectedly, the expansion of the police, reflecting as it did the emphasis of the state's anticrime campaign, was matched by a sharp increase in the numbers of South Africans sent to prison. Between 1985 and 1991, the prison population was relatively stable, but in 1991 it began to climb, from 103,000 to 111,000 by 1993 and 146,000 by 1998. In 2003 the prison population peaked at 182,000 and then began a slight decline, dropping to slightly more than 162,000 inmates in 2009.[42] Overcrowding has also increased, and in 2000 South African prison capacity stood at 100,000, with an inmate population of 171,000; this 70 percent overcrowding rate was 40 percent higher than in 1996.[43] As of the year end of 2009, the Department of Corrections listed official capacity at slightly less than 115,000. Because the court system is so underresourced, the proportion of people in prison awaiting trial has also increased dramatically. In 2004, almost one third of inmates in South African prisons were technically innocent and waiting for their day in court, up from 20 percent in 1996, and by 2007 more than 53,000 inmates in the prison system were awaiting trial.[44]

Trends in policing and in sentencing, matching the "get tough" rhetoric of certain members of the political elite, suggest a future of continued growth in South Africa's imprisonment rate and a worsening of overcrowding. The state in fact acknowledges that it will be unable to build prisons fast enough to accommodate large influxes of new inmates despite its best efforts.[45] It is also unlikely that the drive to make the court system more efficient will be able to keep up with arrests, meaning that the numbers of people in prison awaiting trial will remain high. There have been sporadic releases of prisoners awaiting trial who cannot afford bail, estimated at about 40 percent of the population awaiting trial, and advancement of parole to those who pose no danger to the community, but it remains to be seen whether this will become policy.[46] Even if this were to happen, however, such a policy leaves unchanged the basic trajectory of criminal justice reform; rather, it functions to facilitate that trajectory. As a consequence, South Africa's prison population will remain high until there is a significant and sustained drop in the crime rate or a substantial change in government policy, neither of which seems likely in the near to medium term.

The expansion of the criminal justice system and the considerable resources devoted to the task raise the question of the impact on crime of current approaches. Crime rates and the impact of policing on them are matters of much debate in South Africa, and we will return to this in chapter 4. During the early years of the war on crime, until 2003, serious crimes increased substantially in almost every category, with the exception of murder.[47] The decline in murders, furthermore, was likely due to the decline in political violence after 1994 more than to improvements in policing and the criminal justice system. During the 2001–07 period, official statistics from the SAPS, which are viewed with skepticism by many, show a general decline in serious crime per 100,000 of the total population, with rape dropping from 121/100,000 in 2001–02 to 76/100,000 in 2006–07, attempted murder from 70 to 42.5, assault/grievous bodily harm from 589 to 460, and common assault from 584.3 to 443.2; murder, however, increased slightly in 2006–07.[48] The glaring exception to this downward trend is drug-related crime, which jumped from 120/100,000 in 2001–02 to 221 in 2006–07. The exception to the downward trend in murder had been the Western Cape, where murders increased steadily between 1994 and 2003 and saw their first major decline only in 2003–04; 2004–05 saw a smaller decline in the number of murders from the previous year, a continued significant decrease in attempted murder, a decrease in assault/grievous bodily harm after an increase in 2003–04, and fewer assaults, simple robberies, and aggravated robberies. There was a small increase in reported rapes and a dramatic increase in drug-related crime, from slightly less than 20,000 in 2003–04 to more than 30,000 in 2004–05 and more than 40,000 in 2006–07, when the Western Cape recorded the highest ratio of murders, indecent assault, and common assault by province in the country.

There is some disagreement over the reasons for the increases between 1994 and 2003, as they may reflect political and institutional changes after 1994 more than actual increases in the incidence of crime.[49] The SAPS under the apartheid government was a counterinsurgency force, and its mandate was not to serve and protect black African and coloured township residents. It is very possible, as research by South African criminologist Mark Shaw and others suggests, that crime was equally high prior to 1994 but was not reported to police and was not an object of police investigation.[50] Although mistrust is still a major concern, people may be more likely now to report some crimes to the police, and the state more committed to recording them, although we will see later that these assumptions are problematic. Even with them, however, problems with the recording of crimes do remain. Because crime statistics rely on crimes reported to the police or which come to their attention, figures for murder and car theft, for example, tend to be more accurate than figures for rape, domestic abuse, and child abuse, which usually happen within the home, or for less serious crimes that victims may choose not to report, such as theft of a small amount of money. Reporting of crime will also be more comprehensive in urban areas, where police are concentrated, than in rural areas.[51] With almost 50 percent of the population in rural areas, this could mean that reported crime figures for the country are still very low relative to actual crime.

Caught between demands to address what are still very high rates of crime and demands to accelerate the pace of development, government appears to be in a holding pattern, sticking with the tough-on-crime approach and the basic tenets of growth and development expressed in GEAR and Asgisa. Although the latter suggests some relaxation of the rigidity with which the state has held to its regime of fiscal austerity, there is little chance in the near term for a shift away from some version of neoliberal development strategy; at best we will see a slight increase in social spending, resulting in real but very limited gains for the population. Consequently, the ANC and its partners in government will continue to approach crime from the perspective of control and containment rather than of reduction driven by fundamental structural changes and a reversal of inequality. The next section seeks to situate Cape Town in this drama unfolding on the national stage around the issues of security and development. It provides an overview of the city and its embrace of neoliberalism that will be useful for the more in-depth discussion of crime, security, and development in the following chapters.

Development and the Governance of Security in Cape Town

Neoliberal Governance in the City

According to official census figures, in 2001 there were approximately 3.5 million people living in the Cape Town metropolis, constituting the majority of the 4.5 million residents in the Western Cape province, which in turn represents approximately 10 percent of South Africa's total population.[52] The Western Cape is unique in that it is the only province in South Africa where black Africans are a minority. In 2007, just over 44 percent of the Cape's population was coloured, while black Africans made up approximately 35 percent of the total population; nationally, the figures are 79 percent black African and 9 percent coloured.[53] The Western Cape also has a large white population, which at 19.3 percent is second only to the 20 percent in Gauteng and almost double the national average of 9.6 percent, and a small Asian population at 1.8 percent.

These ratios partially explain why the ANC has struggled in the province. Until 2002, the city of Cape Town was under the political control of either the New National Party (NNP, in reality the old National Party) or an alliance of the NNP and the Democratic Party known as the Democratic Alliance (DA). In 2001, however, the DA fell apart, and the next year, following the introduction of controversial floor-crossing legislation, 27 DA members defected to the NNP, giving the newly formed national NNP/ANC alliance—which shocked many in the country—a majority in the city council. In 2002 Cape Town elected its first ANC mayor, Nomaindia Mfeketo, and in the 2004 national elections the ANC for the first time took control of the provincial government as well. The ANC lost the city to the DA in 2006, and lost the province to them in 2009, making the Western Cape the only one of the country's nine provinces not under ANC control.

Spatially and socially, Cape Town is perhaps the most segregated city in the world.[54] In the west of the city, adjacent to downtown and facing the Atlantic Ocean, are Sea Point, Clifton, and Camps Bay, well-to-do residential and commercial areas. Just to the south/southeast of the city are the southern suburbs, formerly white areas by law, today largely white by economics, which remain predominantly English-speaking. And to the north, across Table Bay, are the northern suburbs, a mainly residential, self-contained Afrikaans area. Far from these largely white enclaves, stretching up to 30 kilometers to the east of the city center, are the Cape Flats. The coloured and black African townships on the Cape Flats were formed by a combination of forced removals and migration. Coloureds and small numbers of black Africans were systematically forced into the Flats from neighborhoods closer to the downtown under the Group Areas Act, which sought to turn the urban centers into white-only areas. The Cape Flats also became home to the many black Africans migrating to the city from rural areas in search of work. Although governance in the city matches that of other cities in the country in broad outlines, these unique characteristics are important to keep in mind.

The reality is that the Western Cape, often referred to as a wealthy province, and the city of Cape Town are highly unequal.[55] The official unemployment rate for the city in 2001 was 29.2 percent, a postapartheid peak, but dropped to 24.5 by 2007. As with national statistics, the total figure hides important disparities, and the unemployment rate in 2007 stood at 38.7 percent for black Africans, 21.8 percent for coloureds, and 4.4 percent for whites.[56] These figures, too, hide important differences, with unemployment highest for black African women at 45.3 percent compared with 34.2 percent for men; and for coloured women, the rate is 23.1 percent compared with 20.6 percent for men.[57] In the metropolitan area of Cape Town as a whole, 42 percent of the households are defined as poor, and 15 percent can be considered indigent, attempting to live on less than R799/month (just over $100). More than 30 percent of black African households and 13 percent of coloured households are unable to afford basic services, compared with about 3 percent for white households. Research does indicate, however, that a number of pro-poor measures adopted by the new city council in 2000 are having a positive, if limited, impact.[58] Still, the socioeconomic situation in the province and in Cape Town is disturbing. A recent study commissioned by city health officials found that poverty and the HIV/AIDS epidemic affecting the entire sub-Saharan region are expected to dramatically reduce life expectancy for many Cape residents. Life expectancy in 2003 was estimated at 55 years for black Africans and 65 years for coloured but in both cases was falling. Whites were not included in the survey because they use primarily private health facilities.[59]

High levels of unemployment partially reflect the nature of investment-driven socioeconomic development over the last decade. The city's own study in its 2002 Integrated Development Plan (IDP) revealed that capital continues to be invested in the more affluent areas and avoided in the less affluent sections of the city, reinforcing existing spatial patterns of inequality.[60] For example, the Central Business District (CBD), Observatory, Simon's Town, and Camps Bay—upscale commercial and residential areas—contain only 10 percent of the city's population but account for 29.5 percent of its formal employment and 33 percent of city business. The Cape Flats, on the other hand, make up 60 percent of the population but only 16.7 percent of formal city employment and 10.8 percent of city business. This is representative of a larger pattern identified by the IDP study, whereby most private capital is invested in areas distant from where low-income residents live. The one major exception is the Cape Town International Airport, which is located on the Cape Flats. The IDP attributed the pattern to the easy freeway access, good infrastructure, high amenity value, and safety of the wealthier areas. This, of course, is a direct legacy of apartheid social planning, which located poor nonwhites far from the urban center as a means of racial segregation, and apartheid capitalism, which sought to control black labor. Not surprisingly, the Human Development Index (HDI) reflects this spatial inequality. In 2005, the HDI for Mitchells Plain, the largest coloured township, measured .71, and for Khayelitsha, the largest black African township, .69. As a point of comparison, the HDI for Durbanville, a northern suburb of the city that is predominantly Afrikaans and was almost 90 percent white according to the 2001 census, was .88, and for the city center, .82.[61] These spatial inequalities are hardly news to local authorities, and the city explicitly included a framework for social integration and targeting zones of poverty in its 1997 strategic planning document.[62] To date, however, the city remains as divided as ever.

The Western Cape suffers from unacceptably high rates of crime, even when compared with other parts of South Africa, most of it concentrated in working-class and poor areas and reflecting the same racial and spatial inequalities observed in measures of development. A survey of 2,000 people in Cape Town conducted in 1998 found that 49 percent had been the victim of a crime in the past five years. Of these incidents, 24 percent were burglaries, 24 percent were robberies or muggings, and 20 percent were car thefts. For wealthier residents, 22 percent of the crimes they experienced were burglary, and 15 percent were car theft. Assault constituted 13 percent of crimes experienced by black Africans, 11 percent for coloureds, and 4 percent for whites.[63] Coloureds are the most likely crime victims, while coloureds and black Africans are both more likely to be victims of violent crimes compared with whites, who are more likely to be the victims of property crimes.

In terms of age, most crime victims were between 21 and 35 years old, somewhat higher than international averages, which tend to show that most crime victims are between 16 and 24.[64] Young people in Cape Town do, however, experience high levels of crime, and in 2001 almost one third of violent crime victims were between the ages of 16 and 25.[65] A 2002 study also revealed that slightly more than one third of children leaving school in the Western Cape had been the victims of sexual assault.[66] The Medical Research Council (MRC) found that 20 percent of Western Cape tenth graders suffered from posttraumatic stress disorder and that 83 percent had been exposed to at least one traumatic event, both due primarily to high levels of sexual assault and gang violence. According to the MRC, the average teenager in Cape Town is more likely to be shot to death than to die from a traffic accident or of natural causes. Analysis of deaths between 1999 and 2000 show that 66.3 percent of deaths of youth in the city aged 15 to 19 were murders and 41 percent of youth under 19 who died that year were killed, 50 percent by gunfire. Dr. Sandra Marais, senior specialist scientist of the MRC's Crime, Violence, and Injury Lead Programme in Cape Town, states that "[i]n every age category for children under 19, firearm deaths were the most frequent cause of violent death. I doubt that children get murdered to this extent anywhere in the world."[67]

Slightly more than half of Cape Town crime victims in a 1998 victimization study by the Institute for Security Studies (ISS) were men. However, the many difficulties in obtaining accurate numbers on crimes against women, especially domestic violence and sexual assaults, make it fairly certain that these crimes are severely underreported. The ISS study did find that in relation to sexual assault, coloured women and women under 25 were at higher risk for victimization.[68] The incidence of victimization of young women in the city is in line with national statistics, which show that 51 percent of rape cases reported to district surgeons between 1996 and 1998 involved women between the ages of 15 and 21. Seventy-five percent of women in an MRC study reported that their first sexual encounter was coerced or against their will.[69] An ISS survey of women in Durban, Johannesburg, and Cape Town found that the vast majority had experienced some form of sexual, emotional, physical, or economic abuse, with 55 percent reporting having experienced all four. Slightly less than 80 percent of serious incidents occurred within either the victim's or the abuser's home, contributing to the invisibility of crimes against women.[70]

Criminals are not the only source of insecurity for Capetonians, and statistics suggest that the tough-on-crime approach may be producing patterns of police abuse that mark these tactics in other places as well. Although interviews I conducted show that productive partnerships between police and communities on the Cape Flats are being formed, the overall picture for the province is less encouraging. Data collected by the Independent Complaints Directorate (ICD), a government body, show dramatic increases in reports of police misconduct and criminal offenses by police in the Western Cape. Complaints of police criminality increased from 192 in 2002–03 to 306 in 2003–04, constituting almost 21 percent of the national total, whereas complaints of misconduct rose from 523 to 910, almost one-quarter of the national total.[71] In the report from 2004–05, the Western Cape registered the highest number of complaints, constituting 22 percent of the national total in a province that contains just above 10 percent of the entire population.[72] At this early stage it is unclear exactly what relationships, if any, exist among the war on crime, the drop in some major crimes, and the increase in complaints against the police. What the ICD figures do suggest is that positive police/community relations upon which long-term crime reduction partly relies remain an elusive goal. We will return to this in chapter 4.

Developing Insecurity

City and provincial authorities are well aware of the inequality and high crime rates with which the city's communities have to contend, and they have generated a number of interrelated approaches to meet these challenges. Although the constraints and opportunities the city faces are mediated by local forces and institutions, they share an overall alignment with the situation facing the nation as a whole. In the shift to GEAR, for example, provinces and municipalities are expected to do more on their own with less support from the national government; hence, the emphasis on attracting private investment. In this sense, GEAR is a key mechanism through which neoliberal governance travels to South Africa's cities. David MacDonald and Laila Smith, of the Municipal Services Project, found that GEAR

> has resulted in significant decreases in intergovernmental transfers from national to local governments in the name of fiscal restraint. Although these cuts began as far back as the early 1990s under the

then-ruling National Party, transfer squeezes continued and escalated after the ANC came to power at the national level, resulting in an 85 percent decrease (in real terms) in intergovernmental transfers to local government between 1991 and 1997 according to the Finance and Fiscal Commission . . . and a further 55 percent in Cape Town between 1997 and 2000.[73]

GEAR's macroeconomic orientation, especially the attention it gives to budget deficit reduction, produced an urban terrain in which generating income emerged as a central task of city government and in practice has meant for Cape Town a strict fiscal regime of cost cutting and cost recovery. These policies, in turn, have created a very strong incentive to privatize government services and have provoked some of the most intense clashes between government and communities in a decade, just as the state was attempting to reassert some control over the townships.[74] Cape Town since the late 1990s has seen frequent and sometimes violent encounters between township residents and law enforcement officials as community organizations mobilize to fight evictions and service cutoffs for nonpayment, independently of which political party happens to be in power. In fact, McDonald and Smith argue that nationally, it has been the ANC-led municipal councils, with Democratic Party and NNP support, that have led the early drive to privatize city services and that in Cape Town, the municipal substructures controlled by the ANC between 1996 and 2000 initiated widespread commercialization and massive water cut-offs for nonpayment.[75] As community resistance increases, the state has frequently chosen to describe this resistance in terms of criminality. References by public officials to community organizations as "gangs of criminals," for example, indicate a potentially dangerous trend that has implications far beyond criminal justice reform, touching on basic issues of state security and social stability.[76]

The complex mix of crime reduction efforts, the mandates of GEAR and Asgisa, and a highly mobilized and politicized civil society, has manifested itself in Cape Town in a variety of ways. Reduced support from the central government compelled the city to seek out new sources of revenue at the same time that it was attempting to address the formidable challenges of socioeconomic development and crime control. The strategy that emerged from this period became evident soon enough in the various campaigns to develop Cape Town into a world-class tourist destination and enlarge the export-oriented manufacturing sector throughout the province, both of which rely on attracting private, and especially foreign, investment. A strategy paper for the city drawn up in 2001 to provide a guiding vision for subsequent planning and budgeting makes it very clear that Cape Town's success hinges on its ability to compete against other cities in the developing world. According to the paper, the city's strategic vision must therefore recognize that the city exists "in a globalising world, where cities compete against each other for events, jobs, investment and tourists."[77]

This vision of development, in which emerging world-class cities compete against each other for the attention of investors, has direct bearing on the question of crime control. The tourist industry in Cape Town is a particularly useful example for illustrating how the governance of security can develop under an unequivocally neoliberal development strategy because the industry's profitability is very much tied to perceptions, and certainly to perceptions of safety and security. Tourism accounts for almost 10 percent of the Western Cape's workforce and GDP, both higher than the national averages, and in 2002 brought in revenue totaling R17.3 billion.[78] Almost one and a half million visitors came to the Cape that year, including more than half of the foreign visitors to the country. The Western Cape Investment and Trade Promotion Agency estimated that the industry would bring in more than R550 million in foreign direct investment in 2002–03, primarily from accommodations (hotels/conference centers, bed and breakfasts, etc.), foreign-owned travel agencies, restaurants, and other entertainment-related industries. The country as a whole saw an 11 percent increase in foreign visitors after two years of decline, and the industry expected to grow from 3 percent to more than 5 percent of national GDP between 2000 and 2010.[79] Not surprisingly, provincial and municipal officials have identified the industry as a primary growth area, and the city's five-year IDP includes tourism as part of its overall vision for economic growth and the primary source of new jobs.[80]

The tourist economy integrates local and national growth strategies in a way that takes advantage of a favorable currency exchange rate, the region's natural beauty, and large surplus of cheap labor. It is Cape Town's climate, geography, capacity, and affordability (for tourists) that make a tourist economy possible, but it is the national growth strategy, the promise of profits, and declining financial support that makes it desirable and ensures that the tourist industry will receive considerable political backing. Tourism fits neatly into market-driven reform, according to its proponents, because it can serve as

the engine of growth, capable of dynamising and rejuvenating other sectors of the economy. It is the world's largest generator of employment opportunities; builds cross cultural relations and is a vital force for peace as well as a foreign exchange generator par excellence.[81]

This rosy perspective is echoed in the ANC's own draft document from October 1998, *A Development Oriented Growth Path for the Western Cape*, where it indicated its own plans for the province:

An ANC-led provincial government will take active steps to boost tourism in our province. Tourism is a major driver for economic growth with enormous potential to create employment and income for our people. In order to maximise this potential it is necessary to develop all forms of tourism.[82]

Although there are tourist attractions throughout the province, the city of Cape Town is the center of the tourist trade, as is evident from the number of restaurants, accommodations, and other tourist-related infrastructure. The international airport is just outside the downtown area, and most travelers, even if they are going on to other parts of the province, will spend at least some time in the city itself. Cape Town has a number of tourist attractions: the city center—a relatively small area of shops, cafés, restaurants, hotels, backpackers, and clubs—Robben Island, Table Mountain, the Castle of Good Hope, Kirstenbosch Gardens, the V and A Waterfront, essentially a large mall close to the city center, and museums and government buildings.

The industry is overlaid on the preexisting organization of space, resources, and state power, which are the legacies of the city's history of political struggle. Concerns over the development potential that tourism holds mirror a wider concern with market-driven growth more generally: that development is being too narrowly defined and that it risks falling into rather than filling the many ruts created by centuries of settler colonialism and decades of state planning. Superimposed upon these deep structures, the tourist industry, whose profitability is dependent on image and an ability to appeal to the fickle tastes of an affluent foreign audience, represents clearly the danger that new development may in fact be reproducing rather than dismantling the apartheid legacy of urban segregation, containment of the poor, and control of their labor. Xolile Gophe, a local councillor from the black African township of Langa, observes that development defined in this way creates "new barriers of social exclusion, reinforces racial divisions, accentuates economic disadvantage and unemployment and forces the poor to squat."[83] These growth strategies, the opposition they provoke, and the state's response are for many of the township social movements reminiscent of a very recently departed apartheid and evidence that the social, political, and economic contradictions of the previous era remain dangerously vital.[84]

The push to further develop tourism has led some critics to argue that the city has become overly concerned with crime that impacts the industry and neglectful of crime that does not. The significance of tourism for understanding the crime/development relationship lies precisely in its reliance on a "clean and safe" image for the city. Indeed, the 2003–04 Annual Police Plan of the Cape Town City Police makes special mention of crime and tourism. The Plan states:

> It is widely accepted that Cape Town is the country's premier international tourist destination. This perception is extremely important for the City. As high levels of crime and grime in the business district and tourist areas pose a direct threat to this industry which represents the livelihood of thousands of Capetonians, its protection will always be a factor that influences the policing environment.

It is in this sense that the tourist economy and its relationship to crime in Cape Town are indicative of a much broader trend in urban planning for the city, whereby crime is identified as the primary obstacle or challenge to development, and in turn shapes—some would say distorts—governance.

There are in fact a number of clearly stated policies and plans for general urban governance, most of which explicitly address the crime problem, and some of which are essentially crime-combating plans that adopt a language of development. The major initiative in Cape Town is the IDP, the five-year plan that guides budget priorities and the overall allocation of resources. The 2002 IDP (and the related City Development Plan) identified four priority areas for the city over the next five years: the prevention of crime, the combating of HIV/AIDS, the promotion of economic development and tourism, and the provision of free lifeline services, i.e., water and electricity.[85] Cape Town police chief Mark Sangster pointed out at the time that the number one strategic priority, as identified by the IDP, was crime prevention and that the continued success of the tourist industry in particular is dependent upon proactive management of "the challenges and problems created by the criminal elements operating within the City and surrounding areas."[86] He then summarizes the four substrategies for crime prevention, which will guide future city spending. They are: securing the CBD, promoting investment in the CBD, optimal utilization of the city's existing law enforcement and traffic services (containment strategy), and enhancement of the city's law enforcement capability through the establishment of the city police service (as distinct from the national police, the SAPS). Sangster's emphasis, which simply reflects the priorities clearly spelled out by city planning documents, is on crime as it impacts the development of the city's more affluent inner core.

This is not to say there are not other priorities, but it does raise questions as to the extent to which a limited budget can address these as well. And already the specific crime/development relationship, the approach to crime reduction, and the definition of development contained within the IDP have all come under heavy criticism by civil society organizations in Cape Town precisely because of these concerns. That many Cape Flats communities and their advocates feel the new development agenda may leave them behind as a renewable pool of cheap labor is now undeniable.[87] As such, what is already a less than amicable relationship between township communities and government threatens to worsen in the near future, especially around the issues of service delivery and policing. This shift, whether on a national or a local level, signals a disjuncture between the stated development/security strategy of government and the direction of criminal justice reform. As we will see in the following chapters, there emerged in the late 1990s dual policing strategies: one for "visible" areas and another for "invisible" areas. Tourists and shoppers in Cape Town's CBD are thus more likely to experience the police as "bobbies on the beat"; in less economically viable areas, on the other hand, whether operations are directed against gangs or against rebellious communities, a very different kind of policing is practiced.

What is emerging is a set of multiple discourses around crime and development, some contradictory, which both reflect and drive the actual practice of crime fighting in the city. Despite a commitment to taking a balanced approach to crime prevention, the evidence suggests that a situation is emerging in Cape Town in which concerns for security in the neoliberal sense are taking precedence over real development for the majority of the city's residents. The various city improvement programs and overall tourist-oriented development have already come under criticism from a number of sectors for channeling energy and resources into geographically small sections of the city, primarily the CBD, the V and A Waterfront, and other commercial areas, while neglecting others. Development is defined in this approach as making tourist and commercial areas clean and safe so that they will attract investment, middle-class consumers, and tourists. In terms of policing and crime combating, this emphasis draws heavily on limited police resources and leads to their uneven distribution, favoring a particular type of law enforcement, one that is driven by market forces rather than the dictates of social development. The CBD, for example, is a relatively small area, but is patrolled by seven different public and private law enforcement agencies. This represents an imbalance in the province as a whole, where the ANC itself has claimed the police per capita ratio is 1/600 in white areas and 1/4,000 in black African and coloured areas.[88] Unequal distribution of this sort can too easily lead to and, indeed, signify already existent discriminatory policing and selective law enforcement agendas, with police disproportionately deployed to places like the city center to filter traffic into high-visibility commercial areas.

Indeed, there is already a belief among many youth workers and advocates for the poor that revitalization of the CBD in particular has taken on an exclusionary character. This is the subject of the next chapter, which looks specifically at the question of urban renewal in the CBD in relation to the controversy over street children and the crimes with which they have become associated. Chapters 3 and 4 then examine the development of policing in the Cape Flats in the context of gang and vigilante violence. Finally, chapter 5 continues the discussion of the Cape Flats but focuses on the developmental aspects of the area and on youth in particular. What emerges over the next four chapters is the picture of a fractured city in which current approaches to crime, development, and security pose the risk of cementing the rifts created by apartheid. Although the opportunities for changes in direction do exist and are being pursued daily by many dedicated community activists and youth workers—sometimes in productive partnerships with officials and police—the push to make Cape Town world class is proving to have considerable momentum. At this point it is still too early to tell how these conflicts will play out, but what is clear is that the struggle over urban space and resources will define the city for some time to come.

2

Children in the Streets: Urban Governance
in Cape Town City Center

*Government has not done a damn thing for me lately. I often wonder
whether we actually exist or whether we're just that almost-half-of-the-nation
that shows up only on sets of stats. Politicians acknowledge me, sure, but
as a nuisance, a threat, a black mark on their dreams. But they don't know
me, they don't feel my needs or understand what scares me. And yet we
simply want what you wanted when you were young. We want to grow up
and live fairly comfortably, without fear, without having to watch our backs
all the time.*

—George Hill Siyaya

One legacy of youth leadership in the antiapartheid struggle after 1976
was that large numbers of young people, by virtue of taking to the streets,
sacrificed their individual futures for that of their country. The continued evocation by politicians of youth development as a national priority
is a reminder of this now historical, as well as historic, reality. A focus on
the apartheid generation and its struggle, however, deserved as it is, may
obscure a much deeper, and perhaps more powerful, current in the country's history, the marginalization of black youth. Although the specifics of
youth marginalization, including responses by young people, have varied
over time, marginalization itself continues to be a defining feature of the
nation's socioeconomic and political landscape. The country seems as far
from overcoming this challenge today as it has ever had been; indeed, the
realignments of South African society in an era of neoliberal governance
are more likely to reproduce rather than reverse the disempowerment and
underdevelopment of youth. Animating this process is a troubling narrative that has shown a remarkable ability to survive and adapt throughout the many periods of South African history, a narrative in which the
tensions, conflicts, and anxieties born of a society organized by white
supremacy are expressed through a language and imagery of danger,
crime, and security.

Black youth in South Africa's cities have played an outsized role in this drama, an ironic situation in which their marginalization is at the same time the source of a particular kind of power. The apartheid state and the opposition forces both recognized this after the youth rebellion launched in Soweto in 1976, in which the older narrative was reinterpreted to celebrate black youth for many of the very same reasons that whites feared them. From the vantage point of the present, however, we can see that this was itself a transition phase; today, the old narrative seems to have returned, transforming youth from heroes to problems. A close look at the intersection of youth, crime, and development in the city thus constitutes an important site for tracing the trajectory of urban governance and the politics of urban inequality across time and political eras. To this end, the following chapters explore this intersection as it currently plays out across the varied spaces of Cape Town, juxtaposing the governance of security in its affluent core to the very different, though intimately related, governance of the underdeveloped periphery. To begin, this chapter opens with a brief discussion of the situation of youth in the country generally and in the Western Cape specifically, providing an overview of what has happened to them since 1994, their current socioeconomic status and their relationship to crime as both victims and perpetrators. The chapter then turns to the affluent city center, the politics of youth representation, and the ongoing efforts to secure what many see as the key to Cape Town's economy and its world class status as we view the urban revitalization of downtown through the conflict over the existence of a modest population of street children.

The chapter provides detailed analysis of neoliberal governance in the urban core, where street children have emerged as central subjects. Although the township *skollie* ("gangster/thug" in Afrikaans) is the more infamous and numerous character from the urban periphery, street children came to play a similar role as a governmental category, retailored for the very different sociospatial realities of the core but similarly representing a target of security governance. Here we see how through categories and vocabularies of neoliberal governance, the black threat is rearticulated in ways more appropriate to a democratic era. The emergent narrative of urban renewal and revitalization—and threats to them—contains embedded, locally understood racial codes that remain central to maintaining tight control over urban space. The state continues to play an important role in providing both policing personnel and legitimate government authority through municipal bylaws, but private and quasi-private governance networks, representing powerful local political actors and economic interests, take a more active and prominent role through the city improvement district model. The use of the improvement district itself, as well as the "broken windows" approach to revitalization and crime reduction that shapes policing within it, underscores the transnational character of this version of neoliberal governance in the central city, replicating as it does, at least in the abstract, forms pioneered in the democratic urban North. Finally, the chapter shows how profoundly urban spaces, physically and socially, can be shaped by neoliberal governance. In addition to attracting a certain kind of investment capital, aimed primarily at tourist and other commercially oriented infrastructure and services, neoliberal governance creates a new sociopolitical landscape, in which citizenship and belonging are mediated by markets as much as by formal political institutions. The examination of street children in the city center raises disturbing questions about the extent to which democracy, as in the right to freely occupy public spaces, for example, has any real meaning for marginalized young black people in a world class city.[1]

Youth in Transition

The changes inaugurated by the negotiations represented a great achievement for South Africa, but as the twentieth century drew to a close, the new state was burdened from the start with the problems of an old society. The government, now led by the African National Congress (ANC), inherited the deep tensions and contradictions that had defined the nation for generations, and was now expected to begin the process of resolving them. The early transition period, though, found the country in the midst of ongoing chaos. Although the struggle against apartheid was officially complete, political violence and the forces mobilized to carry it out were very much alive. However, in the context of shifting political leadership, the absence of clear battle lines, and the uncertainty inherent in the transition process, violence began to diffuse. Clashes continued among covert apartheid security forces, the military, police, criminal gangs, and people's militias, resulting in continued instability and insecurity. More broadly, the nonmilitary organs of people's power remained active and vibrant in township communities across the country, looking to formalize the role of the people and civil society in the transition process. At the center of much of this action were youth, who had in one way or another been deeply affected by the war, as soldiers, as victims, as witnesses. When formal democracy came to South Africa in 1994 and the township rebellions had served their purpose, the country suddenly found itself populated by millions upon millions of young people who had given up or had had normal lives taken from them to join the struggle against apartheid. Many of them, having sacrificed for years to fight white supremacy and endured horrible violence and trauma, now faced the prospect of a future with no jobs and no education and with communities still wracked by crime and violence.

The new government was fully aware of the debt it owed to the "young lions," and as early as 1992's "Ready to Govern" initiative, the ANC committed to taking special care in addressing the needs of these youth. Both "Ready to Govern" and, to a lesser extent, the Reconstruction and Development Programme acknowledged this commitment and recognized that for South Africa to move forward, young people would have to be brought from the margins into the center of the new society, as integral builders of that society. Subsequently, the early years of the transition saw many policy papers, discussions, and committees formed around making these commitments a reality, and public sympathy for the plight of youth was high. As crime came to dominate the headlines, however, and 1994 receded further into the past, much of this sympathy withered, and young people today find themselves largely abandoned by the society around them. In what is probably the most comprehensive evaluation of youth development initiatives and the general commitment to youth, David Everatt tracked the steady demobilization of youth in the early and mid-90s and the eventual bureaucratization of youth organizations by the end of the decade. Already by 1992, youth involvement in political organizations had begun to decline as the nature of the struggle began to change.[2] Everatt argues that as the negotiations wore on, youth began to drift away from the political organizations, because their particular contribution was no longer needed and because political leaders often treated youth mobilization "like a tap that could be switched off and on as the vagaries of the negotiating process demanded," with the result that consistent participation and development of the organizations into poststruggle organs of power were undermined.[3] No alternatives to the political structures were offered, however, leaving young people to find their own way in what was a chaotic and fast-changing climate. By the mid- to late 1990s, perceptions of youth were already slipping back into old channels: "When youth were addressed as a sector, it was generally in the context of the threat they were seen to represent, rather than the complexities and needs of the generation."[4] Overall youth initiatives and structures received little of the support they would have needed to reintegrate young people and prepare them to thrive in the new South Africa; Everatt and others conclude that by the end of the decade, virtually all of them had collapsed.[5]

The abandonment of youth may push them further to the margins of the social order, but as became obvious in the era of late-apartheid, this does not strip them of their power entirely. The sometimes violent response of young people, expressed prominently through Umkhonto we Sizwe (MK, "Spear of the Nation"), the ANC's armed wing, and the township paramilitary organizations, was a response to structural violence committed against them by the state and the daily reality of their lives under apartheid. At the same time, it was also informed by other forms of violence that have received less attention but are proving just as insidious. Neglect, physical and sexual abuse, and domestic and gang violence have generative powers of their own, and these remain entrenched in many communities. This has led a number of observers to note that while youth violence may have played a crucial role in the struggle, now, in the new era, the older generation is reluctant to take responsibility for the fall-out of sanctioned violence and the reality that for many youth, the line between legitimate political violence and illegitimate violence is not, nor was it ever, entirely clear.[6]

After 1994, and especially after the 1996 elections, the relationship between youth violence and the state understandably changed, but many of the conditions young people faced did not: What had formerly been an asset had suddenly become a liability. Although their heroism was being celebrated, at the same time youth were told it was now time to go back to school, back to the townships, and get on with their lives. Graeme Simpson, former director of the Johannesburg-based Centre for the Study of Violence and Reconciliation, commented:

There is an unfortunate irony that in the shift which took place in South Africa, from the politics of confrontation to the politics of negotiation, this very youth constituency—which had carved out a place of belonging through political organization—was once again remarginalised as the struggle moved from the

streets to the boardroom, and from the hands of these young foot
soldiers, to those of a largely grey haired or balding, primarily
male and exile based community of negotiators. On the very eve
of liberation—which so strongly symbolised their victories and
sacrifices—these youngsters, who had grown up on the streets,
were encouraged to go back to school at a time when the snail's
pace nature of transformation meant that little or nothing has
actually changed in the historically oppressive schoolroom.[7]

The problem of youth violence, or the problematization of youth
violence, became a source of tension early on due to the delicacy of the
negotiations and the more militant tendencies of youth political formations relative to the ANC.[8] This tension was recognized and exploited
by the mainstream print media of the day as a way of tempering the
demands and undermining the unity of the mass democratic movement. South African sociologist Jeremy Seekings, based on his research
of a number of major English-language newspapers with a predominantly white readership, argues that the image of violent black youth
was used by the white-controlled media during the transition to
manipulate white anxiety about the ANC, the negotiations, and the
imminent shift of power. This coverage acted as an influence on the
negotiation process, adding pressure on the ANC to exercise a control
over the township rebellions that they did not necessarily possess.[9]

Youth militancy and young people's use of violence were thus complex phenomena, representing a threat not only to the apartheid state but
also, potentially, to the negotiation process, ANC control of that process,
and a smooth transfer of power. The ANC was now in the position of
having to rein in the young lions who had made the townships ungovernable throughout the 1980s. What had recently been understood and
applauded as politically essential radicalism was in the process of transforming into an association with general *disorder*. The same capacity to
make the townships ungovernable, which made the youth constituency
celebrated as heroes, would soon emerge in the new South Africa as the
greatest threat to the democratic transition in the form of crime and gangsterism. As the struggle fades into memory and the youth of that era are
replaced by a new generation, young people are much more likely to be
viewed with confusion, if not hostility. While the image of heroic youth
slips into history, the largely negative perception of young people as out of

control has survived the dramatic changes of the last ten years. According to Everatt, the most frequently asked question in the media among many former activists and others in the decade following apartheid's demise was: "What is wrong with the youth?"[10]

The reemergence of negative representations over the first postapartheid decade speaks to the power of deep historical currents in the country. The imagery of the *swart gevaar,* or "black menace," stretches far back into South Africa's past, and the image of urban, "detribalized" young black man in the late 1980s and early 1990s was only the most recent version of this old figure.[11] The pattern continues in urban South Africa today, with gangs and street children the two most prevalent manifestations of a growing public anxiety related to the nation's large youth population, high crime, social inequality, and the transition process. That youth have become the scapegoat for many of the challenges the country faces is neither surprising nor unique; rather this representation has appeared in many contemporary societies, where youth, especially in times of change or transformation, are constructed as a social problem that gives rise to new forms of social control.[12] The reemergence of "youth deviance" as a postapartheid problem can therefore be linked to the turmoil of the transition as much as to the struggle against apartheid. This phenomenon of stigmatizing marginalized youth is one of the most significant dangers facing South Africa today. What we are witnessing is youth themselves increasingly being viewed in the context of an alleged deviance ascribed to them by others, and being treated as problems to be solved.[13] Whereas the languages used to express these anxieties and through which to create and justify responses have varied over time, the themes of crime, security, and disorder have always figured prominently in the vocabulary.

Youth, Crime, and Underdevelopment in Postapartheid Cape Town

Although political organizations capable of engaging youth on a large scale have slowly fallen by the wayside, gangs and other criminal organizations remain active and well organized. Combined with the abysmal state of youth development, the situation for too many young people today is dire. South Africa is actually a very young country, and according to the 2000 census, 53 percent of South Africans are below the age of 25, whereas in Cape Town 52 percent of the population is under 30. These young people have been particularly hard hit by the economic crisis of the post-1994 period. A national survey of 2,500 youth conducted by the Community Agency for Social Enquiry (CASE) in 2002 found that of those who were economically active, 53 percent were unemployed and only 35 percent were employed full time. The national unemployment rate was a staggering 70 percent for black African youth, whereas the survey reports unemployment at 42 percent for coloured youth nationally, 33 percent for Asian youth, and 10 percent for white youth.[14] When asked whether the job situation had improved or worsened since 1994, 77 percent of black African and 85 percent of coloured respondents said it had worsened.

Seventy-two percent of the young people surveyed by CASE identified joblessness as the number one reason their peers became involved with crime, and another 8 percent blamed poverty. As with the survey of adults conducted by the Institute for Democracy in South Africa (Idasa), jobs were the most pressing issue for black South African youth, and were less of a concern for white youth. Only 16 percent of whites said that jobs were a key problem, whereas 45 percent of black Africans, 31 percent of coloureds, and 35 percent of Asians said so. The proportions are close to reversed on the issue of crime. Thirty-seven percent of white respondents identified it as a key problem compared with 11 percent of black Africans, 20 percent of coloureds, and 18 percent of Asians. Interestingly, given the attention that gangs receive from the media, public officials, and law enforcement, gangs were not mentioned at all by black African, Asian, or white youth, and only 4 percent of coloureds identified them as a key problem.

However, the crime/youth nexus in South Africa, as in so many other places, is considered important not because of what young people think about crime, but because of the relationship between age and criminality. Although it is regularly acknowledged that youth are disproportionately the victims of crime, criminologists argue that they are also responsible for the majority of crimes committed, with young unemployed men in particular singled out as primary perpetrators and victims.[15] While the significant underreporting of crimes against women and girls puts into question the extent to which the latter is true, there is little dispute within the field of criminology on the former. Summing up the conventional wisdom in criminological and law enforcement circles, D. J. Smith writes: "Probably the most important single fact about crime is that it is committed mainly by teenagers and young adults."[16] Blaming most crime on youth, however, uncritically accepts what are to some extent arbitrary, if highly political, distinctions, and with great consequence.[17]

The general drift away from the principles of progressive criminal justice reform and social crime prevention discussed earlier is evident in the juvenile justice field as well. According to criminologist Dirk van Zyl Smit, although juvenile justice received more attention than any other criminal justice issue early in the transition, there was little in the way of measurable results.[18] Some of the most egregious aspects of the old system, such as corporal punishment, have been eliminated, but overall the earlier commitment to an approach to reform driven by human and children's rights is being replaced by the more crime control–driven approach that marks criminal justice reform in general.[19] Most troubling—and telling—was that the numbers of youth and juveniles going to prison began to rise after 1994, despite some admirably worded legislation and the consistent efforts of juvenile justice workers to keep juveniles out through diversion programs and other alternatives to incarceration. The long-awaited Child Justice Bill, introduced only in August 2002, was finally signed into law in May 2009, but it will be some time before we see whether government's commitment to diversion and restorative justice has a different fate than earlier reform measures.[20]

After a period of decline, the overall number of juveniles in prison jumped 158 percent between 1995 and 2000, the highest increase by age category. By 2006, almost half (42 percent) of the prison population was under the age of 25, just as the image of youth was undergoing its own transformation, and media coverage of the enormous crime problem was consistently linking it with the so-called lost generation of black youth.[21] The majority of offenses for which youth were arrested during this time were property related, although the proportion of sentences for violent crimes also increased.[22] By 1999 there were 26,000 juveniles in prison, an increase of 6,000 from 1996, many of them simply awaiting trial.[23] According to the Department of Correctional Services, at the end of 2005 there were 62,000 youth aged between fourteen and twenty five in prison, almost 25,000 of which were awaiting trial; of these almost 3,000 were under the age of eighteen. Statistics for the year ending 2007 showed 63,738 youth in prison, constituting 38 percent of the entire prison population, but by 2009 the number had declined to 57,000, the vast majority of whom are between the ages of eighteen and twenty five. All of these figures are for men and women; however, women make up only 2 percent of the overall prison population.[24]

Figures from the Western Cape indicate that trends there mirror those on a national level. Although it accounts for only 10 percent of the national population, the province incarcerated more than 17 percent of total prison inmates, both sentenced and unsentenced, in 2008, second only to Gauteng, home to 19.7 percent of the total population and 27.7 percent of the total prison population.[25] Many of these inmates are youth. In 2008, of the 18,900 sentenced inmates in the Western Cape, 5,700 were youth, defined by Correctional Services as between the ages of eighteen and twenty-five, and 168 were children, defined as under the age of eighteen. Youth and children in the province thus comprise 17 percent of the national total of sentenced youth and almost one third (31 percent) of all prisoners in the province, slightly above the national average.[26] Statistics on sentenced youth, however, tell only a portion of the story. According to the Correctional Services Web site (which defines youth as between the ages of fourteen and twenty-five), 45 percent of incarcerated youth nationally were awaiting trial in 2009; that is, they had yet to be sentenced. Figures for the Western Cape are not available, but the provincial figure is likely close to this, meaning possibly 2,000 more youth were imprisoned that year than are reflected in the sentenced provincial statistics. Furthermore, youth awaiting trial tend to spend between three and nine months in prison before they are released or sentenced, according to youth workers I spoke with who were active at Cape Town's Pollsmoor prison in 2004, suggesting that the total number of unsentenced youth who spend time in prison in any given year is higher than counts at a certain point in time would suggest. This is especially relevant because the low figure of sentenced children may give a false impression about the numbers of young people below the age of eighteen who experience prison. Based on trips taken to Pollsmoor between 2002 and 2004, the section housing those aged fourteen to seventeen awaiting trial was always very overcrowded, dangerously so according to youth workers, and saw high turnover. Although there may have been only 168 sentenced children in prison throughout the province in 2008, the total number of youth under eighteen who spend at least some time in prison each year is undoubtedly much higher.

Beyond actual imprisonment, the sheer number of young people arrested each year in the province highlights the extent to which aggressive policing and a war on crime in practice means that more youth are brought into contact with the criminal justice system. As with incarceration, youth and children in the Cape, and primarily from the city, are arrested out of all proportion to their numbers in the nation as a whole. Furthermore, these numbers increased during the first half of the decade at the same time that law enforcement and urban renewal efforts, in the wake of the antiterror campaign of 1996–2000, were on the rise. Data compiled by the National Institute for Crime Prevention and Reintegration of Offenders (NICRO), a nongovernmental organization (NGO), show that in 1999 police in the province arrested 36,700 children, defined as age nineteen and under. The number dropped the next year to 31,000, but in 2001 climbed again to 32,900. Halfway through 2002, the last year for which figures were available as of this writing, the number of children arrested stood at 20,000, with predictions that it would hit 41,000 by the end of that year.[27] Although the proportion of children from the Cape arrested dropped from 32 percent of the national total in 1999 to 24 percent in 2001 and 2002, more children are arrested in the province than anywhere else in the country. The rising rate of arrests between 2000 and 2002 and the overall increase in imprisonment indicate that the drop in proportion is more a function of faster rate increases in other provinces than of successful diversions or other interventions in the Western Cape.

The raw number of arrests in the Cape is still sadly remarkable given that according to the census, there are only 1.6 million children in the Western Cape, compared with 2.8 million in Gauteng, 3.1 million in the Eastern Cape, and 4.3 million in KwaZulu Natal. Using the NICRO estimate for 2002, this means that 2.5 percent of children in the Cape had been arrested that year. Because the statistic covers the ages zero years to nineteen, the proportion is obviously higher if we exclude those children who reasonably would not be arrested. For example, using census figures, if we excluded those children age nine and younger, the proportion is 4.7 percent. Although children in the Western Cape make up only 8.5 percent of children nationally, they represent just under 25 percent of those arrested. It is also important to point out that these numbers exclude much of the youth demographic, those aged twenty to twenty-five. The evidence we do have is overwhelming, however, in pointing to the extent to which young people are increasingly being swept up in the criminal justice net as the war on crime drags on.

Increased contact between youth and the criminal justice system, particularly arrest and detention, is of special significance because the evidence suggests that it contributes to the reasons some youth become involved with crime in the first place: violence-related psychological trauma and social marginalization. The available evidence suggests that from arrest to detention, the criminal justice system is a source of trauma for young people, just as it was in the 1970s and 1980s, a troubling reality for a country desperately trying to curb crime. A NICRO survey of children who had come into contact with the system found that "[m]ost of the participants had a negative perception of the police, describing the experience of being arrested as . . . frightening, confusing and humiliating. Physical assault was also reported."[28] Once in prison, where gang rule, sexual assault, and beatings are normal parts of everyday life, the situation only worsens. Sadly, the experiences of children inside the system in many ways mirror the violence they often see or are subject to in their homes and neighborhoods. For those youth who do come into conflict with the law, either because they have committed a crime or because they are falsely arrested, the criminal justice system only exposes them to another round of trauma before they are released. The context in which so many children are brought into contact with the criminal justice system, or simply confronted with the force of urban security structures, is no longer racial apartheid, but a form of security governance that is rooted in a new urban politics, in which the transgressive presence of black youth remains central. In the next section we look at how neoliberal governance through urban revitalization of the city's core contributes to this criminalization of black youth.

Securing the Core: Street Children and Moral Panic in the Central Business District

The city government of Cape Town has openly endorsed a market-driven approach to economic growth since at least the mid-1990s, over the objections of many urban residents and community organizations, and this commitment exercises a profound influence on urban governance. At the heart of the city's vision is the Central Business District (CBD), the affluent downtown at the foot of Table Mountain reserved exclusively for whites under the Group Areas Act. The Act was amended in 1984 to allow for commercial and professional use by all races in the interests of "free trade," but the area has remained predominantly white according to the 2001 census.[29] The CBD was chosen by city officials and the business sector as the flagship of the city's revitalization campaign by virtue of the economic power it represents, a power that is a direct consequence of the privileged status the downtown received under apartheid.[30] According to the influential *Cape Times*, reporting on plans for the city in 2001:

> [I]n as much as other nodes should be accorded equal status, the need to revitalise and regenerate the Cape Town CBD is widely accepted by both the public and private sectors as a major and serious priority. This stems from the belief that central precinct is the main locus of the region's historical, cultural, political and social attributes. It is the principal driver of the Western Cape's economy accounting for 28 percent of all jobs in the metropole, and is accordingly a major area of focus for the [city] council.[31]

Considered by some a "no-go" area as late as 2000, the CBD is now held up as an example of successful urban renewal by the city and its partners in the private sector. Crime is down, investment is up, and shoppers and tourists generally report satisfaction with the overall security situation. The turnaround thus provides an important site for understanding the relationship between urban neoliberalism and the security practices often associated with it in affluent spaces. The change in the CBD is the result of a process that began in the late 1990s, as crime became more and more of a pressing political issue in the city and fears were high that the downtown would degenerate into another Johannesburg.[32] The city's attempt to retake the CBD, spurred in part by pressure from the private sector to safeguard the tourist indus-try in particular, came in the form of Operation Clean and Safe and Operation Reclaim in August 1998 and May 1999, respectively, the latter a year before Operation Crackdown was launched nationally. According to criminologist Bill Dixon, both Cape Town operations deployed large numbers of police into the CBD primarily to target minor offenses, from illegal parking to traffic violations.

Operation Clean and Safe alone involved 400 municipal law officers and 30 members of the South African Police Service (SAPS), who together made more than 20 arrests, gave citations for 2,644 traffic violations, and confiscated more than 3,000 items from traders working in illegal areas.[33] Operation Reclaim, which targeted parking attendants and their custom-ers, was originally slated to last three to six months but had to be called off early because officers were needed in other areas. In both cases, the obvious problem, as Dixon's research has shown, is that these types of operations are unsustainable and require more resources than the city currently controls, even when covering what is a very small, if valued, slice of the city. Furthermore, Dixon points out that the saturation of the CBD with police, although similar in some respects to U.S.-style order maintenance or zero-tolerance policing, was not intended to act as a catalyst that would eventually reduce serious crime. He writes, "Indeed, if any ulterior motive did lie behind the operations it was the preservation and development of Cape Town's CBD as the economic heart of the Cape metropolitan area."[34] Despite their limitations, however, the operations certainly signaled that the city was serious about rescuing downtown and had decided what the primary challenge to this mission would be. From the very beginning, city authorities insisted that establishing security had to precede redevelopment, setting the tone for the following years of urban renewal.

The turnaround process was institutionalized through the formation of the Cape Town Partnership in 1999, the same year as the ill-fated Operation Reclaim. The Partnership is a public/private organization, its membership drawn primarily from the ranks of property owners, business groups, and the city tourism board, although local government and the NGO sector also have representation. Its overarching objective is to transform Cape Town into a world-class city through, in its own words, the "branding, positioning, marketing and establishment of [Cape Town] as a globally competitive city with a globally competitive product offering," although, tellingly, its mandate is confined to the CBD.[35] As part of the transformation process, the Partnership created the Central City Improvement District (CCID) in the center of the CBD in November 2000, designating it as a zone for growth and renewal. Development of the CCID, inspired by international "best practice" from the United States and the United Kingdom, would be achieved by attracting private investment. The Partnership has made clear that accomplishing this goal would require making safety and security the first priority of the renewal effort, primarily in the form of crime reduction.[36] Consequently, in the first year 50 percent of CCID funding went to securing the area, a percentage that has remained consistent up to the present. Six million rand was quickly invested to that end and 120 Community Patrol Officers and other security operatives were assigned to police the area.[37] In that same month, the city's Protection Services Department took full control of the closed circuit television (CCTV) system from Business Against Crime, which had been running the system, and established a 24-hour, 32-member rapid response unit. Business Against Crime was formed in 1996 at the urging of President Mandela to enlist the business community in fighting crime and boosting confidence, investment, and job creation. The Western Cape branch of the organization had initially proposed the CCTV system for downtown in the late 1990s for the failed 2004 Olympic bid, but then reintroduced it into the city council as a measure to improve public safety, especially for tourists.[38] The city's takeover in 2000, however, included an important shift from previous public safety practices focused on crime prevention: "[T]he cameras were now being used to monitor and prosecute not only criminal offences but also a host of traffic offences and municipal by-laws."[39]

This change reflected an explicit focus on "quality of life" policing, and the new approach consciously, and often eagerly, borrows from the experiences of a number of cities in the global North, including New York City under Mayor Rudy Giuliani and police chief William Bratton, who had already visited South Africa as a consultant.[40] These changes were consistent with the city's neoliberal development approach in principle but also reflected the experiences of many who came into the city on a regular basis. For example, in 2000, a survey conducted for the Cape Town Partnership by Roots Research of 600 people who worked in or visited the city found that 74 percent of the disproportionately white respondents said the presence of the homeless, and of street children specifically, was unacceptable.[41] The responses only confirmed what officials had been arguing for some time. Indeed, the subsequent formal and informal policies of the city in the CBD have quite openly asserted the alleged negative impact of homelessness and vagrancy on urban renewal. True to form, Cape Town planners from early on demonstrated an intent to combat both crime and grime, adopting and adapting the aspects of the controversial order maintenance, or "broken windows," policing from the United States and the United Kingdom, attention to relatively minor infractions or violations of "public order" is seen as key to preserving or restoring the integrity of the neighborhood in question, and preventing the emergence of a more dangerous lawlessness.

The borrowing of policing strategies from the United States is in fact part of a broader overlap in approaches to urban renewal, of which security and policing are only one central component. Broken-windows policing was itself conceived of originally not simply as a law enforcement strategy but as part of a more comprehensive development strategy for inner-city neighborhoods in the United States and the United Kingdom that explicitly linked revitalization to a certain form of security.[42] Revitalization, in turn, is defined along fairly explicit class lines that are often expressed most noticeably in debates around gentrification. A 1987 article from *Urban Land* magazine sums up neatly the basic dynamics of this process, and while it does not address the issue of policing directly, the role of law enforcement is not difficult to deduce. In a statement on sociospatial governance that could have come directly from the Partnership in 2000, N. David Miller writes:

> A downtown can be designed and developed to make visitors feel that it—or a significant portion of it—is attractive and the type of place that "respectable people" like themselves tend to frequent. . . . A core downtown area that is compact, densely developed and multifunctional will concentrate people, giving them more activities. . . . The activities offered in this core area will determine what "type" of people will be strolling its sidewalks; locating offices and housing for middle- and upper-income residents in or near the core area can assure a high percentage of "respectable", law-abiding pedestrians. Such an attractive redeveloped core area would also be large enough to affect the downtown's overall image[43]

Thus, when the Partnership looked westward for postapartheid models for urban renewal, what they saw was a fairly well put together package—at the ideological and operational levels—for retaking and remaking ground in danger of being "lost" to the black urban underclass as the national political system shifted from apartheid to neoliberal democracy. It is important to note that the revitalization effort functions not only by pulling in more affluent groups, but also, as Antje Nahnsen points out, by pushing out the poor. In her own work on the central city, she observes that the presence of informal traders and vendors serve to make the CBD functional to lower-income groups who may not be able to afford the upscale consumerism offered to more "respectable" people.[44] Elimination or overregulation of this economy thus has an impact beyond the vendors themselves that undermines the CBD as a social as well as economic space for lower-income people.

Figure 2. Greenmarket Square, an upscale pedestrian mall in Cape Town's central city. Cape Town, 2010. Photograph by Shannon Wentz.

The initial phase of the Partnership's renewal strategy produced results quickly, within six months, according to authorities. City police chief Mark Sangster estimated the drop in crime in the CDB during that brief period at 40 percent. Overall, the city claimed a 60 percent drop in crime and R4 billion in new investment between 2000 and 2002. By 2003 the police were making up to 700 arrests a month, mostly for offenses such as vagrancy, loitering, public drinking, urinating in public, and causing public disturbances, while investment continued to pour in.[45] The Partnership's contention that the area was well on its way to recovery was given an additional boost when a major foreign investor, Howard Eurocape, purchased seven major downtown properties that it planned to transform into residential and retail units, as well as a "six star" luxury hotel. According to company chairman Frank Gormley,

I have visited Cape Town many times and have been very impressed by what has been a remarkable turnaround in the CBD. We have had a great deal of experience and success in investing in property developments in CBDs of cities that have blossomed as a result of urban renewal, and we are absolutely committed to this project.[46]

Despite these accomplishments, however, the cleanup of the CBD was apparently not complete. A number of surveys conducted during this time found that while people generally felt safer, many nuisances remained, from petty crime to the petty hassles created by the poor who continued to live and/or attempt to earn money in the same places tourists and more affluent residents stay, shop, eat, and recreate. One survey conducted in 2002 found that 52 percent of respondents in the CBD felt that security was acceptable, up from 16.7 percent in 2000. However, when asked what their greatest complaint was, 71.6 percent singled out street children, with "vagrants and undesirable elements" the number two complaint. Street children had in fact, in the words of one local paper, become public enemy number one, occupying ground zero at the intersection of youth, crime, and development in the city's affluent core.[47] Even as safety and investment improved, city authorities and Partnership representatives spoke of street children using increasingly strident rhetoric.

"Street children" are children who live or spend a significant amount of time on the street, earn their livelihood from the street, and are inadequately cared for, protected, and supervised by responsible adults. Some may be permanently homeless, some may have occasional family contacts, and others may work the streets during the day and return home at night.[48] A report by the Cape Metro Council in 2000 put the number of street people in the city at 4,133, most of these women. Overall, according to the report, 782 of these were children, primarily between the ages of seven and eighteen.[49] In and around the CBD, the number of children on the street at any given time varies, and the Partnership in 2002 put the number at 120, while the estimate of the Department of Social Services was 250.[50] One experienced youth worker I spoke with said these numbers are largely guesswork and that reliable figures do not exist.[51]

Street children in Cape Town are predominantly boys of either black African or coloured background, mostly the latter, and they come to the CBD and surrounding areas primarily from nearby townships.[52] Given their relatively small numbers, it may seem surprising how much of the blame they bore for the CBD's renewal challenges in 2002. However, as the "urban terror" of the Cape Flats war among gangs, the police, and the vigilante group People Against Gangsterism and Drugs (discussed in the next chapter) was driven back onto the Cape Flats and urban renewal in the inner city began in earnest, the Partnership turned its attention to petty crime and grime, which it increasingly linked to the presence of street children and other destitute black people. The Station Commissioner for the Cape Town Central Police referred to street children and vagrants as the CBD's biggest problem, and Michael Farr, chief executive of the Partnership at the time, blamed more than half the crime in the area on these children. The Partnership stated in 2002 that street children and informal parking attendants had cost the city R300 million in investment.[53] These and other reports as well as coverage by local newspapers often served to reinforce this link between crime and street children. When the city deliberated on the need for a now established municipal police force, street children and vagrants who "make people fearful" were cited as primary reasons by security experts for the need for such a force.[54] The emerging politics of urban renewal in the CBD and the menace of street children seemed to once again rest on the specter of a black menace in the heart of downtown. The resulting moral panic marked a crucial point in the wider social conflict over urban resources and the use of urban spaces that continued to scar the postapartheid city.

Sociologist Jeremey Seekings, in his work on media representations of black youth during the negotiations, explicitly refers to white anxiety during that period as constituting a moral panic and notes that South African historians have often used the concept to describe urban and rural white anxieties about black masses. The concept of a moral panic employed by Seekings and others is informed by the work of criminologist Stanley Cohen. According to Cohen, a moral panic occurs when

> a condition, episode, person or group of persons emerges to
> become defined as a threat to societal values and interest; its nature
> is presented in a stylized and stereotypical fashion by the mass
> media; the moral barricades are manned by editors, bishops,
> politicians, and other right-thinking people.[55]

More recently in South Africa, researchers have begun to use the concept to refer to renewed anxiety by higher-income, still largely white urban and suburban residents in the face of high crime, the HIV/AIDS crisis, and a perceived general social disorder.[56] The following story is illustrative: On

May 10, 2002, the *Independent on Saturday*, a Durban-based paper, ran a story with the headline "AIDS' Legacy—Orphan Gangs Roam Inner Cities." The next day a Cape Town paper, the *Weekend Argus*, ran virtually the same story, this time with the headline "SA Cities under Threat from AIDS Orphan Gangs." The stories cited researchers and welfare agents warning of dire consequences if dramatic action were not taken immediately, and stressed the general threat with which society is faced, especially in urban areas. The *Argus* story warned, "Time is running out for South Africa to come to grips with the spectre of feral AIDS-orphan gangs roaming our city streets," while the *Independent* predicted that the deaths of parents from AIDS would turn city streets into no-go areas because of "bands of lawless children, armed to the teeth and rampaging for food and shelter, waging a war of survival against each other and society at large, much like a page from Lord of the Flies." The language of lawlessness and the evocation of *Lord of the Flies* are instructive. As Rachel Bray points out, the threat posed by street children emanates in large part from the fact that they thrive outside adult authority. The perception of youth criminality and deviance, she argues, is part of an underlying notion among (adult) society that

> childhood, and particularly youth, is a dangerous period of life. Young people are considered vulnerable, but also rebellious and potentially delinquent. For these reasons, there is a perceived need to organise and control the young in order to prevent social disorder.[57]

In the case of children, Bray continues, the source of disorder is the fact that they exist not only "outside" of society in general, but outside the primary institution of socialization, the family. Street children's existence outside the "family norm" thus makes them especially vulnerable, but also especially dangerous and powerfully symbolic of social breakdown. She further points out that, as with similar panics in the 1980s and 1990s, the evidence presented often relies on a relatively small number of sources, in some cases relying on one article that is cited again and again, resulting in a "circular, self-perpetuating discourse around cause and effect that is isolated from other relevant social debates."[58]

To get a better sense of how perceptions of black youth in the CBD were changing during the renewal period and how the "black menace" was being rearticulated post-1994, I surveyed Cape Town newspapers from 1999–2002, and again from 2004–05, after the Partnership had declared victory in the effort to reclaim the CBD. The survey was done through a search for stories about street children in the electronic archives of Independent News and Media (INM), an international media conglomerate based in Ireland and the largest newspaper chain in South Africa, publishers of the *Independent on Saturday* and the *Weekend Argus*. INM papers claim more than a 60 percent share of English-language newspapers in the country and a 64 percent share of metropolitan newspaper readers. Although there are newspapers published in various African languages and in Afrikaans, the English-language papers are read largely by higher-income urban residents, including decision makers and policymakers, and have substantial influence on the non-English-language papers.[59] In Cape Town, INM publishes three major English-language papers: the *Cape Argus,* the *Weekend Argus*, and the *Cape Times*, in addition to the *Sunday Independent* and fourteen smaller community papers; the readership of the three major papers is disproportionately white and affluent.[60] INM also publishes the Pretoria-based *Sunday Independent* and Johannesburg-based *Star*, both of which are fairly accessible in Cape Town as well.

The search was limited to the news section of the three primary English-language Cape Town papers. What it revealed was that there was a clear shift in the type of coverage that street children received during the first survey period. To capture the shifts, the stories were divided into three categories: those that portrayed street children as victims, those that portrayed them as part of the crime and disorder problem, and those that were either balanced or relatively neutral. All of the surveyed stories fit into one of these categories, although, significantly, many of those in the first category actually focused on those providing care to street children rather than on the children themselves (see Figure 3).

As Figure 3 shows, the period in which crime was decreasing and investment increasing was accompanied by sharp changes in the portrayals of street children. Negative stories jumped from just 28.6 percent of the total in 1999 to 60 percent in 2002, whereas stories framing them as victims fell from 71.4 percent to 30 percent over the same period. A closer look at the stories themselves reveals other points of interest and more detail on the links between the images and stereotypes of street children that readers of these papers were consuming, as well as continued marginalization of black youth. For example, although 1999 and 2000 both saw a high percentage of what can be considered sympathetic stories, many of these nevertheless portrayed street children as deviant: as child

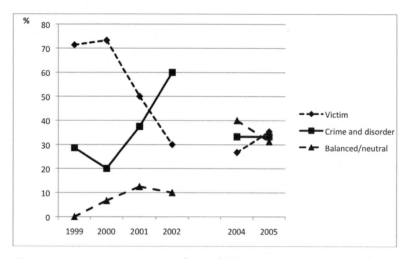

Figure 3. Newspaper representation of street children, 1999–2005. N = 110 (total sample size for all years combined). Data not available for 2003.

prostitutes and victims of sexual assault, drug addicts, and potential carriers of disease. Of the eleven victim stories in 2000, six involved child sex abuse and prostitution, including four stories covering one specific case of alleged pedophilia. Although it is clearly important that these abuses receive coverage, it is also true that such one-dimensional coverage, which defines street children within the context of abuse, addiction, and victimization, reinforces the stereotypes readers already have of them, perpetuating their status as a problem.[61] This in turn can contribute to their further marginalization and increase the chances for their coming into conflict with the law.[62] The majority of the sympathetic stories in these years focused on those individuals or organizations providing care to street children. Thus, for the most part, street children tended to be portrayed as passive victims, or their ability to act was reduced to their alleged propensity to commit crimes. In both cases they are constructed as subjects whose presence downtown is problematic and, more specifically, antithetical to the vision of who populates a world class city.

Stories that linked street children to crime generally discussed the types of crimes they are said to commit (muggings and smash-and-grabs, for example), the impact of these crimes, and therefore of street children, on the CBD's revitalization, or the general danger to public order that street children represent. The Cape Town Partnership and especially its chief executive at the time, Michael Farr, were often quoted in the Cape Town press blaming street children for much of the CBD's crime. In February 2002, when much of the CBD was in fact under Partnership direction and crime had reportedly dropped by 60 percent, Farr criticized authorities for failing to control street children, whom he referred to as "the greatest perpetrators of crime." The headline for the story in which he is quoted reads: "Homeless Children Holding City Centre in Grip of Crime."[63] In another story from the *Cape Times* of December 6, 2002, the headline reads: "Smash and Grab Attacks—Are You Next?" In this article, smash-and-grab attacks, robberies in which a car windshield is broken and valuables taken, often while the driver is waiting at a traffic signal, are blamed largely on juveniles and an overly lenient criminal justice system that fails to deter and detain. Farr is again quoted here, this time singling out "strollers," street children who come into the city in the morning and, in his words, "get up to no good during the day," as primary perpetrators. The cumulative effect of the presence of street children, as pointed out in the city security report I have cited, is to "make people fearful," and it is this aspect of their presence that was most prominent in media coverage of the issue during the 1999–2002 period.

Another of the themes throughout these stories, closely related to the power that street children are said to exercise over public space, is the negative impact that street children and other street dwellers were having on the area's revitalization. This theme, importantly, complements the position taken by a number of key city documents relating to renewal and the city's emphasis on the central role of crime reduction. A story from the November 9, 2000, *Cape Times* cites a poll of business owners in the CBD and reports that in general they agree that "reducing street children is imperative" if the area is to be made safe and "if Cape Town hopes to meet its goals of stimulating investment, ensuring business confidence and encouraging tourism."[64] A year later, on December 19, the *Times* ran another story on the CBD's revitalization, which reported that the city had attracted more than R9 billion in investments, including a large world-class convention center and a new five-star hotel. However, despite these achievements, city shopkeepers agreed with Michael Farr that "the next step would be to rid the city of street children and vagrants." One antique dealer in the CBD pressed the Partnership to realize that "this time of year [summer] is hunting season for the street kids and vagrants."[65] One year later, another *Cape Times* story carried the Partnership's claim, cited earlier, that informal parking attendants and street children had cost the city R300 million in investments, even as the Partnership reported in June 2002 that investment in the CBD had reached a record R11.5 billion.

The degree of criminalization of street kids reaches its most extreme in the evocation of gangs, used in the story on AIDS orphans and then again in a story about street children in the city from the *Cape Times* in December 2002: "Iron Fist Comes Down on Street Gangs." Experts on street children have already argued that in addition to general perceptions that street children are manipulative troublemakers, the public and police already often equate street children with gangs.[66] Well-organized and deeply entrenched township gangs represent an enormous challenge to the Western Cape, and its poor communities in particular. The language of gangs and gangsterism is a powerful one here and no editor can possibly be unaware of its impact on newspaper readers. Whatever the reasons for the use of the terminology in relation to street children and AIDS orphans, conflating groups of street children with the gangs of the Cape Flats represents irresponsible sensationalism of two discrete, though not unrelated, phenomena.

That changes in media coverage of street children occurred during the same period during which crime in the CBD was plummeting and investment increasing, according to Partnership and police figures, suggests that the attention given to street children cannot be reduced to any substantial or building danger they pose in any literal sense. In fact, running through a number of the news stories is a more figurative theme of street children not simply as perpetrators of specific crimes or as obstacles to private financial investment, but as manifestations of a more general threat or danger to the social order. These stories often evoke the imagery of citizens under siege by violent (black) intruders, including street children, a resonant theme in the history of South Africa. Two examples from the period, both involving the issue of electric fences as anticrime tools for private homes and communities, provide a sense of how the threat is being portrayed and how it is informing the emergence of new governance forms across affluent parts of the city. The first, from the *Cape Argus* of June 29, 1999, is entitled "Now City Intruders Get Shock Treatment." According to the story, more and more families are buying electric fences from private security companies to replace or supplement private guards and private armed response companies. A representative from Cape Electrified Fencing remarks that this is a shift from the pre-democracy period, when most inquiries came from businesses. The story concludes with a representative from Chubb Armed Response, a Western Cape–based private security company, commenting that criminal gangs are recruiting young people because "they know that these youngsters will be out on the streets 48 hours after their first court appearance. Many of these intruders are street children."

The second story, from the *Cape Times* of March 25, 2001, is headlined, "Suburb under Siege Wants Anti-Crime Fence," in reference to a community that bordered an informal settlement. Homeowners from the community of Capri Village said that rampant crime in their area had them living in fear and, according to the *Times*, with a "virtual siege mentality." Claiming that the police were overwhelmed, residents were trying to have a 4-kilometer electric fence installed, which they argued would reduce crime by up to 80 percent. One community member, in a letter to residents, stated: "Our police and municipal law enforcement units, for various reasons, are unable to cope with the influx of vagrants, street children and criminals, and this results in escalating crime in our area." Here street children are not only conflated with increases in crime and criminality but are also part of an invasion overwhelming homeowners and creating siegelike conditions. As with the previous story, the issue at hand is not simply a straightforward criminal justice one, but one that taps into deeper fears and anxieties born of the past.

Another significant, related subtext to all of these stories is a commonsense notion of when it is appropriate for whom to be where, linking the presence and absence of certain social groups to general feelings of safety and security. Street children may or may not commit certain crimes in certain quantities, but even more important is that their very visibility in certain places becomes the source of fear, drives away investment, and threatens public order. Their visibility as threat becomes a de facto representation of crime/disorder/danger in a time when the needs of increasingly invisible youth are still at least a rhetorical concern of South African society. There is, arguably, not a more vulnerable sector in the city, forcing the question of whether public sympathies are reserved perhaps for unseen children, for children in the abstract, rather than the children in the flesh standing at traffic intersections and begging for money. By using the language of sieges and invaders, by speaking of reducing the presence or ridding areas of street children who make people fearful, these stories both reflect and reproduce the old social anxieties felt by some sectors of the population in the new Cape Town regarding threats to and conflict over urban space. They do so by manipulating the relatively powerless or, put another way, by manipulating their power. As Charlotte Lemanski argues, within and through the discourse of a fear of crime:

> the criminal is constructed as a member of the collective other (usually poor and black) seeking to penetrate "our" socio-spatial purity. This incites an "us" and "them" mentality, giving rise to exclusionary mechanisms legitimised as a reaction to fear of crime, but actually a consequence of (prejudiced) fear of "other". Fear of crime is thus an expression of powerlessness due to loss of control over territory and urban order.[67]

It is interesting that Lemanski mentions race in relation to criminality because only one of the stories in the entire sample makes any significant mention of race at all, and that instance concerns charges of racism against the Capri Village residents for wanting their 4-kilometer electric fence. As Lemanski points out, however, the fear of crime, in South Africa and elsewhere, is often part of a more complex set of racial codes. The race of street children, vagrants, and the informal parking attendants is no more a mystery to the readers of the city's newspapers than is their socioeconomic status; they are racially coded black African and coloured from the outset. It is precisely the thinly coded nature of race in the discourse around street children that is important for understanding the "postracial" nature of neoliberal urban governance.[68] As Lemanski reminds us, in the new, "nonracial" South Africa, these codes—expressed, for example, through moral panics—often serve as new ways to talk about old problems, interests, and conflicts in ways that reflect new sensibilities, a concern that frequently appears in criticisms of urban renewal by NGOs, researchers, and community groups. One Cape Town parastatal organization, the Western Cape Provincial Development Council (WCPDC), commenting on the draft Integrated Development Plan and private sector–driven renewal, writes that these initiatives

> appear to be mainly concerned with improving the appearance of the CBD through addressing issues of "crime and grime". "Crime and grime" is associated with vagrancy, street children, homeless, and informal traders. Hence, the private sector response is ostensibly

about the brutal eradication of these "unwanted"/"bad" elements to stem capital flight from the CBD. The City is not an innocent bystander in this "eradication" programme. The initiatives overlook the fact that the poor constitute the majority of the city and that the vagrants/street children/informal traders are surface manifestations of deep-seated problems; viz. poverty, unemployment and social breakdown in the underdeveloped areas.[69]

What informs this and similar critiques is the concern that in the single-minded focus on attracting investment and removing crime from targeted zones, the new development plans risk ignoring or underestimating the deep-seated problems that constitute the real challenges facing the city. The result would not only be continued underdevelopment in the majority of the city, but also the resurfacing of very recently buried, though not necessarily dead, mechanisms of ordering, securing, and utilizing urban space. This new crop of media representations of street children is, therefore, neither new nor independent of much deeper currents in South African society.

As I have demonstrated elsewhere, since 2002 the moral panic around street children has subsided, and the reclamation of the city center is complete, as is reflected in the change of coverage between 2004 and 2005.[70] The lasting impact of the moral panic has, however, been institutionalized in the form of "quality of life" municipal bylaws that proscribe behavior associated with the urban poor. Through the physical demarcation of valuable space, with the creation of the CCID, and the deployment of private security to police the uses of that space, "order" and "security" have been established in the city's heart. This process relied heavily on the image of the criminal street child, who, his "performance" in the public eye now complete, recedes into invisibility.[71] In the following section we turn to this process and look more closely at how the governance of security developed alongside and through the moral panic around street children in the rarified urban space of the CCID.

Neoliberal Governance and the Reproduction of the Fragmented City

Behind the ideological and racial formations of moral panic lie the more mundane practices and policies that do the work of shaping urban space on a day-to-day basis. During and just after the moral panic years, seven different law enforcement bodies patrolled the CBD, and CCTV of the area was continuously monitored by armed rapid response units. According to the CCID administration, security in the CBD consisted of resources provided by a combination of the CCID, the Cape Town Partnership, the city council, the Municipal Police, and the SAPS. The CCID provided 160 personnel working in shifts, five patrol cars, ten horse-mounted patrols, and a 24-hour operations center maintained in conjunction with the SAPS. The city council provided traffic backup, 32 security personnel, a 72-camera network, and 24-hour rapid response. The Partnership contributed 50 parking marshals, and the SAPS made an additional 45 personnel available to the CBD at any given time. Managing security for the CCID during its early years was Derek Bock, a former lieutenant with the South African Defence Forces with 18 years of military experience and a background in intelligence gathering, counterterrorism, and hostage negotiation.[72] Bock has since moved to the private sector, as head of operations for Howard Eurocape's South African subsidiary, Eurocape Holdings, one of the largest owners of property in the CBD.

The task of these security forces is to police the CBD but in ways consistent with democratic law enforcement practices and the precepts of urban renewal that the Partnership believes have been successful in many cities of the global North. In effect, this means that police and private security become de facto social development workers and frontline agents of urban renewal because they are the ones who enforce the quality-of-life bylaws through which urban space in the city center is reclaimed and security established; in practice, however, the result has been an escalation of harassment and even violence against the homeless by security forces employed by the CCID.[73] During the revitalization period, the City of Cape Town began to debate the implementation of a municipal bylaw targeting so-called quality-of-life offenses. The bylaw is in line with the vision for the development of the CBD in that it empowers law enforcement to confront both crime and grime. It is at this juncture, where the security forces, the poor, and criminals come into contact, that the power of moral panic is most evident. Although it is a physical space that is policed in a literal sense, policing practices occur in and are shaped by the context of struggles over urban space in a deeply divided city.[74]

The Cape Town municipal bylaw regarding quality-of-life issues, enacted in 2007 after a protracted battle between city officials and civil society organizations, is similar in content and controversy to municipal bylaws from New York City to Sydney. The source of the controversy is precisely the claim that the bylaw is antipoor and provides the city and the security forces with useful tools to legitimately remove or banish, in the words of the Roots survey cited earlier, undesirable elements, as part of the larger project of urban renewal. The major document on the bylaw during the controversy was "Promotion for a Safe and Secure Urban Environment," twenty pages of proposed municipal bylaws drawn up prior to the ANC–New National Party (NNP) alliance, when the city was still run by the Democratic Alliance (DA). The list of prohibited activities is extensive and covers everything from planting trees to digging holes and holding protests. A number of subsections in the bylaw, however, will clearly impact the city's destitute population disproportionately. These include prohibitions in public places against begging, urinating, spitting, consuming or being under the influence of liquor or drugs, storing belongings, and washing, cleaning, or drying any objects, including clothes.

The document also includes a prohibition against directing cars to parking spaces in exchange for money. This is an explicit move against what Police Chief Sangster has referred to as "parking terrorists," Cape Town's version of New York's infamous "squeegee men." These are black men, often refugees, who try to earn a few rand on the city's streets by guiding and watching cars, an activity the chief and Partnership officials refer to as extortion. News stories in 2002, when early drafts were circulating, also reported that some versions included prohibitions against begging within 6 meters of an automated teller machine, at bus and rail stops, within 3 meters of the entrance to a building or vehicle, or in a public road, but these do not appear in the draft from 2003 or in the final version of the bylaw passed by the city council, which make an exception for beggars who sit or stand passively, with or without a sign, and who do not address any solicitations at other people specifically. The bylaw does, however, make it a crime for individuals in a public space to refuse to move at the order of a peace officer. Violation of city bylaws will result in a fine, up to six months of prison, or both, although courts have discretion to impose alternative sentences.[75]

Explaining the reasoning behind the proposed bylaw in 2003, Michael Farr argued that mugging, robbery, drug dealing, and other serious street crimes "flourish where disorderly behaviour goes unchecked."[76] Speaking in May 2003, well into the CBD's renewal, Farr continued:

Therefore, illegal refuse dumping, illegal informal trading, urinating and defecating on the street, informal parking

attendants and harassment of the public are classified as the
first problem to be addressed in creating a safe and secure
environment. . . . Apprehension and/or prosecution for bylaw
infringements are the first step in crime prevention. While these
may seem to be minor charges, they do frequently lead to more
serious crime.[76]

In theory the bylaw applies to everyone, but it is questionable how strict
and even the enforcement will be across the many populations within
the city. For example, on most weekend nights the streets outside the
many clubs and bars located within the CBD are full of visitors and more
affluent residents under the influence of liquor, but zero tolerance does
not appear to be part of managing this population. On the other hand, the
bylaw provides a perfectly legal rationale for security forces to pick up any
street children who are suspected of being under the influence of alcohol
or glue and other inhalants. Furthermore, it is unlikely that any affluent
person will find it necessary to beg, wash, and dry their clothes in public
or work as a parking terrorist while visiting the CBD. It will, therefore,
require careful monitoring—of arrest figures, for example—to determine
to what extent the bylaw is in practice being used as a mechanism for
regulating the presence of the poor within the CBD.

Revitalization hit a bump in the road at the end of 2003, when the
city's new mayor rejected the proposed bylaw, saying it would criminalize
homelessness and lead to the mass arrests of street children. In place of
the bylaw Mayor Mfeketo proposed a more developmental approach that
would address the socioeconomic roots of homelessness. The move was
embraced by the Partnership, now led by Andrew Boraine, who replaced
Michael Farr in 2003. Striking a new tone for the Partnership, Boraine
commented, "We don't have a problem with making the city safe, but we
can't criminalise social problems."[77] The reversal did not go over well with
the DA, which continued to support the bylaw and claimed that the ANC
and NNP councilors in the safety portfolio committee had given their
approval to the policy before it was sent to the mayor. Indeed, when the DA
regained control of the city in 2006, the bylaw was quickly reintroduced,
resulting in renewed objections by a number of NGOs working in the city.
In part this suggests that the steady criticisms made of the antipoor direction the CBD is moving in have intervened in the debate around the area's
development and forced a discussion of how the city's practice is veering

away from rhetorical commitments to inclusivity. At the same time, it is also worth considering that from the point of view of reclaiming the area, the CBD has already been secured, without the use of the bylaw, through decreased accessibility from the townships, for example.[78]

Prior to the flap over the bylaw, a number of youth workers observed that street children were being increasingly harassed and beaten as a way to teach them to stay away from the downtown area. Reports in local media about the crackdown on vagrants and loiterers in the CBD indicate that street children are being chased into surrounding areas and shelters; these neighborhoods have reported increases in the numbers of children they see as the cleanup campaigns sweep them out. Other street children allegedly have ended up in prison because of the crackdown, and one youth worker was told by a child to work in prison, because that was where most of the children were.[79] Renewal authorities deny there is any abuse by the security forces. Derek Bock, responding to criticism that zero tolerance was contributing to abuse, stated, "I categorically deny that we have ever used strong-arm tactics and if anyone is abused, it is our personnel," while police spokesperson Andre Traut admitted receiving complaints but did not think these are part of a tendency.[80] These views are not supported by those who work with street children, however, who saw both an increase in harassment of people living on the street and a sharp reduction of their numbers in the CBD during the revitalization period.[81]

In 2002, Michael Farr commented on the improvements in the CBD and the remaining challenges: "We're obviously delighted at the achievements from all the CCIDs [in the CBD], but crime prevention and the *proper control of public space* remains the number one priority [emphasis added]."[82] The desire to control space has fueled efforts by the Partnership and city authorities to expand the CCID itself and promote the City Improvement District (CID) model in other parts of the city and to strengthen its position within the downtown governance network of the post–moral panic environment. Within the CBD, the CCID has tried to expand its borders into the rapidly gentrifying coloured community of Woodstock adjacent to the CBD, its regulatory powers through the bylaw, and its management of the downtown infrastructure, particularly the rail and taxi station deck, the largest remaining working-class black space in the CBD.[83] Beyond the CCID, plans currently exist to create up to sixty more CIDs over the next few years in Cape Town, and already the downtown areas bordering the current CBD have established CIDs or are applying for CID status. Commenting on the expansion of CIDs, Clinton Osbourne, a former coordinator for social development at the CCID, told me: "Everyone's getting one, it's the new trend. Woodstock, Obs [Observatory], they're just spreading like wildfire all over the Cape."[84] Looking at a map of the city, with the existing or proposed CIDs outlined, one sees a city divided into increasingly contiguous and predominantly white areas inside the CID fold, with the middle-class, working-class, and poor black areas on the outside. If the same security and development practices being carried out in the CBD are repeated in the new CIDs, then it is likely that undesirable elements will be pushed farther and farther from downtown.

The Partnership and CCID authorities say they recognize that street children are themselves victims and require help from their organizations as well as the relevant government departments and NGOs already working with these children. In acting on this recognition, however, the CCID has generated concerns that it is interested primarily in consolidating its control over downtown governance and sidelining organizations critical of its commitment to socioeconomic development. In 2002 the Partnership established a program of service delivery for city street children in conjunction with provincial and municipal government agencies. The program would establish an umbrella organization to pool funds from the Partnership, government, business, and civic groups and authorize a board of trustees to distribute the funding to NGOs. In effect, this would bring the street child service sector in the CBD under the control of the Partnership. In explaining the reasoning behind the program, Farr said that although many NGOs were doing good work, they had become businesses competing for resources. He stated, "They employ a lot of people—you're talking about an industry with expensive overheads, executive directors and salaries."[85] The program worried some in the NGO sector. Pam Jackson, chair of the Western Cape Street Children's Forum Alliance, argued at the time that it duplicated work already happening and that the board would need neutral people who understood the issue. Furthermore, she says, "I think the [Partnership] has too much of a vested interest to manage the project."[86] The issue appears to revolve around a mistrust of the Partnership's experience and interest in addressing the needs of street children outside of the larger priorities of the development of the CBD. This concern was expressed to me directly by Clinton Osbourne, who resigned from the CCID precisely because he believed that its commitment to social development was largely rhetorical and that its administration was much more concerned with "security" and getting the poor out of the downtown.[87]

Although the creation of CIDs can certainly revitalize certain areas, it is at best an open question whether CIDs are a practical development solution to the city's poverty and joblessness, even within the confines of the CBD. Indeed, the critique from many corners of civil society and community organizations is that the CCID concept turns what should be public space into literal or de facto private, heavily policed enclaves. The WCPDC has argued that the CCIDs "nodalize" the city, resulting in continued sociospatial fracture that flatly contradicts the city's stated commitment to integration. The WCPDC remarks that the CID concept is an inappropriate import from the global North that approaches the problems of underdevelopment from the perspectives of the overdeveloped.

> To lose ourselves in the fog of comparison, largely to the USA and "world cities" paradigm/s, would mean us denying the poor access to the city; destroying the livelihoods of the most vulnerable segments/sectors of society; and reinforcing the divisions of old that would be an outcome of deploying particular types of urban regeneration/renewal vehicles. Worse still, we could re-create a city of old premised on an "inclusion within rejection"; i.e. the city as playground of the elite that admits the poor only as labourers, domestics, gardeners and the like.[88]

The "particular types of urban regeneration vehicles" being deployed, however, contain within them a very clear logic of security governance, especially if we view the media representations of street children as a part of this deployment. Jeremy Seekings made the important observation that moral panics give rise to new forms of social control, which emerge as reactions to anxiety over economic and social disorder.[89] Whereas the panics themselves do the work of defining the phenomenon in question as a problem and identifying causes, the new forms of discipline arise as attempts to solve or contain the problem. At their core, these problems in Cape Town are defined in terms of race and deviance, if not outright criminality, and the solutions involve the imposition of control. Invariably, the mechanisms of control bear the marks of the panic itself and the social conflicts that lay beneath it. In South Africa, moral panics have tended to focus on young black men, whose visible presence in urban South Africa is represented as a problem. It then becomes these young men who must be controlled if urban social order is to be maintained or restored.

Although there are broad outlines within which a historical continuity exists between different outbreaks of and responses to moral panics, the conditions in each case have their own uniqueness. In the case of street children in the CBD, the forms of control are an outgrowth of the logic of a development strategy that is predicated on the reduction of crime and grime and an era of fiscal austerity and which is itself a characterization of the development problem linked to another panic around foreign investment and the opinions of global creditors. A moral panic is in fact a form of social control and, in the present case, one that is intimately linked to the politics of urban renewal and the drive to make Cape Town world class. Particularly in a group as vulnerable as street children, the ease with which others can define them and the meaning of their presence in public spaces constitutes a form of control. However, the act of representation is at the same time a precursor to the mobilization of, in this case, newspaper readers' emotions and a whole range of institutional resources to "deal with" the problem. In a post–Group Areas Act Cape Town, the law cannot bar certain people from certain areas based on their race, class, or age, but the CCID can create and enforce new conceptions of belonging, even citizenship, mediated by the market and property owners, yet still clearly rooted in race and class conflicts. The rhetoric of revitalization-cum-development provides an incredibly fluid and flexible tool through which to contain, or at least attempt to represent, old conflicts as development problems, including the unwanted presence of black vagrants and street children in the city's core.

The political economy of urban renewal and the emergence, or reemergence, of a moral panic that expresses deep anxieties around the possibility of racial change are contributing to a situation in which embedded notions of race and criminality combine to produce new mechanisms of social control at a number of connected levels, from representation to the actual practice of policing in the CBD, whose combined effect is to reenclose affluent urban space through the use of coercive cordons. In place of real social development and urban renewal, Cape Town is already witnessing new or expanded forms of control and fortification. As economic inequality and crime in Cape Town increase, and small inner-city areas are carved out as protected habitats, the city risks reproducing the spatial divisions inherited from the days of National Party rule.

What I have suggested here is that urban renewal is, in relation to the poor of the CBD, positioning them as unwanted trespassers rather than as citizens entitled to all of the rights that the new constitution guarantees. What this criminalization suggests is that choosing this development path in the midst of overwhelming poverty and stratification necessitates new forms of social control that are able to secure the borders between the affluent nodes and the still underdeveloped areas on the other side. This is an inherent feature of borders under modern conditions of inequality and "surplus" labor. In Southern Africa alone, we see a number of concentric circles of affluence, each representing a border of sorts, with South Africa's urban areas at the core. Rural domestic migrants head for the cities, and immigrants from neighboring countries try to cross the national border. As resources are poured into targeted zones, economic migrants will follow, provoking precisely the kinds of anxiety and panics among affluent residents we are witnessing in Cape Town. We can therefore expect to see continual increases in public and private resources being channeled into forms of social control to fill the gaps left by ill-conceived renewal strategies and contain the poor within the peripheries of developed urban cores. By evoking the emotional issue of crime, a very real problem for Cape Town, an urban renewal agenda that serves a very narrow slice of the city's population can introduce this new urban segregation under the guise of development. The response to street children in the CBD constitutes a moral panic that rearticulates race and class tensions in terms of threats to order and mobilizes resources (emotional, organizational, and financial) to confront these threats.

That public and private security forces become central to the city's response is far from surprising given that even under the best of circumstances, insufficient time has passed to overcome patterns that are more than a century old. What is noteworthy, however, are the ways these patterns of panic and repression are becoming intertwined within discourses and practices of social crime prevention, urban renewal, and development in a city committed to urban entrepreneurialism and a country committed to multiracial democracy. There emerges a "split personality" of sorts, as officials speak aggressively about the need to crack down on crime and show zero tolerance, but at the same time routinely embrace the progressive sentiments of "Ready to Govern." The case of street children in Cape Town's CBD is important because it gives some indication of how the resolution of this contradiction is influenced by a number of complex factors. Urban renewal in the CBD is shaped by development agendas that are simultaneously local, national, and transnational, by the political history of the city, and by a conviction that crime reduction must precede development. It also provides a useful case study of how important the struggles over the meanings of crime and development are to this conviction. Defining development as turning the city into a world class city, a definition made with little consultation with the city's residents, contributes to an understanding among city planners and police about not only the importance of crime reduction, but of what crimes are to be considered priority crimes. Underneath these policy and planning questions lies the legacy of apartheid, from the distribution of resources and space to deeply embedded racial anxieties, which, if left unresolved, will continue to exercise their power over any attempts to make the city new again.

3

Gangsterism and the Policing of the Cape Flats

The Council of the City of Cape Town is outraged by the continuing violence and murders committed by gangs, against the citizens of Cape Town. The Council recommits itself to fighting for a safe city and commits its resources in support of SAPS to bring a halt to the action of gangs.

—Cape Town City Council, February 14, 2001

In May 2002, the police and army rolled into several areas of the Cape Flats in response to a gang war. The conflict was between the Americans, allegedly the largest gang in the Cape, and the 28s, an entrenched prison gang that has spread out to the townships, but also included the many smaller gangs lined up on either side of the rivalry. In the course of a month, thirty-seven people were killed and thousands of children had to stay home as schools were closed in five different neighborhoods and army trucks stood guard over taxi routes. In the Lotus River neighborhood alone, seven schools had to be put under heavy police protection.[1] The gangs were at war over a number of things, from control over *shebeens* (drinking establishments), drug trafficking, and taxi routes to members visiting girlfriends in rival areas. According to police intelligence reports, the violence was fueled by the recent release of some gang members from prison looking for revenge. The war was part of a larger conflict sparked by turf battles and recruiting drives that had been taking place across the Flats for weeks, hitting the coloured communities of Mitchells Plain, Manenberg, and Hanover Park especially hard. Philippi police spokesperson Rodney Martin reported that in Hanover Park eight people were killed and eight attempted murders were reported in the battles between the Americans, the Ghetto Kids, and the Laughing Boys.[2]

Less than a year later, in March 2003, gang violence on the Cape Flats claimed the lives of four children caught in the crossfire over the course of little more than a week. Officials from the Democratic Alliance, the police, and the African National Congress responded by pushing for military deployment into what the provincial Member of the Executive Committee (MEC) for Community Safety Leonard Ramatlakane of the

90

ANC called "areas where gangsterism was rife."[3] Speaking after the third shooting death, of ten-year-old Desmoné Smith, Western Cape minister for education André Gaum issued the following statement

> [d]rastic action is needed to save our schoolchildren from the ongoing open violence of ruthless and murderous gangs. The tragic death of Desmoné Smith is the third time that a child's life has been ended by gang violence in the last few days. I therefore wholeheartedly support the Premier's request that the Army be urgently called in. There is no other choice but to fight fire with fire. This is clearly the only language understood by the gangs, whose members care less than nothing about our children. The swift approval of military action to stabilise the situation has now become an urgent necessity.[4]

Incidents like these are constant reminders that concern over crime on the Cape Flats cannot be reduced to the outsized fears of residents in affluent white areas, although crime there certainly figures into the larger discourse of crime and insecurity beyond the township borders. They also provide a glimpse of how the state responds to the crime and gangsterism on the Cape Flats that deeply affect the everyday lives of millions of people, by far the vast majority of the city's population. As we will see, the approach to the very real and complex challenge of gangsterism risks falling into the well worn channels of the apartheid-era approaches to security, with marginalized youth ignored until they come into conflict with the law, at which point they are dragged into a criminal justice system as unsuited today as it was ten, twenty, or thirty years ago to deal with them. Central to this process on the Cape Flats, as it is in the city's core, is the combination of a fundamentally unaltered approach to the question of security and development and the reinforcing effect this has on the ideology and practice of policing.

The result is that many of the core features of apartheid policing remain, despite sometimes successful, if limited, attempts to transform the basic structure of community/police relations. Although the scope of the problem is much broader on the Cape Flats than it is in the Central Business District, and despite many stark differences in the apartheid and postapartheid climate, at the center of the politics of crime and urban renewal in the city we still find young unemployed or marginally employed black youth. To date, democratic South Africa, while it perhaps has more of an incentive to end the marginalization of these young people, has yet to demonstrate the required political will. Indeed, anxiety over the damage crime can do to the city's image appears to shape the actions of economic and political elites in the city to a much greater degree than concern over youth development. The urban renewal challenge on the Cape Flats is very different from that in the city center, as is the relationship of the area to the vision of Cape Town as a world class city. Still, an important link exists between the downtown and the townships in the form of young black people, who, in both areas, remain largely invisible from the point of view of urban governance except as potential threats to personal safety and economic growth outside of the townships. More specifically, with regard to youth, street children and gangsters are products of the same circumstances and, for similar reasons, become a part of the alternative, if often overlapping, social structures of the life on the street and in the gangs. Although the structures themselves may be discrete, the boundaries between them are rather fluid.

Over the course of the next three chapters, we will examine exactly how and when resources are expended on township youth. The picture that emerges is of a city genuinely frustrated and outraged by violent crime but whose response is often misdirected and counterproductive if the goal is transformation of the lives of its young people. This chapter opens the discussion by briefly introducing the issue of gangsterism on the Cape Flats before turning its attention to the practices of the apartheid security forces that have managed to survive the transition into the democratic era. The importance of this continuity is that since 1994, the commitment by government to more social development–driven approaches to security has eroded, and urban renewal strategies are reduced to anticrime and antigang operations led by police. In the process, the narrative of townships as problems is reinforced, and the black menace revived in the form of the Cape Flats gangster. As we will see, this increasingly institutionalized approach has a devastating impact on youth and on their communities more generally, and is derailing even the modest efforts at genuine social development. The fact that the practices involved are for the most part not new cautions us against simply attributing aggressive policing to neoliberalism. However, we must also be attentive to the reality that current approaches to the governance of security on the Cape Flats, driven more by the state here than in the city center, have an undeniable containment rationale that is well suited to the overarching neoliberal governance strategy of pursuing world class status in a highly unequal and unstable environment. Central to this strategy is the deployment of a particular kind of policing that, familiar as it may be, has acquired the trappings of technocratic reform and a vocabulary of international "best practice," and it is to this strategy that we turn our attention.

Gangsterism in Historical Context

Crime on the Cape Flats is generally understood within the context of gangsterism, which in turn is viewed as a young man's game. The challenge of gangsterism is therefore very much central to the oft-cited "challenge of youth" in Cape Town. At the same time it is also part of a theme running through the history of the country and the Cape, one in which race, masculinity, urbanization, and the notion that young people are a problem all intertwine. Similar to the presence of street children in urban areas, the existence of and danger posed by gangs in South Africa's cities has often been explained through reference to youth who thrive on or beyond the edges of normal society and adult control. As discussed earlier, the fear of black people and young black men in urban areas throughout the twentieth century was most often articulated through the language of disorder and criminality, functioning to mobilize social control mechanisms that served to reinforce racial boundaries constantly in danger of being breached. Somewhat ironically, perhaps, the attempt to control how black people moved, where they lived, and where they labored—through the pass laws, for example—laid the groundwork for the emergence and growth of the gangs that today operate within the coloured townships of the Cape Flats and are blamed for much of the area's insecurity.

The precursors to today's coloured gangs appeared in Cape Town's coloured neighborhoods prior to the forced removals that followed the Group Areas Act, as overcrowding increased competition for hawking and the *shebeen* markets in places like District Six, leading to the emergence of youth groups that engaged in criminal activity for income.[5] It was the removals, perhaps apartheid's greatest "development project," however, that generated the more organized and sophisticated gang structures we see today. The expulsion of entire coloured communities from the inner city and surrounding suburbs of Cape Town to the Cape Flats was incredibly destructive and caused enough disruption to provide the kinds of spaces in which gangs could grow and eventually flourish. Cape Town journalist Marianne Merten, in the *Mail and Guardian*, writes:

> Gangsters were part of District Six and coloured communities
> such as Bo-Kaap and Simon's Town. Mostly they fought each other,
> played numbers, bet and smuggled alcohol. For a long time they
> remained on the peripheries of these close-knit communities that
> for the most part looked after their children and the needy. Nearby
> churches, mosques and amenities such as shops, parks and the
> beach countered many of the gangsters' negative influences. But the
> apartheid-era forced removals ripped apart the social fabric. When
> people were dumped on the bleak, sandy stretches of the Cape Flats,
> there was nothing and jobs were no longer a walk or short bus ride
> away. Gangsters were quick to take advantage of this vacuum.[6]

The impact of the removals on the growth of gangs in coloured communities is widely acknowledged. Captain Kishor Harri, formerly of the Western Cape Gang Unit before becoming Superintendent at Manenberg Police Station, points to the removals as a catalyst for gang growth, particularly because of the huge increases in unemployment and the social instability they provoked. The introduction of the addictive drug Mandrax to the Western Cape in the 1970s further entrenched the gangs in the local economy and Cape Flats' communities, generating income but also exacerbating social instability in the form of substance abuse and related problems and leading to an increase in gang violence. According to Harri, drug lords began to make use of the gangs to safeguard drug markets, resulting in sharper conflicts and the emergence of endemic gang warfare. The problems associated with gangsterism were deepened through a combination of government negligence, as drugs and gang violence on the Cape Flats were not seen as a white problem,[7] and the state's active collaboration with the gangs and the drug trade as part of the counterinsurgency war in the 1970s and 80s.[8]

With the growth of political activity and political organization sparked by the Soweto uprisings of 1976, gang activity subsided for about a decade across black communities, as political organizations provided alternatives for township youth and acted as counterweights to gang growth. In the mid-1980s, however, as state repression and the destabilization campaign escalated, gangs took advantage of the chaos and began to reorganize, becoming increasingly involved with planned murders, extortion, bribery, theft and robbery rackets, and drug and gun syndicates, their activities often overlapping with the state's counterinsurgency agenda. Benjamin Haefele, with the Centre for Military Studies at the University of Stellenbosch, identifies this period of renewed activity as stretching from approximately 1983 to 1993, the period during which state repression and political violence was at its most intense. Gangs benefited from a state that largely ignored or encouraged their criminal activities and capitalized on the access they provided as eyes and ears within the rebellious townships, using the time to strengthen their organizations. The destabilization campaigns of the late apartheid period, while destructive to black communities generally, at the same time provided crucial space for gangs to grow.[9]

Since then, gangs have taken advantage of the many opportunities provided by the negotiated transition and the reconfiguration of South Africa's relationship to the global economy to diversify their illicit activities and form partnerships with legitimate businesses, generally for money laundering purposes. The result of the gangs' ability to adapt to and capitalize on changing political, social, and economic conditions is that gangsterism remains an embedded socioeconomic feature of the Cape (and a development challenge) that, according to Haefele, has "become increasingly ruthless and business oriented" over time.[10] Researchers and members of law enforcement are in general agreement that the opening of South Africa politically and economically as well as, quite literally, the opening of its borders contributed to the growth of opportunity structures for organized crime and, therefore, the growth of the gangs. Not only did the end of apartheid allow international syndicates to penetrate the South African market, it has also exposed South African criminal organizations to the global economy, resulting in significant changes in gang structures and activities. However, that the transition provided new opportunities for the gangs does not mean that their growth is explained by the transition, as some researchers claim. Criminologist Irvin Kinnes, an expert on gangs in the Western Cape, has pointed out that political and economic uncertainty, such as existed during the early transition period, often contributes to the growth of organized crime, a critical factor in the earlier period of growth in the 1970s as well, and by no means unique to the transition.[11] The "gang problem" is in fact part of the living legacy of the apartheid system itself; it remains because many of the conditions that nurtured it also remain.

The decade preceding the transition, when gangs reorganized in the wake of massive political mobilization, was also a time of political and economic uncertainty, and so it is likely that changes in the mid- to late 1990s were as much a consequence of an opportunity to reorganize in the earlier period as they were of the turbulence of the transition itself. Whether gangs grew because of the transition or their growth has simply been shaped by the transition while its causes lie elsewhere is at the very least unclear. Furthermore, it is well established that the first major period of gang growth and the origin of the gangs themselves also occurred during periods of social and economic uncertainty, in the contexts of overcrowding and forced removal of coloureds to the Cape Flats. What we have then is a series of developments in gang structure and size, from emergence to growth, associated with the removals, reorganization, during the violence in the 1980s, and growth again during the transition. Each of these periods was marked by economic, social, and political disorder, although of different, if related, sorts. Gangs have proven their ability to adapt through all of these changes.

But it was not only gang activity that increased during the social and economic volatility framing the late apartheid era. The increase in crime nationally and provincially, so often linked simplistically to the gangs, also began long before 1994, dating back to the intensification of resistance and repression in the mid-1980s. The overlapping and mutually reinforcing structural crises in the townships during this period provided fertile ground for increases in crime generally and gang activity in particular.[12] The opening of South Africa in the early 1990s functioned not so much as catalyst where there was none; rather, it presented a series of new opportunities for criminal activity to mutate under conditions of uncertainty that had been present in one form or another for at least two decades and to which gangs were well accustomed. In fact, organized crime in the country, including gang crime, can be directly related to elements of the apartheid state's counterinsurgency strategy, with the older regional smuggling networks created by the security forces and intelligence agencies now being utilized and expanded upon by criminal enterprises in a more global environment.[13] What this suggests is that many of the analyses offered by local and international law enforcement experts, which attempt to correlate the crime and gang crisis with the transition as part of the growing pains of liberal democracy, rely on overly reductionistic comparisons with transitioning societies in eastern Europe, which are also contending with high crime, and a preoccupation with the narrow framework of the transition itself.[14] A more comprehensive and historically grounded approach, in contrast, would focus not only on what has changed and is changing, but also on what remains the same. Underlying the formal transfer of political power is a situation of continued social and economic inequality in Cape Town. To see crime as an obstacle to development because it results in insecurity while largely ignoring the structural constraints and processes of active underdevelopment and their role in the crime problem is to set the stage for short-sighted and abstract anticrime measures based on a fundamental misunderstanding of the relationships among crime, criminals, and the communities from which they come and upon which they prey. Most obviously, it produces law enforcement solutions based on the mistaken ideological assumption that crime is essentially external to the proper functioning of a neoliberal democratic state.[15]

New Opportunities: Gangs in the Neoliberal City

Operating in an environment full of new opportunities, the gangs from the Cape Flats have developed an impressive portfolio and reach over the last decade. Locally, gangs from the Cape Flats are involved in, among other things, the alcohol and drug trades, prostitution, trafficking in stolen cars, gun smuggling, and large-scale theft. The gangs have also become more involved in legal businesses, putting money into hotels, night clubs, public transport, shops, and commercial fishing boats.[16] Partly in search of new markets and partly as the result of police crackdowns, gangs have also spread to other areas of the Western Cape and to provinces as far away as KwaZulu Natal. Experts in law enforcement also believe that gangs from the Western Cape have begun to work with foreign syndicates, one of the primary reasons that organized crime on the Cape Flats has drawn the attention of international law enforcement agencies.[17] In communities frustrated by deteriorating socioeconomic conditions and a lack of opportunities, gangs not only survived the transition but appear to be thriving.

Although the actual number of gangs in the Cape remains relatively stable, they have grown in size. Authorities on gangs in the Western Cape claim that there are approximately 80,000 to 100,000 gang members in the city in 100 to 120 gangs, and some city officials estimate that gang members make up approximately 5 percent of the total population.[18] Given these numbers and the periodic outbreaks of gang violence, it is understandable why many people in Cape Town see them as intrinsic to both the crime problem and the seemingly intractable development challenges the city faces. Determining the extent to which crime in the Cape is gang related, however, is not simple even at the level of crime statistics. A crime victim survey conducted by the Institute for Security Studies in 1998 found that victims often were not sure whether the perpetrators were gang members. In the case of robbery, for example, 41 percent of respondents said their attackers were gang members, while 41 percent said they were not and 18 percent could not be sure; the ratio was similar for murder. Forty percent of respondents who had a member of their household murdered identified the perpetrators as gang members, 40 percent were not sure, and 20 percent did not believe they were. Assault and sexual assault had even higher numbers of respondents unsure of whether or not their attackers were affiliated with gangs.[19] Nonetheless, involvement of gangsters in recorded crime is said to be high, and criminologists estimate that up to 60 percent of serious violent crime on the Cape peninsula is gang related.[20] For their part, the police attribute up to 70 percent of total crime in the Province to gang activity, and Kinnes notes that the Western Cape has more convictions for gang-related crime than any other province in the country.[21] One important exception to these estimates is a more recent claim by the new provincial police commissioner for the Western Cape, Mzwandile Petros, that less than 10 percent of serious violent crime is gang related.[22]

Despite their growing reach, the majority of Cape Town's gangs are still territorially bound and entrenched on the Cape Flats, where the majority of the city's recorded crime generally and violent crime in particular take place. It is also their activity in and around the city that authorities see as a barrier to urban renewal because of the impact they believe crime has on the city's global reputation. Gangsterism is also prevalent in rural communities of the Cape, but there are fewer resources in those areas to combat it, and perhaps less incentive to commit them there.[23] Unfortunately, the emphasis on the negative impact of gangsterism on urban renewal neglects a more complicated and inconvenient relationship it has to the city's political economy, one that undermines the logic of security-centric, law enforcement–driven responses to the challenge. High unemployment, social instability, and poverty on the Cape Flats not only provide gangs with new growth opportunities, they reproduce the social and economic conditions from which they first emerged. The continued strength of gangs is not a reflection of lax policing and an inefficient, underresourced criminal justice system, but is the legacy of a half century of state neglect and underdevelopment in the majority of the city's communities. Over many years the gangs have come to occupy a prominent place in the local economy, filling gaps created by the state. Andre Standing, a researcher at the Institute for Security Studies in Pretoria, has conducted research on organized crime on the Cape Flats and found that the criminal economy is increasingly central to socially excluded communities. He writes that organized crime is "a rational response to governmental and economic crisis. Organised crime provides income that is increasingly seen as . . . necessary. It supplies commodities and services that are in demand and have become normalised."[24] Standing adds that criminal elites in these situations often gain significant social status, becoming both regulators and benefactors of marginalized communities. Organized crime not only provides an alternative economy but can generate alternative forms of institutionalized power as well. Citing Susan

Figure 4. Government-built low-income public housing blocks for those forcibly removed by the Group Areas Act. Hilda Hof in Manenberg. Photograph by Shannon Wentz.

Strange and Letizia Paoli, Standing argues that gangs can in fact function as a form of "countergovernment" in the face of state retreat from certain areas of social, economic, and political life.

Poor communities, although they are the primary victims of gang violence, therefore have a complex relationship with gangs. High unemployment rates, upward of 60 percent in some Cape Flats townships, often mean that many city residents have come to rely upon the illegal economy. One youth worker I spoke with, active in some of the hardest-hit coloured communities, said that the cordon and search operations that police sometimes conduct on the Cape Flats may shut down the drug trade for a few days, but they also cut off much-needed income, making conditions harder for residents and, for some, increasing resentment toward the police. When the police leave, the situation returns to normal, leaving many residents to wonder what the point was in the first place.[25] In one coastal Cape Town community, a law enforcement crackdown on abalone poaching, in which gangs are heavily involved, increased community cooperation with gangs because the community depended upon poaching for income.[26]

On the Cape Flats, gangs not only provide income, they also support schools and sports teams and lend money to help people pay rent and avoid evictions, a constant threat for many in the townships. According to researcher Steve Kibble, "People may realise that they are being coopted by the gangsters, but often have little choice if they want to avoid eviction or need to buy food."[27] Gangsters are also able to use their resources to build relationships with young people. In one example, the Americans gang—by many accounts the city's most powerful—gave out hundreds of silver scooters to kids in Tafelsig, a Mitchells Plain neighborhood where unemployment and gang activity are particularly high. Thus, although community relations with gangsters are contradictory and gangsters have many negative effects on their communities, the relationship is such that gangsters have in the past been able to produce 3,000 people for a march on Parliament.[28] Urban renewal strategies whose leading edge is the criminal justice system and, more specifically, the police risk underestimating this kind of dynamic by ignoring the many key aspects of the gang–community–crime relationship, many of which the police are not designed to address. The city, however, has elected to implement an urban renewal strategy whose primary focus is not youth development but, instead, the crippling of gang structures. The deployment of police and military forces to the Cape Flats to fight gangs today may share key similarities with the previous era, but is now shaped by a different political and economic reality, in which gangsterism, if it is not contained, could shatter the fragile stability and conscribed prosperity of the new neoliberal democratic city. Neatly elided, at least in practice, in this approach to governance is the deeper socioeconomic crisis from which gangsterism has drawn nourishment for decades.

Policing Underdevelopment in the Townships: The Cape Flats Renewal Strategy

Just as the Cape Town Partnership was overseeing the implementation of the city's first city improvement district in the Central Business District, local and provincial authorities were busy drawing up plans to confront the biggest crime challenge the city faced, the gangs on the Cape Flats. The result of this process, unveiled in February 2001, was the Cape Flats Renewal Strategy (CFRS), a joint effort led by the provincial government and involving also the municipal government, local communities, and the private sector in implementing an integrated and multisectoral approach to development on the Cape Flats. The CFRS was intended to combat crime on the Flats in line with directives laid out in the National Crime Prevention Strategy (NCPS) and to complement the National Urban Renewal Programme (NURP). It was linked, at least conceptually, to the urban renewal process under way in the city center through its incorporation of the spatial governance model of reclaiming and revitalizing key geographic nodes. The CFRS, like the central city's improvement district model, also foregrounds crime and security, making very clear that its primary task of urban renewal is to address the "gang phenomenon." The goal here, according to law enforcement and political authorities, is not simply a "cleanup" for which a "broken window" strategy will suffice, though it will have a role to play. Instead, the most pressing need is to break the backs of deeply entrenched criminal organizations that have thus far survived—and, indeed, thrived under—the war on crime. A strategy-related document from a May 2001 meeting of the city's Executive Council (EXCO) declared that

> [t]he majority of security threats a year ago were defined as being urban terror, transport violence and gang activities. Whilst some measure of success has been achieved in respect of the first two categories, it would also be fair to reflect that the said two categories of crime are fairly recent phenomena and of a more temporary

nature, as it were. The scourge of gangsterism, on the other hand, has been prevalent for decades and has, up to now, not been successfully combated.[29]

The EXCO document, which provides the estimate that 5 percent of Cape Town residents are gang members, puts the number of gangs at 280, by far the highest estimate circulating. In outlining the nature of the gang problem, it also points out that it is an old one, while emphasizing that most of its members are young. EXCO makes direct reference to the gang problem being a youth problem, asserting that most gang members are between the ages of twelve and twenty-five and that most come from the coloured communities of the Cape Flats. EXCO information on gangs is taken directly from the budget speech made by then MEC for Community Safety for the Western Cape Hennie Bester two months earlier, at which he also introduced the CFRS. Although the numbers tend to vary, these assertions complement those made in other city documents regarding youth involvement with crime and the perceptions of many police. The Integrated Development Plan from 2002–03 puts the number of youth (defined as those between the ages of sixteen and thirty) associated with gangs at over 100,000, though it is not clear whether "associated with gangs" is meant to imply gang membership, some other relationship, or both combined.[30]

Research by Jean Redpath published in 2001, consisting of interviews at almost all of the Western Cape's 150 police stations, including those on the Cape Flats, revealed that police generally consider youth crime to be either relatively constant or on the increase, while some respondents attributed almost all crime to youth offenders.[31] What these different sources indicate is a perception by city officials that many youth are affiliated in one way or another with crime and gangsterism. The equation of youth with gangsterism, the latter then identified in turn as the primary obstacle to development, parallels what is happening in the city center in the sense that urban renewal problems in both cases are—sometimes directly, sometimes indirectly—blamed on young black people. And as holistic as the CFRS attempts to be, it does not entirely escape implying that youth are a problem to be solved; indeed this could be read as being the central thread of the entire strategy.

Acknowledging that the province and the city do not have the resources to roll out the initiative to all the areas of the Cape Flats simultaneously, the CFRS focuses on seven specific locations. Two of the chosen areas are the predominantly black African township of Khayelitsha and the coloured township of Mitchells Plain, both also selected as priority sites of the NURP. Unlike the NURP, however, the CFRS covers only subsites within the two townships, Site B in Khayelitsha and Tafelsig in Mitchells Plain, whereas the NURP covers the areas in their entirety. The other sites are the largely coloured areas of Elsies River, Bonteheuwal, Hanover Park, and Manenberg, and the mostly black African townships of Philippi and Nyanga. Sites were selected based on official crime data and intelligence assessments of areas most affected by gangsterism provided by the South African Police Service. Khayelitsha and Mitchells Plain, whose selection by the NURP preceded the CFRS, were chosen in large part, because they are on a national SAPS list of priority areas responsible for most of the country's recorded crime; the subsites identified by the CFRS are also known crime "hot spots."[32]

The strategy has three operational components intended to work together as part of an integrated and synergistic approach to urban renewal, each of which is to contribute to the broader goal of neutralizing the gangs. The aim of the first, *economic renewal,* is to create a safe environment through, for example, housing development, graffiti removal, upgrading of parks, installation of closed circuit television cameras, job placement, and repair of derelict buildings and broken windows. The second component is *social renewal,* and its goal is to foster community development projects, including Department of Social Welfare programs; enlist the participation of religious organizations and churches; and establish neighborhood watches and a SAPS Youth Leadership project. The third and final component is *community safety and law enforcement.* The outcomes here are crime prevention, visible policing, and the arrest and conviction of gang leaders. The methods include cooperation among different police agencies and traffic and bylaw enforcement, building of gang leader profiles, strengthening of local police stations, and zero tolerance policing.[33]

Explaining the thinking behind the strategy during its unveiling, MEC Bester stated that it

> envisages that all government agencies pool their resources and align their strategies so that law enforcement is underpinned by urban and social renewal. . . . Too many of our communities have become economically dependent on the proceeds of crime and are

forever condemned to a life of poverty and subservience because of it. If we want our people to be truly free, we must break the criminal economy. Simultaneously we must put in place measures to fill the gap left by the gang economy.[34]

The EXCO strategy document admits that previous efforts to combat gangs have failed, largely because they were not sustained over the medium and long terms, with the result that gangsterism actually worsened. In particular it mentions that although a police presence can reduce gang activity, once the police leave, the problems return, a dilemma that has consistently undermined anticrime actions on the Flats. This is one of the key reasons behind strengthening local police stations as a core feature of the law enforcement component of the strategy. The document goes on to acknowledge that the social and economic renewal components have never been successfully implemented because they "have normally lacked a focused and suitable delivery mechanism,"[34] an important insight that foreshadowed the fate of the CFRS as well. The hopes for the new strategy, then, were that the law enforcement component would be sustained in the long term, with successful implementation of social crime prevention measures aimed at ameliorating the socioeconomic causes of crime.

As a strategy, the CFRS therefore made a commitment to approach the crime problem as a development problem, notwithstanding the unifying theme of antigangsterism. Focusing on sites determined by police intelligence, it sought to secure crime "hot spots" through the combined pressure of social, economic, and law enforcement measures, mirroring the approach of the NURP and NCPS. As the following discussion details, however, even in the early stages signs emerged that what had been conceived of as an integrated, multipronged urban renewal approach was slipping into a narrowly focused crime control and security campaign that did not adequately address the developmental needs of the communities generally and young people in particular; central to this shift was the overly narrow focus on gangs as the primary obstacle to development. The form of governance emerging from the Cape Flats urban renewal efforts suggests that underdevelopment is likely to remain a problem for the area and unequal development a perennial feature of the greater city, barring significant changes in the short and medium terms. If this is indeed the case, then current approaches to development-oriented policing represent an adaptive rather than a transformative feature of politics in the city today.

The new South African government, and the ANC in particular, acknowledges that the repressive policing of the apartheid regime piled insecurity on top of instability. The effort to put that recognition into practice through the Community Policing Forums (CPFs), the NCPS, and various pieces of supporting legislation represents not just a break from South Africa's past but also an embrace of "progressive" international standards. Naturally, the reforms generated great optimism and hope for a new kind of approach to criminal justice, one which understands that meeting the security needs of the people means more than just removing criminals from the community. The NCPS and the more recent NURP, although not without problems, at the very least articulated visions of crime prevention that are embedded in larger discourses of development for the people and communities of South Africa. The CFRS made additional headway in identifying meeting the needs of youth as a crucial crime prevention intervention.

What troubled people from a variety of sectors, however, was the extent to which the process was driven by law enforcement. Critics from township communities and from many civil society organizations that were focused on crime reduction, rehabilitation, and development claimed that implementation was tilted from the start in favor of police priorities, with social crime prevention efforts losing out to aggressive, deterrence-oriented hard policing tactics that leaned too heavily on the use of overwhelming force. In the process, social development, including youth development, while still a goal of urban renewal on the Flats, was neglected in practice. For too many young people in the townships, as the arrest statistics in the preceding chapter indicate, the primary experience they had with the new strategy was through the police. Policing was quickly becoming the central mechanism in the urban renewal program and a primary institution mediating relations between the state and the people, as the police not so quietly slipped into the role of de facto agents of underdevelopment. Understanding how and where young people fit into urban renewal on the Cape Flats—the focus of the next chapter—thus turns on an understanding of how gangsterism and policing have come to largely define the parameters of development practice in this vast territory to the east of the city's core.

Central to understanding this process is the concept of social order. Urban renewal under conditions of neoliberalism is best understood as a sociospatial ordering project, but one that manifests differently in different urban spaces. The role of policing in developing the city center mirrors urban renewal in South Africa as a whole, where both conceptually and practically it provides for the police to play a central role in the transition away from the urban geography of apartheid, in whose creation and reproduction they also figured prominently, and toward a new democratic division of space and distribution of resources. Unlike in the past, however, the role of the police is not to enforce an urban renewal whose goal is to pacify the population. Rather, law enforcement is meant to participate in a process of reform that incorporates less militaristic, human security perspectives in approaching crime and security challenges. Social crime prevention speaks to both these aspects of reform, representing a new understanding of the police role in communities and of the relationships among crime, severe deprivation, and inequality. The new role for law enforcement is not to police communities so much as it is to work with communities in developing effective strategies for making them safe. The change in emphasis requires a reconfiguration of the relationship between the police and urban communities, one that is captured in the emphasis on social crime prevention. A more human security–oriented approach to crime recognizes that police and the criminal justice system cannot solve development problems. What they can do is contribute to a more broadbased, or multipronged, development strategy. It is the apparent contrast between the ideals of policies such as the NURP and the actual practice of urban renewal in the city, however, that throws into question exactly how much police reform is actually occurring and to what extent social crime prevention, as opposed to sociospatial ordering, figures into the renewal process.

Efforts to implement social crime prevention and police reform did not come to the Cape Flats with the CFRS, but arrived earlier, with the establishment of the CPFs and the attempt to introduce various forms of sector policing, seen by law enforcement experts as an integral component of democratic policing.[35] These innovations were part of national efforts related to constitutional mandates, federal legislation, and SAPS policy changes, the desire to comply with and improve on international trends in police reform, and the local need to maximize scarce police resources. As Bill Dixon has documented, sector or cluster policing came to the Cape Flats in 1996, as part of an attempt to fit early 1990s London-style sector policing to the unique features of South Africa. The project took place in Philippi/Nyanga, which would later become an urban renewal site, and involved dividing the area into ten residential and three business areas, each with its own police and community anticrime force, and clustering police station areas into larger units.[36] Dixon emphasizes that because of local hostility to the police and a lack of resources, law enforcement was compelled to work with community patrols in ways he says would be unthinkable in London. He goes on to note that a similar constraint imposed by scarce resources contributed to the implementation of sector cluster policing in Elsies River, also on the Cape Flats, in the late 1990s. Not only did a lack of resources encourage police to try and work with communities, it also influenced how they dealt with the gangs, forcing police to negotiate in the absence of superior force. Indicating how tenuous these partnerships could be, one officer Dixon interviewed, then Elsies River station commander William Pienaar, commented: "If I've got enough manpower, if I've got enough resources, I don't have to try and talk to you, I'll go straight and . . . But I haven't got manpower, so I use another strategy."[37]

Of interest here is the reference to resources; specifically, Pienaar identifies "manpower" as a resource but does not appear to view the community as a resource, potentially a much greater one than a few more officers. Although the discourse of community as resource is evident on the Flats, as I will discuss in a moment, Pienaar's response is indicative of what many community residents see as problematic attitudes on the part of police with regard to area residents—for example, in relation to the CPFs. It also points to the issue of preexisting attitudes on the part of some police and the impact that increasing budgets for the criminal justice system and for policing in particular may have on fault lines running through fragile police/community relations. With cooperation already an effort, more resources could inadvertently act as a disincentive to future partnerships. As Dixon notes, the resources available to London police makes this kind of intimate interaction between law enforcement and communities unnecessary, even though precisely these kinds of partnerships are often heralded as key to successful crime reduction. This raises important questions about the definition, role, and pursuit of resources in the police reform process. Given the emerging reality of social crime prevention being sidelined in pursuit of hard-edged law enforcement and the concern with an overemphasis on technical reforms and systemic efficiency, it is arguable that the problem of resources is not the most pressing one. These problems existed in the old South Africa but, just as importantly, are endemic in the Western democracies whose models inform transformation in the SAPS and where reliance on technocratic solutions to crime are core features of the war on crime. To some extent the need for police and communities to work together because of scarce resources is an opportunity more than it is a liability. The current mindset of the state, however, at the national, provincial, and municipal levels makes it likely that the opportunity will be squandered. This is certainly suggested by the evolution of antigang strategies in the Cape since the mid-1990s.

Local experts point out that the greatest deterrent to crime is good relations between the police and the community.[38] Because the communities are the ones that have to live daily with the gangsters and the crime problem, and because of their unique position in relation to gangsters and the police, they represent the greatest resource that law enforcement could ask for. What this suggests is that the definition of resources in the discourse of criminal justice reform, and police reform specifically, prioritizes those resources that facilitate a law enforcement approach rather than a social crime prevention one. The result is a problematization of resource scarcity that reflects and reproduces technocratic as opposed to social crime prevention. The point is not that officers do not need reliable equipment in sufficient quantity to do their jobs and to keep safe. Rather, the belief that the solution to crime lies in overcoming scarcity of resources suggests an ideological predisposition to law enforcement strategies at odds with many of the principles contained in the NCPS, the 1998 White Paper on Safety and Security, and the CFRS. It is also important that we understand how this predisposition shapes policing and police interactions with people in gang areas. In Dixon's examples of sector policing, it becomes evident that police commitment to community-oriented policing is not at this point secure, and could in fact weaken if police have access to resources to "go straight and . . ." The implications for urban renewal on the Cape Flats is significant, as urban renewal is steadily becoming a process of disciplining youth who have been largely abandoned by other, more supportive state initiatives. The police become in this situation the state workers thrown into this gap between what government cannot provide but the criminal underground can.

Arguably, the most troubling indication of the direction urban renewal is headed is the growing of the divide between the stated commitment to social crime prevention in principle and the actual practice. This is likely to have an enormous impact on renewal initiatives like the CFRS because, being fundamentally antigangsterism strategies, they cede a great amount of power to law enforcement to act as agents of urban development. One of the challenges these strategies create, though, is that they increase the already substantial pressure on the police to break the back of gangsterism through a combination of social, economic, and security initiatives. The pressure to take decisive action conscribed by the principles of social crime prevention in the face of what has up until now proven to be one of the Cape Flats' most intractable challenges presents a contradiction of sorts between the parallel processes of police reform and getting tough on crime. Police are expected to participate in social crime prevention and be frontline soldiers in the war against crime, a balancing act that is proving to be difficult for already "democratized" police in places like the United States.[39] Had the gang problem been one that could be distilled out from the community, isolated, and attacked, there might be cause to think that narrowly focused antigang strategies could work. But, as experience is showing, the process is quite a bit more complicated and the police are proving to be a rather blunt instrument for township revitalization. In many cases police strategies for targeting gangsters are counterproductive from the standpoint of improving police/community relations and for reducing crime; and in the effort to come down hard on gangsters and show results, many innocent people end up getting trampled. The result is further alienation of two parties already estranged for good reason, and an increased reliance by the police on more "resources." This can become a mutually reinforcing cycle of mistrust, in which police/community relations, in terms of partnerships in crime fighting, often degenerate into law enforcement viewing communities instrumentally as simply sources of information and intelligence and communities viewing police with ambivalence, as sources of insecurity as much as remedies.

An incident from 2003 illustrates some of the ways these complex dynamics are playing out on the Cape Flats. The story, reported in the *Cape Argus* on January 8, involved a shooting war between the Americans and Dixie Boys in Athlone/Kewtown, a working- and middle-class coloured area that was for a brief time considered as a site for the city's 2010 World Cup stadium. Shooting began on a Saturday night and continued into the next day, and violence between the gangs continued until Wednesday. Police responding to the scene on Saturday reported being fired at and called for backup units. According to the *Argus*, "Other units arrived and chaos erupted. Policemen, apparently chasing runaway gangsters, allegedly kicked in residents' doors, ran into houses, threw food out of fridges and cupboards, overturned beds and assaulted law-abiding people."[40] One resident who spoke to the *Argus*, 29-year-old Llewellyn Brown, says he was beaten by a group of police after warning them that they were shooting in the direction of his wife and three children. Brown was then thrown in the back of a police van, driven around for awhile, and eventually released. Reflecting on the incident, Brown commented: "Most of the people living in Kew Town are decent, law-abiding people, most wanting to help police fight crime. But I have lost my respect for the police after they assaulted me." Brown estimates that there were approximately 200 police "running around acting crazy," and other residents reported that the officers were attempting to hide their identities by not wearing their name tags. Residents also allege police assaulted young and old, called protesting women "whores" and their children "bastards." One woman, speaking anonymously, related her experience:

> I was sitting on our balcony when I saw the police assaulting
> people with batons, helmets and butts of shotguns. Our door was
> kicked down when 10 police rushed inside. Instead of searching the
> house, they trashed our house by throwing out our food from the
> fridge and cupboards, and broke eggs. I heard my baby crying and
> ran to the room where I saw a policeman lifting up the bed with
> my baby lying there. I tried to stop him but he smacked me and
> threw me on to the bed. I thought he was going to rape me, but my
> older six-year-old child ran inside and was also smacked by the
> policeman, who laughed and told me I was a whore. . . . We might
> live in the slums of Cape Town, but the majority of us are good,
> decent, law-abiding people and not animals.[40]

Residents filed numerous complaints and an internal probe was scheduled.

The *Argus* story mentions, only in passing, a potentially important element to the events in Athlone/Kewtown. According to some residents who spoke to the paper, the Dixie Boys were protecting the community against an attempt by the Americans to take over Kewtown, and police officers reported that some residents refused to tell them where gangsters who had run into their homes were hiding out. What these reports suggest is that the circumstances surrounding the shootout and ensuing police effort to stop it go deeper than simple law enforcement, to say nothing of the broader context of community/gang relations in the community. The basic dynamic present in extreme incidents like this is widespread and routine in the views of youth workers I spoke with, as we will see in the next chapter, indicating a potentially counterproductive consequence of aggressive policing in anticrime and urban renewal programs that, in theory, are meant to center social crime prevention and development.

The prevalence of conflict between poor communities and police and the numbers of young people being swept into the criminal justice system relatively early on in the nation's transition demonstrate clearly the dangers lurking in law enforcement–driven urban renewal. The pressures on police to produce results, or at least to take bold, tough action, together with the power police have been granted by the state pose a credible threat to social crime prevention efforts because of the questionable effectiveness of hard policing in reducing crime, paving the way for socioeconomic renewal, and improving community/police relations. While in the CFRS the rationale for social crime prevention and zero tolerance rests on a relatively clear-cut distinction between criminals and residents, in practice the distinction can become blurred, as is evident in these examples. Thus, while in principle the city continues to speak in the language of social crime prevention, in practice it is slipping further into an all too familiar approach to policing the townships.

Postapartheid Roots of Hard Policing: The Cape Flats War

The direction policing is taking should be situated in relation to the continuity of institutions, practices, and, in many cases, personnel from the pre-1994 era, even as we remain attentive to the more contemporary forces that breathe new life into this historical trajectory. The belief that the period from the late 1990s to the present consists of a reform process in danger of being derailed, although accurate in many respects, does not adequately take into consideration the significance of these continuities, the reasons for them, and their impact on new challenges to police reform and the implementation of social crime prevention. In particular, the use of quasi-militaristic operations, often carried out in conjunction with the South Africa National Defence Forces (SANDF), have been endemic in the city and on the Cape Flats since 1994, arguably defining visible policing in the townships since then. Democratic reform of the criminal justice system is meant in principle to include an end to these kinds of operations and to the deployment of the military domestically;

both, however, have remained relatively constant features of policing in the province. The post-1994 roots of these operations lie primarily in the Cape Flats war that erupted in 1996 among the vigilante group PAGAD (People Against Gangsterism and Drugs), gangsters, and the security forces, and that helped to institutionalize in the new democracy an approach to policing that many hoped would recede into history along with the apartheid state. As the Cape Flats war began to wind down in 2000, these operations have been absorbed into the war against crime and gangsterism and have become integral aspects of urban renewal initiatives on the Cape Flats—sometimes, as we have seen, with horrible results. The Cape Flats war is therefore an important period in the evolution of security operations and structures in the city, representing a bridge between the counterinsurgency campaigns of the apartheid era and the war on crime of today.

On the surface, the involvement of the military in crime fighting and the militaristic nature of policing in the late 1990s are understandable. The political violence associated with the transition, much of which has since been confirmed as linked to state-directed provocation, was just beginning to subside. Crime and violence, however, continued to plague working-poor and middle-class areas and fed into the emergence of PAGAD as a community response to perceived police apathy, ineffectiveness, and even complicity with gangsterism on the Flats. Emerging from working- and middle-class coloured communities in the mid-1990s, PAGAD was, importantly, a response not just to high crime rates but also to perceived deficiencies in the state's ability and willingness to protect vulnerable communities during a tumultuous period in the city. The growth of a powerful vigilante group posed two significant challenges to the new state: On the one hand it was a direct challenge to the state's monopoly on the legitimate use of force, and on the other it exposed and publicized the state's inability, and to some its unwillingness, to protect the average citizen. As PAGAD became more militant and violent, it posed a third and a fourth challenge: to state security, at least at a local level, and to the nation's image. In 1996 PAGAD very publicly executed Rashaad Staggie, one of the leaders of the Hard Livings gang, in Salt River, very close to the city center, and in 1999 it was blamed for a series of bombings at Cape Town police stations in and around the city center. The campaign of "urban terrorism," as it was referred to in local media and by government, constituted a direct threat to the city's ability to attract foreign investment and tourists just as the drive for world class status was taking off, and heightened the perception that police were unable to contain the multifaceted threats emanating from the townships.[41]

Although PAGAD, at least at the outset, was primarily concerned with gangsterism and drug dealing, its views of the police ranged from disdain to hostility, a spectrum that mirrored differences within the organization itself. The escalating conflict between PAGAD and the police, however, is often explained in terms of the growing influence of militant religious fundamentalists within the organization. But, as researcher Anthony Minnaar has pointed out, this militancy was also partially fueled by the police decision, as far back as 1996, to treat PAGAD as "just another gang."[42] According to Minnaar, clashes with police and one PAGAD leader's declaration of a war on drug dealers *and* police, prompted the deputy national commissioner of the SAPS, Zola Lavisa, to respond:

> PAGAD's naked aggression, especially against the police, shows quite clearly that it has deliberately embarked on a policy of criminality. As far as the SAPS is concerned, PAGAD has degenerated into just another gang, and is now firmly part of the crime problem in the Western Cape.[43]

These kinds of attitudes frustrated some people within PAGAD and contributed to the perception that the police were indifferent to the grievances of Cape communities and were ultimately an obstacle to crime reduction and to their safety. The state, in turn, missed a potential opportunity at a crucial moment in the city's history to defuse the situation before it got out of hand. Thus its aggressive, militaristic response to PAGAD cannot be explained solely by the militancy of PAGAD, as it preceded the shift and may even have contributed to it. This pattern was repeated in the state's stance toward gangsters around the same time, when 3,000 of them and their supporters famously marched on Parliament in September of 1996 demanding a hearing as part of the Community Outreach Forum (Core).

Formed largely in response to PAGAD, Core was an umbrella organization made up of gang leaders from the major Cape gangs, as well as current and reformed gangsters from most gangs on the Flats. Core presented itself as an opportunity to reduce gang violence and defuse the growing conflict. Its position and demands were intriguing, as the organization called for "previous and present governments" to "take responsibility for turning them to crime," a reference to the violence and neglect of the apartheid system, the active use of gangs by the security forces against the antiapartheid movement, and the continued failure of the state to address the demands of the coloured population.[44] Summarizing Core's proposal, Wilfred Schärf writes that in response, they would contribute to

> development programmes for gangsters who wished to get out of the gang life-style. . . . The threat that CORE tagged on to their offer was that they would set the prisons alight if the government did not talk to them by a particular deadline. In exchange the "reformed" gangsters wanted total amnesty and the withdrawal of all charges against arguably the biggest drug wholesaler in the Cape, Colin Stanfield. A notable omission from their offer is a convincing undertaking that they will cease dealing in drugs or other illegal activities, either directly or indirectly.[45]

As Schärf and others point out, there were understandable concerns over the sincerity of Core's commitment to leaving gangsterism behind, concerns that were to some extent later borne out. But Core, like PAGAD, was not a homogeneous organization, especially in its early days, and contained both militant criminal factions and elements apparently sincere about addressing social and economic development. At the very least, there was reason to believe that the dialogue was worth pursuing. The state, however, was having none of it and refused to talk to Core. This decision to squeeze the complex and often contradictory phenomena of PAGAD and gangsterism into a law enforcement box foreshadowed many of the problems the Cape faces today in the struggle against continued violence. In framing the conflicts of the mid- to late 1990s as primarily a violent challenge to the state, authorities fell back on an overreliance on the blunt and well-worn instrument of force. This moment was thus a crucial point not only for the trajectory of postapartheid policing, but also in the much broader and more complex struggle over socioeconomic development, spatial governance, and political transformation that the Cape Flats war exposed.

Conditions in late 1996 were such that the escalation of the violence, if not inevitable, was at least not surprising. Attacks on gangsters and drug dealers, attributed to PAGAD, took out many senior gang leaders, as well as innocent bystanders. Increasingly, attacks and counterattacks between PAGAD and the gangs began to spill out of the Cape Flats into the more affluent parts of the city, and the state security forces themselves became the targets of sometimes successful bombings and shootings.[46] Not without controversy, city authorities blamed the spike in violence mostly on PAGAD and the increasing militancy associated with the rise of the fundamentalist Qibla faction. Indeed, the tendency, certainly on the part of the police but also among researchers on urban terrorism in the Cape, has been to focus on PAGAD militants as bearing a disproportionate responsibility for the violence of the Cape Flats war. Although PAGAD clearly shares significant responsibility, it is important to stress that certainly in 1995 and 1996, when PAGAD emerged, the SAPS had virtually zero credibility in the crime-ridden communities, which it had more than earned over the course of more than four brutal decades. The state violence of the apartheid counterinsurgency campaigns, carried out largely by the SAPS, was hardly a memory at this point, and police reform was still drying ink on paper. The feeling that police were part of the problem cannot be dismissed as unfair harshness or impatience and propaganda on the part of "militants" but had a strong foundation in practical knowledge based on years of firsthand experience. Furthermore, not only were communities aware that the police had covertly cooperated with gangs in the very recent past, but evidence began to surface in the media in 1997 and 1998 suggesting that the relationship between the two continued and that elements within the police were in fact stoking violence between the gangs and PAGAD.[47] The militancy of PAGAD and the violence associated with the war need to be seen in this light, as a reformulation of continuous violence, both political and criminal, that stretched back decades, and the ongoing struggle between the state and society. As with the growth in crime, it would be shortsighted to view the group and the conflict surrounding it as products of the transition or challenges unique to democratic consolidation. However, much of the state's response to PAGAD and the associated violence did just that, seemingly blind or powerless in the face of the unresolved and in some sense now heightened contradictions of the apartheid period.

The SAPS took an early and aggressive approach to the escalating war centered around the Cape Flats in 1996 but was overwhelmed before the end of the year. Consultations between authorities at the national and provincial levels sought to quickly address the weaknesses of the police by bringing in the SANDF and the national intelligence agencies, underscoring the militarized nature of the state response to unrest in the city.

The response took the form of a series of special counterterrorism operations directed through a SAPS/SANDF partnership established early in 1996, the National Operations Coordinating Mechanism (Nodoc). Nodoc allowed authorities to coordinate provincial and national intelligence and carry out joint operations involving the various security and intelligence agencies brought in to quell the spiraling violence.[48] Although fighting a different enemy, the operations were structurally and institutionally similar to the apartheid counterinsurgency campaigns, and the state was able to draw on the experience of well-trained cadres to meet this new challenge.[49] The operations are especially important because, over time, as PAGAD and the wave of urban terror were brought under control, they survived, morphing into the anticrime and antigangsterism initiatives that continue to structure current urban renewal strategies on the Cape Flats.

The four operations carried out during the Cape War are described in a monograph published by the Institute for Security Studies (ISS) in July 2001. The first, Operation Recoil, was introduced in October 1997, and although modifications were made to subsequent operations, it contained within it the basic characteristics that would define these campaigns up to the present. What emerged were a series of operations that blended with seeming ease key components of apartheid policing with "cutting edge" policing practices from the Western democracies.[50] First, the operations were largely intelligence driven and mobilized intelligence gathering and analysis structures to produce tactical intelligence for use in identifying crime "hot spots," against which high-density crime prevention operations would then be launched. The use of intelligence also served another purpose, providing evidence for court-directed investigations that would help to ensure prosecution, especially of higher-ranking PAGAD leaders. The operations also made use of high-density policing, mobilizing a range of specialized units, including the visible gang unit, the public order police, and the army, for rapid interventions and saturation policing. They were coordinated between the provincial and national levels, and regular meetings were held for joint planning and evaluation. Weekly briefings were then held with the national director of the SAPS and the chief of SANDF. They, in turn, would brief the NCPS's ministers committee on a monthly basis or as needed. According to the authors of the ISS monograph:

> The concept of Operation Recoil was based on the principle
> of flooding flashpoint areas with high-density security force

deployment by way of mobile visible patrols as well as cordon and search operations, in order to flush out criminals at such flashpoint areas. This strategy also improved the SAPS's ability to synchronise and focus high-density deployment in flashpoint areas, as determined by weekly crime pattern analyses submitted by crime information managers at SAPS station and area levels, as well as strategic crime tendency analyses conducted by the intelligence coordinating structures.[51]

Instead of using the quality-of-life approach to catch small-time offenders, most likely a pointless task given how vast the Flats are and the many "broken windows" across it, the strategy here is to catch the "untouchable" criminal elite and break their organizations through the careful collection of intelligence. According to one senior police official interviewed by Bill Dixon, high-profile criminals would be taken even if the offenses were relatively minor, as a way to exert constant pressure on the organizations.[52] Intelligence also drove another important aspect of the attempt to break the organizations through constant pressure: civil and criminal asset forfeiture laws successfully introduced through the Prevention of Organised Crime Act (POCA). Both of these strategies, intended to work in tandem and maximize the reach of the criminal justice net, rely on solid evidence and court prosecution, marking a radical departure from the sweeping powers granted the security forces under apartheid. Intelligence played a central role in the more traditional aspects of the operations as well; especially as PAGAD's bombing and assassination campaign escalated in 1998, quick collection and analysis of reliable intelligence was crucial to preventing attacks or tracking down perpetrators after they had been carried out. The emphasis on intelligence is a significant part of the evolution of policing in the Cape. It allows for the knitting together of the aggressive, security-driven methods in which the SAPS was well versed with modern democratic techniques and discourses newly available with the opening of the country to the global marketplace, all within the complex and contradictory contexts of criminal justice reform and urban renewal, the pressure to end the violence and the legacy of apartheid policing, and fractured relationships between communities and the police. At the same time, as we will see in the next chapter, the reliance on intelligence-driven policing would also come to constitute a barrier to overcoming strained community/police relations once the Cape Flats war concluded.

The state responded with modifications of its strategy as the war intensified through the late 1990s. In January 1998 Operation Saladin was introduced as part of Recoil but with the specific goal of responding to shifts in PAGAD targets, including high-profile attacks on security forces and Muslim businessmen. Administered at the provincial level, Saladin was essentially a detection, rapid response, and interception project that involved the SAPS, SANDF, and the National Intelligence Agency. In January 1999 the two operations were merged into Operation Good Hope, again in response to further developments in the war, specifically to the targeting of police and businesses in and around the city center and other more affluent areas. Bombings at the upscale V and A Waterfront mall downtown, including Planet Hollywood, and the Cape Town Police Station were clear signals that even the commercial heart of the city was not immune from the troubles spilling out from the Flats. Good Hope is notable for what the ISS calls an increase in force levels and the attempt to mobilize community projects to gather intelligence for the security forces, an approach in many ways increasingly indistinguishable from classic counterinsurgency warfare, save perhaps in its rhetorical alignment with the language of democratic policing employed in the West.[53]

Good Hope led to a sharp increase in accusations of police brutality reported to the Independent Complaints Directorate (ICD) in just its first month. Operation spokesperson Anine de Beer, speaking to the *Cape Times*, acknowledged the unpopularity of the operation but said that police remained committed to the zero tolerance approach: "We know that some of the criminals and the community are not happy. We will continue to do our job, but we know that the people who are complaining are also the suspects."[54] But given the frayed relations between the communities and the police that contributed to the rise of PAGAD in the first place, the state's reliance on harsh measures should be seen as a consequence of limited options for the police as much as of an ideological commitment to the efficacy of a zero tolerance approach. Criminologist Wilfred Schärf, quoted in the same story, remarked: "It seems as though they [the police] are going back to what they did in the old era, not only with Operation Good Hope but also at other police stations. It seems that the police are frustrated." Schärf's observation here is significant. For the SAPS in the Western Cape, the rise of PAGAD, the ensuing cycle of violence, and the bad publicity this was bringing the city and nation at a time when economic growth had been pinned to the country's international image increased the pressure the police faced and, understandably, contributed to a sense of frustration. The renewed determination to take decisive action that would yield immediate results was a rational response to this set of circumstances. In addition, the rise of PAGAD as a vigilante group compounded the difficulties facing the government in its attempt to establish legitimacy in areas where its control and authority were already tenuous. Continued ineffectiveness in the fight against crime and violence could reasonably have been expected to further erode faith in the state's ability on this front and seriously worsen the growing problem of vigilante justice around the country.[55] At the same time, the resort to force had its own risks, as Schärf and others have pointed out, leaving the government and security forces open to charges, particularly in the wake of incidents like those in Athlone/Kewtown, that nothing had changed. It is not a surprise, then, that authorities were feeling frustrated and that, as Bill Dixon and Jill Marie-Johns observed:

> Long-accustomed to reaching for their familiar hammers, the security forces saw PAGAD as just another nail—a threat to the authority of the new State much like the [United Democratic Front], the ANC and the others had been to the old.[56]

All indications, however, are that wielding the hammer against PAGAD was initially a success, as the number of serious incidents attributed to the vigilante group began to decline in 1999 and throughout 2000 with the introduction of Operation Good Hope. Although PAGAD is still active, its reach has been greatly reduced for the time being. By the time Operation Crackdown came to the city in April of 2000, the Cape Flats war was on the wane and the shift in focus of these operations from urban terror to more conventional crime, still apparently on the increase, was well under way.

Crackdown, unlike the other operations, was part of a national campaign and was developed under the national urban renewal priorities laid out in President Mbeki's opening address to Parliament in June 1999. Reflecting key aspects of the NCPS, these priorities included taking a multifaceted approach to crime reduction that would bring together all the relevant departments and agencies in implementing social crime prevention as a complement to more aggressive strategies. The first action carried out under Crackdown was the massive cordon and search operation in Johannesburg in March 2000 discussed in chapter 1, the main targets of which were Nigerian crime syndicates and illegal immigrants in the Hillbrow neighborhood. Crackdown came to the Western Cape the next month, and although it had a different target than its predecessors, the structure was fairly similar: It was intelligence driven, emphasized high-density swarm and storm operations targeting national crime hot spots, and relied on crime data analysis and resource clustering. Two of the marked hot spots included the Cape Flats communities of Mitchells Plain and Manenberg, both of which would also become sites for the CFRS the next year. Crackdown also differed from the older operations in that it sought to involve as integral elements social development and social crime prevention measures to soften its hard edge and harmonize the operation with the principles of the new urban renewal program. In this sense it was a bridge of sorts, linking the antiterror operations to the increasingly central anticrime operations.

The last major operation against PAGAD, Operation Lancer, came in September 2000 in response to the assassination of Wynberg magistrate Pieter Theron, who had presided over a number of PAGAD-related prosecutions. Lancer was specifically geared toward urban terrorism and PAGAD, and its activities included providing 24-hour protection to all investigators, prosecutors, magistrates, and judges involved in PAGAD investigations.[57] Like the other operations, Lancer was also intelligence driven and focused on gathering information that could be used to obtain indictments. After the September 11, 2001, attacks on the United States, Lancer was adjusted to include in its mission the protection of U.S. interests in the Western Cape and nationally from PAGAD strikes.[58]

The most recent special operation, Slasher, was introduced in March 2001 with a clear antigangsterism focus and again adopting the "hot spot" strategy of spatial governance.[59] The five areas included in Slasher overlap significantly with the national crime spots in the Western Cape referred to by Mbeki in his 1999 speech and the locations in the CFRS, introduced that same month in MEC Bester's budget speech: Mitchells Plain, Elsies River, Manenberg, Philippi/Hanover Park, and Bishop Lavis. Slasher is a direct outgrowth of the older urban terror operations and of Lancer specifically, with the operational team from Lancer taking charge of the new program, and has been folded into the CFRS as the operational component of the strategy's law enforcement prong. Significantly, its stated role, as part of the strategy, is to pave the way for urban renewal. Illustrating the thinking about security and development under urban renewal, police argued: "Once law enforcement, in terms of visibility, and widescale arrests has been achieved, urban renewal and social upliftment will gradually begin to show in the five demarcated zones."[60]

In keeping with the priorities of the older operations and the CFRS, Slasher's primary targets are high-level gangsters, whose arrest and successful prosecution, it is believed, will break the backs of the gangs and thus reduce violence. The operations carried out under Slasher followed virtually the same patterns seen in other operations, such as Crackdown. For example, in mid-2001, four months after it was introduced, a high-profile cordon and search was carried out in Manenberg, resulting in the arrest of a leader of the Clever Kids gang, his wife, and a drug dealer in their car. Police made six other arrests, two for serious crimes, and issued 28 summonses for traffic violations. The sweep was based on crime data intelligence analysis provided by the new station commissioner for Manenberg, Senior Superintendent Harri, a former member of the gang unit and also a U.S. Department of Justice intern who had advocated the implementation of U.S.-style antigang measures back in 1998.[61] It was part of a weeklong series of similar operations that saw more than 700 arrests and involved 400 police and soldiers and two helicopters and traffic officers setting up roadblocks and conducting searches of persons, cars, and homes.[62] These types of actions continued over the next two years, in the Cape and around the country as part of Operations Crackdown and Slasher and the provincial and national urban renewal efforts, leading to a massive intervention of police into the daily lives of township communities.[63] And as pronouncements by National Safety and Security Minister Charles Nqakula in 2002 made clear, the operations are still seen as a response to security threats to the state, this time in the form of gangsterism rather than urban terrorism.[64]

The operational and discursive transition from counterterrorism to war on crime has been a fairly smooth one at the level of the state and its security forces, but it has at the same time created or reproduced serious problems for the communities on the Cape Flats. In the next chapter we look more closely at some of the consequences of this approach to policing for the broader project of social crime prevention and development it is ostensibly intended to support. What becomes clear, in contrast to the governance of security in the city center, is the different relationship of policing and crime reduction to the respective populations. Whereas in the city center, governance structures are responsive to the concerns and interests of residents and certain visitors, in the townships, communities often feel they themselves are being policed. The differences are important for making the case that even within one city, although neoliberalism may be the overarching governance regime, its actual expression can vary significantly according to variations in the social terrain.

4

The Weight of Policing on the Fragile Ground of Transformation

The policing of township communities has always been central to the governance of the urban poor in Cape Town and is therefore central to understanding how the insecurity of the periphery is reproduced. The following chapter thus examines some of the consequences of hard policing for the fight against crime and gangs and for township communities. Proponents of the law enforcement approach have an almost singular focus on crime rates, and this is where the discussion here begins. Crime rates, however, are only one aspect of the security equation; at least as important are the immediate and long-term effects of hard policing on communities more broadly, and its ability to prepare the ground for future development, as per the governance strategy the city has embraced for more than a decade. The discussion of crime rates is therefore followed by a closer look at the realities behind the statistics: complaints of police misconduct, interactions between police and young men in the townships, the institutionalization of hard policing via the embrace of "international best practices," and finally, the related lack of effective social crime prevention strategies. Taken together, policing in the townships is in effect reinforcing the wedge that exists between police and residents, deepening mistrust and cynicism and eroding the ground in which genuine long-term crime prevention, and therefore social development, could potentially take root. Instead, Cape Town's peripheries are plagued by a harsh, if erratic and partial, form of policing, which has a questionable impact on many serious crimes and a negative impact on others while further insinuating violence into the fabric of everyday life.

Policing of the townships is the counterpoint to neoliberal governance of security in the city center. It contributes to the reproduction of the conditions of insecurity from which it draws its legitimacy, both actively (e.g., in further marginalizing township residents) and passively (e.g., neglecting genuine security for township residents). Instead of withering away or being dismantled after 1994, the old form of policing has been absorbed into and is now articulated through the structures and processes of neoliberal governance. The neoliberal dimensions of this policing and its consequences are found in discursive and spatial articulations where they are framed as necessary to protect fragile growth and national/municipal images. They are legitimated through reference to the "best practices" of liberal democracies, and often hidden from view through their implementation across the particular geography bequeathed by apartheid, all the while being quietly celebrated by boosters of Cape Town as a world-class city. The consequences of this approach to the governance of security are directly linked to very old and very local as well as to the authoritative power of transnational approaches that are a hallmark of reclaimed world-class city spaces and cutting-edge neoliberal urbanism.

The Implications of Hard Policing for Crime and Gangsterism on the Cape Flats

The success of vigilante campaigns of the People Against Gangsterism and Drugs (PAGAD) helped to legitimize and institutionalize a standard operating procedure for anticrime units based in special counterterrorism operations.[1] They therefore form an important backdrop to the emergence of a war on crime in the Cape and the insertion of these specific law enforcement approaches into the center of postapartheid urban renewal programs, themselves centered on anticrime and antigangsterism measures. As the previous chapter demonstrated, the war on crime did not suddenly emerge so much as evolve over almost a decade of special operations that functioned along military lines from the start and often included military forces. It is not altogether surprising, then, that law enforcement and many government officials continue to evince scepticism or even hostility toward policing reform along progressive lines meant to displace traditional approaches. The benefits of social crime prevention can be somewhat slow to reveal themselves and may even be indirect from the perspective of measures such as annual crime rates. Unlike cordon and search operations, social crime prevention is also unlikely to attract significant media attention because it generally does not involve newsworthy events and its effects on crime rates are difficult to measure.[2] The anti-PAGAD operations, on the other hand, were highly visible and highly effective in diffusing the organized violence of the vigilante group. They also boldly announced that the police were in fact "doing something" about the violence and lawlessness sweeping the peninsula at a time when many were watching to see if the city would stabilize or spiral deeper into chaos. By so doing, however, they may have inadvertently compounded the difficulties involved in shifting over to social crime prevention approaches that treat crime as a multidimensional phenomenon and craft solutions in line with the security paradigm spelled out by the African National Congress in its "Ready to Govern" resolution, their apparent success narrowing room for alternative approaches to crime.

Revisiting the issue of crime rates is a useful starting point for assessing the consequences of the anticrime campaigns that began in the wake of the Cape Flats war as they relate to crime itself and to the communities in which they are concentrated. Although officials and the police defend the campaigns and their results, the claims of success raise two basic, related questions: Are they reducing crime and are they making communities safer? The overall crime picture for the Cape between 1997 and 2003, based on annual crime statistics of the South African Police Service (SAPS), show that non-terror-related crime increased, including a 30 percent jump in the murder rate. Attempts to capture the impact of current police approaches on crime and security after 2003, however, reveal a complex picture and show the unintended, if not completely unexpected, consequences of current policies and practices. Statistics for 2003–04 provided by SAPS do generally show impressive drops in the murder and attempted murder rates and small decreases in the incidence of rape. At the same time, assault with intent to do grievous bodily harm, common assault, and carjacking increased. These patterns, with some exceptions, hold for the city as a whole and the Cape Flats specifically. Since 2004–05, the incidence of crime in the city has decreased, although crime across Cape Flats communities continues to seesaw, with the exception of the steady and dramatic increase in drug crimes. The government understandably points to declines, when they occur, as proof that the country has turned a corner on crime and that its intelligence-driven "get tough" approach is bearing fruit. Whether this is in fact the case or whether the changes reflect a temporary dip or stabilization at what are still unacceptably high levels remains to be seen.

Beyond the debate over the relationship between the statistics and aggressive policing lurks a more troubling issue that could pose a major challenge to building the strong community/police relations upon which long-term crime reduction and social development depend. Despite the official statistics, people over the years from the youth development sector on the Cape Flats, youth workers in the Central Business District (CBD), and representatives of nongovernmental organizations (NGOs) involved with youth diversion programs were uniformly, and often strongly, skeptical of claims that crime was on the decline. As some of the reasons for the apparent drop, they point to political manipulation of the figures, a decreasing likelihood of people reporting many crimes, and police discouraging people from reporting crimes (particularly rape and domestic violence). Their views were supported when a scandal erupted across three provinces in 2009, including in coloured and black African communities of the Western Cape, concerning charges that police at a number of stations had manipulated crime statistics to create the appearance of a decline.[3] Among the strategies allegedly used by senior police at some of the stations in question were burning case dockets, changing or bringing a lesser charge for crimes that were on the rise, dropping cases that might be difficult to prosecute, and, in the instance of Cape Town's Lansdowne police station, recording rape cases as "enquiries" rather than as crimes and therefore excluding them from crime statistics. Concerns over the manipulation of crime statistics in Cape Town surfaced as early as 2006, when police reports on the issue were leaked to the media, but at the time no action appeared to have been taken despite evidence uncovered by the SAPS national inspectorate.[4] As of December 2009, however, the Independent Complaints Directorate (ICD), a government body that is meant to investigate complaints against the police, said it would demand to see more than 1,000 case dockets in the province possibly related to the manipulation of crime statistics, and a number of senior police had already been fired, suspended, or charged with crimes.[5] Regardless of the outcome, the scandal is likely to further strain relations with township communities whose trust the police, and the state more generally, will need if anticrime measures are to have any lasting positive impact. The manipulation of crime statistics not only clouds the issue of whether current approaches are working, but it also suggests that the narrow focus on crime statistics may in fact compete for the attention of law enforcement and the state more generally with the focus on actually making communities safer.

Further compounding the difficulties in building trust and relationships is the direct impact of police operations and the interactions of law enforcement with people in targeted high-crime areas. Although interviews conducted show that communities and police are in some cases forming productive partnerships on the Cape Flats, the overall picture is less encouraging. Data collected by the ICD for the years 2002–09 show dramatic increases in reports of police misconduct and criminal offenses in the Western Cape in the early years, after which criminal complaints remained steady and misconduct complaints declined; over the same period, deaths in custody and as a result of police action rose steadily (see Table 1).

Beyond these numbers, two important aspects of the ICD data stand out. First, at the national level, police brutality constitutes the vast majority of criminal complaints. In 2008–09 for example, 69 percent of criminal complaints related to some form of police brutality (attempted murder, common assault, and assault with intent to commit grievous bodily harm). Second, complaints in the Western Cape tend to make up a disproportionate percentage of the national total. Complaints of police criminality in 2002–03 constituted almost 21 percent of the national total, whereas complaints of misconduct made up almost one quarter.[6] The next year the province registered the highest number of total complaints, constituting 22 percent of the national total in a province that contains only 10 percent of the entire population.[7] It is unclear exactly what relationship, if any, exists among the drop in some major crimes; the aggressive, law enforcement–driven strategy credited for the decline;

TABLE 1.

Number of Complaints Against Police to the Independent Complaints Directorate, Western Cape, 2002–2009

	CRIMINAL	DEATH	MISCONDUCT
2002–03	192	57	593
2003–04	306	73	910
2004–05	295	65	897
2005–06*	NA	NA	NA
2006–07	338	79	375
2007–08	339	95	546
2008–09	356	82	399

Source: Independent Complaints Directorate Annual Reports
*No data available on Web site for 2005–06.

and the increase in complaints against the police in the Western Cape, but what the ICD figures and the crime statistics scandal suggest is that police/community relations currently rest on extremely weak foundations, which we return to in the discussion of social development in the next chapter.

Interviews conducted in the city with youth workers provide a glimpse behind the figures and reveal how interactions between police and youth in high-crime areas can mirror incidents like that in Athlone/Kewtown from the previous chapter. Mike, a former prisoner who works with at-risk youth in Pollsmoor prison and in their communities, provides some insight on the experiences that lie behind these figures. Speaking of the police, he told me:

> They're too scared to patrol two people in a car. They patrol three vans at a time, ten, fifteen policemen. So whoever they stop, it's going to be an antagonistic situation. When you're fifteen policemen you can't make a nice inquiry. There's too many eyes on you, you have to be hard core, and that's your role as a policeman in your officer's eyes.[8]

Commenting on police behavior in communities, he makes an observation often heard about individual officers who want to make a difference but are unable to do so in their professional capacity:

> You get the individual policeman who really wants to make a difference. They come from the community, they see what is happening, they want to do something. You can speak to them, they're eager to assist. But once again, their hands are tied, there's nothing they can do as representatives of the SAPS. They'll do it in their personal capacity.

He contrasts this with the institution of the police and of policing:

> But you as an individual in the community, you are still the victim of abuse. There's no nicety about it. It's all this raw, fucking, in-your-face "get the fuck out of my way, arrgh!" . . . There's a lot of anger and fear. They're [police] so scared to be nice because, "Hey, I might get shot here."

Valda, another experienced youth worker, makes a similar observation:

> They're not trained properly, they have no way of dealing
> with communities, I've seen some of them become really angry
> and fairly abusive, I mean just around here alone. . . . You don't
> get the sense that it's an institutional change. . . . Now maybe
> there's a couple of captains, maybe one or two at a police
> station, but the general attitude is not necessarily an
> institutional attitude that's changed, you know, "We now
> approach things differently."[9]

She describes how one of the boys she works with was treated after being
picked up by the police on the train for not having a ticket:

> They arrested him for the weekend, they kept him for seventy-two
> hours. [He] was beaten up by security police on the train. . . . It
> affected the hearing in his ear, the way they beat him up. He went
> and laid a charge [filed a complaint] and they [SAPS] said to him
> that he should go back to the railway station where it happened
> and hang around there until he sees these guys, and he should
> follow them.

The situation is especially bad for young people who have been to prison,
who often are easily identifiable because of their tattoos.

> Especially the prison boys, with their tattoos and things, they just
> get arrested, you know. It causes turmoil with their parole, but no
> cognizance is taken of that. . . . They've been arrested for looking
> suspicious, being suspicious in a place.

Kevin, from an organization called Youth Leaders Against Crime in the
Grassy Park area, remarks:

> I feel sorry for them [police] but they're also to blame because of
> how they handle the people. Even now, when it comes to crime
> issues, the smacking and the . . . and also the corruption that is
> going on. So from the youth, already what happened in apartheid,
> now they see still this thing is happening, it's not yet been . . . there's

nothing like, "We want to come and help, we want to support. We still see you almost like we are afraid of you."[10]

According to Llewellyn Jordaan, a social worker in the Flats community of Lavender Hill:

> The kind of mentality of the approach is to have a complete zero tolerance—towards crime, fine, that's good—but in terms of how they are going to behave towards finding youngsters on the road, they are very aggressive. And if the youngsters are very well built and all that, they will not be pushed around by the police. In that sense, it can become quite contentious. And I've seen a lot of conflict between the youth and the police.[11]

The experiences of these youth workers and those they work with give some sense of how current approaches to the governance of security in the townships can operate at the micro level today. Beyond the problems at this scale, however, the war on crime in the city is having a more structural impact on crime and gangs as well, one whose roots lie in the Cape Flats but which is being reproduced through their increasing institutionalization against a background of steady public pressure.

One of the unintended consequences of the approach to PAGAD by the police, which, ironically, mirrored PAGAD's own approach to gangsters, was to give the gangs an opportunity to organize. The emergence of the Community Outreach Forum (Core), for example, which united most of the Cape Flats gangs, was a direct response to the growing power of PAGAD and its increasingly uncompromising stance toward gangsters. Although not a homogeneous organization, Core, over time, increasingly came to act as a cover by the Hard Livings and the 28s prison gangs to take control of and consolidate gangs and syndicates within and outside the province, using defense against PAGAD and community development as its political cover.[12] Core fell apart after much of its leadership was assassinated, allegedly by PAGAD. However, this too had important unintended consequences. The assassinations, by eliminating the older, upper levels of gang leadership, opened up space for increased competition among younger members for power within and among the gangs, leading to renewed and increasingly violent clashes in a scramble to fill the vacuum. Gangs became more decentralized as a result. One observer interviewed by Jill Marie-Johns stated that because of PAGAD's "success,"

> [g]angs have decentralised and that's . . . much more dangerous for us in the community, because when the gangs decentralize, then you don't know who's doing what. Then you can take eight or nine or ten people and they can form their own section of the gang, they can specialize in armed robberies, for instance. Whereas under centralization you could detect . . . immediately what's going on—now you can't do that.[13]

One of the lessons the state could have learned from both PAGAD's and their own role in the war is that isolating and coming down hard on the leadership may lead to some high-profile convictions and disrupt the organization, at least for a time. But the other side of that success is a clearing of the slate, so to speak, that sets the stage for new gang conflicts and reorganization so as to adapt to the new circumstances. The obvious point here is that while a layer of leadership is removed, the conditions that gave rise to the organizations remain. Jean Redpath refers to the problem as a "hydra phenomenon" and points to examples from Athlone, Grassy Park, and Philippi in the late 1990s, when the arrest or death of gang leaders in these areas of the Flats often led to the emergence of several smaller leaders and failed to result in reduced levels of crime.[14] She and Irvin Kinnes also point to the spread of gangs to rural areas as another unintended, if unsurprising, consequence of heavy-handed law enforcement tactics, as gangs seek new, less policed areas in which to operate. As a consequence, organized crime, the exploding drug trade, and the violence and instability associated with them are scattered over a greater area.

This counterproductive approach to combating organized crime has since been institutionalized through the transfer of U.S. technologies, coded as "international best practice," to the local South African context. In 1998, the national government passed the Prevention of Organised Crime Act (POCA), mentioned in chapter 3, which was modeled directly on the Racketeer Influenced Corrupt Organizations (RICO) Act from the United States and drafted with U.S. assistance.[15] A key advantage of the new legislation, according to proponents, is that it facilitates coordinated attacks on gang leaders. One of the problems with POCA, however, is that it will simply add to the pressure on gangs to decentralize, making it harder to track leaders. Instead of one or a handful of leaders giving orders and issuing weapons, for example, the organization hierarchies will flatten.[16] Organizational adaptations to police crackdowns are changing this structure. Instead of increased security, police operations designed to hammer the gangs may be perpetuating conflict and proliferation, pushing gangs to adapt and survive. It does not appear that the lessons from these experiences have been learned, and the more recent Cape Flats Renewal Strategy (CFRS), relying on the POCA legal framework, explicitly made targeting gang leadership a centerpiece of its law enforcement strategy.

The institutionalization of law enforcement–driven antigang approaches in POCA goes well beyond the targeting of gang leaders through POCA's definition of gang membership. This portion of POCA is also borrowed from the United States. The POCA section on gangs provides five criteria, taken directly from the separate but very similar California and Florida Street Terrorism Enforcement and Prevention (STEP) Acts. One of these criteria, contained in chapter 4, sec. 11(c), defines a gang member as one who "resides in or frequents a particular criminal gang's area and adopts their style of dress, their use of hand signs, language or their tattoos, and associates with known members of a criminal gang."[17] Given the prevalence of gangsterism on the Cape Flats, virtually any part could be considered a criminal gang's area, and many youth not associated with gangs in any significant way are likely to "associate" with known members of a criminal gang. The criteria also assume a clear and obvious distinction between "normal" and gang youth cultures among young people who have grown up in the same neighborhoods, one that adults (i.e., the police) can easily identify. Because this assumption is often incorrect and ignores the reality of prejudice in the public against coloured youth, POCA-based gang identification reinforces the idea that gangsterism largely defines coloured youth on the Flats. Brian van Wyk, with the Medical Research Council's Health Systems Research Unit, argues that the reality on the Flats is that "[y]outh dressed in a certain way hanging around on street corners are always labelled as gangsters."[18]

Sec. 11(c) of POCA is a verbatim reproduction from the Florida STEP Act, which has itself already been challenged inside and outside the U.S. courts because of its arbitrary definitions of gang membership and the related problem of racial profiling of black and Latino youth.[19] As with the various STEP Acts, chapter 4 of POCA gives authorities wide latitude to determine which youths are gang associates and members. The POCA clause also confers state legitimacy on highly politicized and problematic definitions of youth criminality, translating stereotypes into legal code. Taken by itself, racial profiling describes an unconstitutional law enforcement practice, but more important it is at the same time an exercise of social control insofar as it combines state power and social prejudice under controversial security strategies that empower police to deal with youth "deviance" in communities where relationships among gangs, residents, and the law are already tense. Control is exercised through the implicit evocation and reproduction of deeply racialized notions of criminality that still infuse South African society, legitimated by their basis in "international" law enforcement practice and operationalized in the antigangsterism focus of urban renewal. Not only does a war on crime funnel more young black men into the prison system, the antigangsterism crackdowns also mean that more youth in general come into contact with the system through their interactions with the police in their communities as suspects, potential suspects, and arrestees. Even for young people not involved with gangs, the experience of racial profiling can make concrete the criminal identity ascribed to young coloureds in general by the public. It was a member of the Americans gang who said to me that in his experience, protection from the police is actually one reason some youth join gangs in the first place. Seeking protection, however, the new recruit also now becomes part of the problem and a legitimate target of urban renewal operations. Racial profiling in particular, especially under conditions of a war against crime, is thus implicated in a chain of events, beginning with the assumption of criminality and proceeding to harassment, arrest, gang membership, and, ultimately, prison. Most youth are involved in this chain, if at all, only at the first and perhaps second steps (no hard data on profiling appear to exist at this point), but as the arrest and incarceration rates suggest, many are propelled along further.

The critiques of current approaches to gangsterism are important because, in addition to explaining a key component of gang growth in the post-1994 period, they complicate the more conventional explanation offered by some experts that gang resurgence is a function of decreased repression after the fall of apartheid and the introduction of democracy. Rather, increased gang activity can just as easily be understood as the result of continued repression and continued instability in the townships in the context of shifting political and economic conditions. This misunderstanding informs many of the critiques of soft policing and the notion that South Africa is too concerned with human rights–oriented policing.[20] The failure thus far of what is really quasi-military policing begs the question of its appropriateness as the hinge around which urban renewal turns. Because of the central role given to law enforcement in the CFRS, this question is crucial, as it touches on a core issue in police reform and police practice on the Cape Flats, namely, whether hard policing simply needs to be fine-tuned or is an inherently unsuitable framework for crime reduction and the challenge posed by gangsterism. The opinion of most criminologists and criminal justice researchers who have studied crime and policing on the Cape Flats is that the theory of hard policing reducing crime and paving the way for urban renewal is deeply flawed at the conceptual level and is an ill-matched solution to the development problems on the Flats.[21]

The institutionalization of law enforcement approaches to crime and gangsterism certainly has roots in the Cape Flats war, but the process is supported by various forms of public pressure that, somewhat ironically, work against the kinds of policing that might make residents safer. The pressure on law enforcement to produce results comes from a number of different quarters, from the communities most impacted by crime, from more affluent areas less impacted but equally or more frightened by the specter of crime, from the business community frightened by the impact of crime on economic growth, and from political leaders concerned about perceptions of their competence, the realities of electoral politics, and the need to secure the investment environment. Although all of these groups are undoubtedly interested in real reductions in crime and violence, they also have differing interests, options, and perceptions of what crime reduction should be. We saw, for example, the role that crime and the fear of crime played in political campaigning in both the 1999 and 2004 national elections and the subsequent "tough on crime" stance taken by the various parties and then by the national government. The renewal of Cape Town's city center provides another example of how urban renewal is shaped by particular kinds and combinations of pressure, this time from local government, certain sectors of the public, NGOs, and the business community, and how these can produce a particular kind of policing and development in a relatively short period of time. On the other hand, although less affluent communities of the Cape Flats have consistently voiced their interests in crime-reduction efforts and their complaints about the police and police operations, change has been much slower in coming on these fronts of the reform and urban renewal processes. It is true that the gangsterism and development challenges on the Flats are more vast and complex than those faced by the Central City Improvement District (CCID; see chapter 2), but this should not obscure a more fundamental problem: the relative weakness of the political pressure on the police and, by extension, the state that these communities exert. In other words, the inappropriateness of the antigangsterism/urban renewal approach is linked both to an absence of mobilized political power in the communities that can drive different approaches, an abundance of power in other quarters, and the institutional genealogy of the SAPS. The unfortunate situation this creates is that the communities most affected by crime exercise the least influence over how the problem is addressed.

Referring specifically to support for hard policing in political circles, Carl Niehaus, formerly executive director of the National Institute for Crime Prevention and Reintegration of Offenders (NICRO), puts it this way:

Operation Crackdown can play a part, but it is not the answer. Operations like this are easy for politicians to support—they want short-term results, to gain votes in the next election. As a politician unless you can plug into the prevailing public opinion and present yourself as a person of action and delivery, your political career is in trouble. In the call for tough action against criminals, people do not take into account that many offenders are young, the prisons are overcrowded, and there is no segregation in prison between younger and older prisoners. Dealing with crime in a different way requires the political will to take steps which may not be popular with the voters.[22]

Dr. Bernie Fanaroff, adviser to the Minister of Safety and Security and former head of the National Crime Prevention Strategy (NCPS), speaking at the same forum as Mr. Niehaus, concurred, stating: "The public and politicians like to see cordon and search operations, roadblocks, and lots of arrests—military-style stabilisation." He also criticized the rationale behind operations like Slasher, that "stabilization" would necessarily lead to renewal and development, directly contradicting the logic of the CFRS: "Once an area has been stabilised, a normalisation process is necessary. However, we must avoid a simplistic idea of normalisation—for example, the idea that jobs will be created once the stabilisation operation is over."[23] What Fanaroff and Niehaus suggest is that the primary relationship at work here is between the operations and public perceptions, not between anticrime initiatives and subsequent crime reduction, much less social development.

As hard policing approaches become institutionalized, some suggest that policing that could contribute to genuine security for residents is neglected. A number of gang members from the Cape Flats interviewed in August 2002 remarked on the lack of real crime prevention in their neighborhoods, even as the high-profile antigang operations were in full swing. One group said they thought crime reduction was just talk by police and politicians. When media attention or high-profile crimes created enough pressure, the police would "do something," but eventually the efforts would fade. They said there was little consistent action by police to actually make communities safer.[24] The creation of the municipal police force was in part billed as an attempt to remedy the lack of regular visible policing in high-crime areas, but its deployment outside the city center and in the

Figure 5. Bishop Lavis, Cape Flats. Overcrowding, neglect, and poor construction have led to the steady deterioration of these flats. Photograph by Shannon Wentz.

Cape Flats has been slow.[25] Referring to the new deployments, however, one gangster said that municipal police would often set up roadblocks at the borders of townships but did little real patrolling to make the streets safer. Echoing some of the comments made by youth workers, this was because the townships "were too dangerous for them."[26]

Llewellyn Jordaan, the community and youth worker from Lavender Hills, was even more dismissive of the municipal police. When I asked him about community/police relations and the new force in his community, he replied:

> I don't even want to talk about the municipal police. . . . I even forgot what they call themselves. [T]hey were recruited, and many of them have criminal records. . . . So there's still a hell of a lot that needs to be done. The municipal police is fighting one another, in terms of the black uniform, the blue uniform, the brown, they still have their differences. And there's a lot being said about . . . but they still have that old mentality. That robust approach.[27]

A leader of the Americans gang in Athlone agreed that police are too scared to do regular patrols. He said they end up driving around a lot "doing nothing," scamming (i.e., running protection rackets), shopping, and eating lunch. When I asked him about the new municipal police, whom he referred to as "pizza boys" because their uniforms are similar to those worn by the employees of a local pizza chain, he said they spend most of their time in the CBD and are there every day, whereas they come to the townships only once or twice a week. For the most part, he added, all they do is hand out citations for bylaw and traffic violations. Speaking to the politics of policing a divided city, he claimed that "as long as Cape Town [city center and suburbs] is safe, they don't care about the townships." In fact, he admitted that since the so-called cleanup of the CBD, committing crime there has become more difficult. The police, he observed, were serious about keeping the area safe and protecting the tourists.[28]

Social Crime Prevention, Security, and Police Priorities

Beyond concerns with the direction of policing lies a greater concern with the broader reforms that the postapartheid era was meant to introduce in approaching crime and security. Although our primary interest here is with the consequences of existing anticrime policy, it is useful to look also at the absence of social crime prevention in postapartheid Cape Town, as this was originally intended to provide the context within which new criminal justice and policing policy would be formulated. Taken together, what is present and what is absent from current approaches helps to explain how they work against the formation of strong partnerships between law enforcement and communities by translating conceptual weakness in the governance of township security into a counterproductive distortion of priorities at the level of implementation. Social crime prevention targets the causal factors of crime through policies and practices determined by existing research rather than prevailing political winds or punitive moralities.[29] To this end, the ANC-led government released a white paper in 1998 outlining what social crime prevention meant for South Africa, stating that its aim was to "reduce the social, economic and environmental factors conducive to particular types of crime."[30] The white paper, citing the NCPS, went on to list gender inequality, the proliferation of firearms, inadequate support to victims of crime, youth marginalization, and underdevelopment as some of the key factors conducive to crime.[31] However, since the release of the white paper, social crime prevention has largely gone the way of the NCPS framework from which it emerged.[32] To the extent that non–law enforcement prevention measures outlined in the NCPS and white paper have been implemented, they consist largely of environmental design, or spatial governance, including extensive use of closed circuit television (CCTV) camera systems, visible policing, the establishment of CIDs and the regulation of informal traders.[33] As discussed in detail earlier, these measures have been used extensively in governing the Cape Town CBD; for the townships, however, the only crime reduction measure of any note has been law enforcement.

Social crime prevention languished in the city even as tough-on-crime policing was on the ascent and being institutionalized at all levels of government. Although the CFRS and the city's many Integrated Development Plans (IDPs) explicitly foreground social crime prevention measures derived from the NCPS and white paper, much of the effort at this point is in the form of passive crime prevention, especially in the form of environmental design of public spaces to minimize the opportunities to commit crimes. As part of its Integrated Safety and Security Strategy, the 2003–04 IDP outlined a dual strategy for social crime prevention, including the developmental approach of the UK-inspired Safer Cities Programme, proactive policing, and the installation of CCTV.[34] Safer Cities at the time included plans to deploy more police and to expand the use of CCTV systems into areas under the CFRS and the National Urban Renewal Programme (NURP), specifically in Khayelitsha, Mitchells Plain, Manenberg, and Bonteheuwel. By mid-2003, many of the systems were in place and city police claimed they had already curtailed gang activity in some areas, and over the following years the CCTV system underwent significant expansion, particularly in the CBD and other commercially valuable economic zones.[35] The latter are thus poised to act as a formidable, yet routine, complement to the more intense, targeted operations of Slasher and similar operations sure to come, as well as to entrench an intelligence-driven spatial governance model of urban crime reduction.

What the institutionalization of this model likely means is that social crime prevention is effectively dead at this point as policy at any significant scale in the city. More pointedly, the gulf between official priorities, in practice if not in rhetoric, and meaningful action to address the types of crimes that plague so many communities will remain, and perhaps grow wider. Instead of social crime prevention acting as a bridge between law enforcement and urban development agendas, enhancing both in the process, its absence signals the ascendance of a new governance regime better suited to an old, divided city. Sociospatial segregation will be further reflected in security priorities, and policing on the Cape Flats will become structurally incapable of addressing the crimes that make most residents insecure. This trend is most evident in the formulation of policing priorities. Although drug trafficking, gangsterism, and other high-profile criminal activities rank at the top for city officials and police, the prevention of other crimes is just as important to many residents. Wilfred Schärf explains how this tension has unfolded in relation to the development of community policing and sexual violence in the city:

> The second phase in the development of community policing was one that focused on the communities expressing their priorities to the police. This was again a learning curve for the police, seeing that they had expected the hierarchy of needs to coincide with the most serious crime, such as murder, armed robbery, and the like. But when some communities in poor residential areas expressed the view that rape constituted the crime which worried them the most, they were floored, seeing that rape, and any form of sexual or

domestic assault, was considered entirely peripheral to the interests of the police. They certainly didn't constitute "real crimes" as far as the police were concerned.[36]

This deprioritization of crimes committed primarily against women and children in the community policing debate is far from unique, and supports criticisms leveled at the implementation of the Domestic Violence Act: a lack of consultation with women, of dedicated resources, and of implementation and commitment.[37] Writing in 1998 on this theme, researcher Lillian Artz observes:

> [For victims of domestic violence] police continue to be the most discouraging contact with the criminal justice system. . . . Police continue to regard domestic violence as a "domestic problem" . . . and obviously consider it peripheral to and insignificant in the greater domain of police work. . . . It appears that the patriarchal ideology of police, welfare and justice still exists and exacerbates the problem for victims of domestic violence in that they actively support non-intervention into the "private sphere" and insist that wife battering is a civil rather than criminal affair."[38]

Current approaches to crime reduction, which reify and reproduce these types of distinctions, are unlikely to have any impact on offenses that are often committed between intimates and in the home. But even with "real crimes" such as murder, it is fair to question whether cordon and searches, roadblocks, and other resource-intensive hard policing approaches are appropriate as long-term reduction measures, and whether the distinction between serious crimes and crime between intimates is, even at the level of prevention measures, a false one. A report released in 2001 by the late minister Tshwete, who personified the state's commitment to waging war against criminals, shows that in South Africa 87 percent of victims knew their killer, 25 percent were killed at home, and more than 50 percent were killed during an argument.[39] Just a few months later, however, the minister announced plans to increase the police force from 127,000 to 140,000. In response to the plan, ISS researcher Martin Schonteich commented that social factors such as poverty and drugs, which contribute to these crimes, are largely beyond police control: "Even if one were to double the police force it wouldn't make much of an impact in the murder rate. . . . The majority of people who are affected by violent crime know their perpetrators.[40]

As Jean Redpath found in her interviews with police, most violent crimes in the Western Cape are assaults linked to alcohol and domestic violence, with weekends and holidays showing the highest rate of assaults.[41] So-called hard policing, however, may in fact contribute to these crimes while pulling resources away from more effective, but less muscular, forms of policing. One police station captain admitted that although zero tolerance policing in his station areas had reduced street crime, it also contributed to increases in crimes that happen behind closed doors and in the home, where women and children are disproportionately the victims.[42] The issue of police priorities demonstrates how current approaches can contribute to exactly those problems with policing and real community safety voiced at the close of the previous section. Wilfred Schärf pointed out in 2002 that in Mitchells Plain on the average weekend there are only four police on patrol, and the stations are on skeleton crews with the most junior staff supervisor on duty; yet, although this is when most crime happens, it is only very recently that efforts have been made to address this gap. Llewellyn Jordaan made a similar observation about police resources at the Steenberg police station, which services his community of Lavender Hill:

LJ: The police station is servicing an area of approximately
    280,000 people—but it could be more—with eight policemen.
TRS: The Steenberg police station serves 280,000 with eight police
    per shift?
LJ: Ja, you've got two on the vans, two vans. So that's already four.
    You need personnel in the office, that's six, so it's impossible,
    it's unrealistic.[43]

These critiques touch on a related set of concerns regarding high-profile operations and the immense amount of resources they absorb. The problems faced by Operation Reclaim in the city center, called off because officers were needed in other areas, are not unique to the CBD. The challenge this poses for the Cape, which, unlike New York City or Los Angeles, does not have a seemingly unlimited budget, is how to allocate existing resources among hard policing, soft policing, and socioeconomic renewal approaches to crime reduction. In just its first year, for example, Operation Crackdown had used up all projected police personnel overtime costs set aside for the financial year within only six months of being introduced at the national level.[44] This tendency is troubling because it places stress not only on the SAPS budget but also on personnel involved in other policing activities, e.g., disrupting local police work so that station-level officers can participate in road-blocks and cordon and search operations.[45] Raising broader questions of balance in the CFRS, the Western Cape Provincial Development Council, in its critique, writes:

> If the strategy is not just an "antigangsterism/zero tolerance" intervention, why is it that the R6.33 m budget committed by the Department of Community Safety is so heavily weighted towards law enforcement? Is this bias in the budget due to the fact that the strategy has its roots in Operation Lancer, the campaign used to tackle urban terrorism in the Western Cape? . . . Where are the concrete and tangible economic development programmes and projects that will reduce the dependence of communities on the illicit/criminal economy?[46]

Importantly, the perception that policing priorities diverge from, and may even contradict, the priorities of residents is not limited to Cape Town. The director of an organization working with youth in Westbury, one of Johannesburg's coloured townships, agreed that police also flood the community where he lived and worked and then move out. In stark contrast to the impression created by the many complex and coordinated operations carried out by the police over the years, he told me bluntly: "Police have no plan for dealing with crime." He added that police just wanted to make arrests, and some had even complained that the work of his organization with local youth was affecting arrest rates.[47] This last observation touched on the concern voiced by other youth workers as well, that police were too concerned with arrests and not attentive enough to whether this was a strategy that actually made communities safer. Here again, we are confronted with the disconnect between what many from the communities themselves see as their needs, and the actual crime prevention they receive; this provides us with important insight into the relative power of different constituencies to set policing priorities.

Political pressures that police and government "do something," operational continuities from previous years, and the institutionalization of law enforcement approaches can help to explain the absence of adequate social crime prevention, but in this closing section of the chapter we look at another crucial aspect that first emerged in the discussions of crime statistics and police interactions with young people: the deep rift that exists between the police and the communities being policed. The continued reliance by the state on aggressive law enforcement as a centerpiece of urban renewal and the imbalances this creates is to a great extent an expression of this rift, even as it contributes to its reproduction. The rift produces frustration on both sides, with police seeing some communities as "uncooperative" and some communities claiming that the role they are expected to play amounts to little more than passive "eyes and ears" for a security force they still do not trust to keep their neighborhoods safe. Without this trust, however, social crime prevention programs will not work, and the police, frustrated and under pressure, will likely continue to return to the practices which they know best.

Serve and Protect? Community Mistrust of the Police

It is clear that large portions of the communities of the Cape Flats simply do not trust the police and do not believe that the well-being of their families and communities is a state priority. This view is expressed by community members, community organizations, and gangsters, and is also confirmed by research.[48] It is also true that there are and have been exceptions and even moments when real change on this front seemed possible—for example, during the early days of the Community Police Forums.[49] As recently as 2004, youth workers and other local activists working on the Cape Flats expressed hope that productive partnerships with police and local government that do exist could be expanded and sustained, often with individual officers rather than with the institution itself. However, the overall impression is that the relationship in general is badly deteriorated. The context for community suspicion of the police is, of course, rooted in the recent past of apartheid, but it can by no means be considered an inertia effect. As the statistics provided by the ICD suggest and the experiences of many of the youth workers interviewed for this project support, the problem of police misconduct nationally and in the Western Cape is substantial and may even be on the rise as police are ordered to hammer down on the criminals.

There are two criticisms that are especially relevant to the relationship on Cape Flats. One complaint heard frequently has to do with the ability of police to do their jobs, which is subdivided in the following into issues of corruption and competence. The other criticism is one that stems from a perceived lack of change in the police themselves. As will become clear, these are not neat divisions; problems with both corruption and competence, for example, are intricately linked with problems inherited from the past. More accurately, they simply represent different and overlapping aspects of the challenges facing communities demanding a changed police service. The significance of these rifts is enormous. If reducing crime is the linchpin of the urban renewal strategy and a deep mistrust still exists between police and residents, the prospects for social and economic development, even assuming the urban renewal strategy is a sound one, are dim. The troubled status of police/community relations is therefore a useful indicator of where the renewal process stands, one which has not received the attention it warrants, and goes a long way toward explaining an important aspect of evolution under way in the controversial war on gangsterism.

Arguably, the aspect of police corruption that receives the most attention is police cooperation with the gangsters; this was certainly the case when people were asked to assess police efforts to deal with crime and gangsterism. Active collaboration between the two during apartheid and, as some evidence suggests, even during the Cape Flats war continues today and is acknowledged by the police and by politicians as a significant challenge to the reform process. As journalist Marianne Merton has written with regard to the Flats, "Most residents regard police officers—with a handful of exceptions—as unhelpful, conniving with gangsters whose *shebeens* and homes they frequent, or even as being on gang payrolls."[50] Community workers and gangsters made similar statements, claiming that police often drink with gangsters, deal drugs, and accept bribes. One gangster alleged, for example, that police will confiscate one hundred Mandrax pills, report that they seized twenty and then sell the remaining eighty.[51] A member of the Americans told me, when I asked him if there was corruption among the newly deployed municipal police, that it was mostly small stuff, like taking fruit from stands. But in his considerable experience, this is how more serious corruption begins.[52] Recent research by Liza Grobler confirms that this strategy is often used by gangs to recruit police in the Western Cape—giving small gifts such as meat and alcohol for parties at the police station is only the first stage in a process of binding officers to the gangs.[53]

A major problem is the apparent flow of information between some police and gangsters. Law enforcement sources cited in Merton's article said of raids conducted during the Cape Flats war that "gangsters seemed to know when [we] were coming." In May 2002, I was invited to a meeting between residents of Tafelsig, a neighborhood in Mitchells Plain, and representatives from the police gang and crime analysis units at the Mitchells Plain Detective Branch. In attendance were approximately thirty community members, some of whom belonged to community organizations, several members of the police force, and a representative of the Provincial Department of Community Safety for the CFRS in the Tafelsig area. In their presentation to community members, the police laid great stress on the importance they placed on relaying information about crime and gangsterism to the authorities. Addressing the assembly, the superintendent of crime intelligence underscored the vital role this played in law enforcement efforts to reduce crime, and a spokesperson from the Crime Information Analysis Centre encouraged people to act, in his words, as eyes and ears. In response, a number of residents said that they did not feel they could trust police to keep this information away from gang members, which could lead to retaliation. One woman stood up and explained that she had once called the police to report a stash of guns being kept in a house nearby. By the time the police arrived, she said, the guns had been removed and hours later shots were fired at her house.

A similar issue came up in relation to the importance of individuals testifying against gangsters in court, also mentioned by the officers, and the inability of the police often to protect those who do. People pointed out that when someone testifies against a gang member, it is not uncommon for the whole gang to show up for support, which is very intimidating to the witness. Gangsters I spoke with about this were even more blunt, saying that there is in reality very little protection for witnesses. The gangsters simply wait for police protection, if there is any, to end and then beat or kill the witness.[54] In the eyes of the community, police expectations that they will act as information outposts as their primary contribution to intelligence-driven policing, an expectation shared by provincial authorities, do not adequately appreciate the dangerous, and largely passive, position this puts people in and the role that corruption within the force plays in the reluctance of many to participate. In many cases, with some high-profile examples over the last few years, attacks have also been directed at magistrates, judges, and police officers involved in criminal proceedings. Under these circumstances it is understandable that the people who have to live in the areas in which the gangsters operate are skeptical about the ability, much less the commitment, of the authorities to protect them. A further complication on this point is that police often rely on their relationships with gangsters for information, creating useful but problematic relationships, especially within the context of law enforcement–led development. In looking at this particular dynamic, Schärf finds that the use of informers, usually against rivals, has benefits for both the handler and the informant. For the latter, these can include immunity, the ability to obtain gun licenses, tip-offs about impending busts, and expanded territory, whereas for the handler more arrests can lead to job advancement. Consequently, senior SAPS investigators protect informants because they "depend for their success on having the most senior gang leaders in the province as their informants and close 'investigative' allies."[55]

The use of informers is not unusual and, as Ethan Nadelmann documents, has been a core feature of the U.S.-style policing which has come to Cape Town, sometimes directly, and sometimes refracted through the European nations.[56] The spread of this model across the Atlantic, modern and democratic as it may be, is deeply problematic to many analysts because of the very real and well-known danger of the corruption this type of policing entails. In a place like the Cape Flats, and the nation as a whole really, such codependence is unlikely to contribute much to improved perceptions of the police by the people. This reasonable mistrust then leads to considerable frustration. Reluctance on the part of residents to provide information is often read by police as obstructionist, and the push by law enforcement for people to act as eyes and ears is viewed as opportunist, if not with outright suspicion. The fallout is that police and the residents of the areas they serve become more estranged, reinforcing for law enforcement the "need" to rely on intelligence, informants, and force in bringing crime under control.

Contributing to this estrangement is the role that police/gangster relations play in flooding the townships with guns. The provision of arms to the gangs by police has come up in earlier periods, most recently during the Cape Flats war. One internal investigation police conducted in the late 1990s, for example, implicated some members of the SAPS with providing hand grenades to gangsters.[57] When I asked a group of four gangsters, one of whom said he was involved in gun smuggling, where they got their weapons, they mentioned theft but also said that they purchased guns from the police and that weapons were sometimes smuggled into communities from the army, via the police, as well. In some cases, they claim, police will confiscate weapons and then resell them.[58] The availability of firearms is a serious problem for obvious reasons—it contributes to the high murder rate, especially of young people, and to the power of the gangsters and, in turn, lends credibility to the arguments for a tough, zero tolerance approach. The fact that police may be actively involved in supplying guns, something of which many in the community are apparently convinced, not only complicates efforts to rally community support and cooperation, but also undermines any effectiveness policing strategies actually could have. The Western Cape Provincial Development Council, in its own critique of zero tolerance on the Cape Flats, suggests that in some areas the police are already outgunned and that there is little reason to think that any kind of long-term zero tolerance policing can be carried out, regardless of whether these are actually effective or not.

Police incompetence is another complaint often heard in relation to the ability and commitment of law enforcement, one which has been acknowledged nationally by officials as a legitimate concern. Much of the problem here is out of the hands of rank and file officers insofar as deficiencies in training, equipment, literacy, morale, and other areas that prevent them from performing their duties are largely structural, but the experience of this incompetence by residents contributes to the distrust of local stations and individual officers nonetheless. One pressing issue is the low rate of cases that are successfully completed, with the perpetrator caught and convicted. The statistics on this topic from the South African Law Commission are dismal; for example, only 6 out every 100 murders, rapes, and aggravated robberies reported to police result in conviction two years after the incident has occurred.[59] Not surprisingly, it is this kind of problem that drives much of the demand for criminal justice reform, in particular the more technical reform in which the Western powers are interested, including the formation of the Scorpions, modeled after the U.S. Federal Bureau of Investigation, and the training of prosecutors and forensic specialists.[60] These are just a few examples of attempts to streamline the criminal justice system, boost the conviction rates, and chip away at the sense of impunity many feel is behind the nation's high crime rates. But the low conviction rates, and perceived police incompetence generally, have unintended consequences that can fuel instability and drive police and communities further apart, as is apparent in the various forms of vigilantism and street justice that frequently appear in the townships, as well as efforts at restoring traditional and alternative justice systems.[61]

At the meeting in Mitchells Plain, residents related their own experiences with the kinds of incompetence that contribute to frustration in the community. In some cases officers did not even know how to take reports; or once they were taken, reports would occasionally be lost. The latter may actually not always be the result of poor policing. According to the leader of the Americans gang, police can be paid to sell case dockets or make them disappear, a charge that is given considerable weight in light of the recent crime statistics scandal discussed earlier. Unreasonably long response times are another complaint. Gangsters told me that in their neighborhood, it could take up to three hours for police to respond to a call. Residents from Tafelsig also said that police do not know the appropriate information when people come to them and try to pass people off, claiming matters are out of their jurisdiction. Finally, a number of people remarked that police sometimes arrive at the scene with alcohol on their breath. Based on reports received by the ICD, which says misconduct cases are underreported by the SAPS and municipal police, these experiences are not anomalies.

Advocates of police reform also point to the troubling lack of change within the police themselves from the previous era. A degree of continuity was essentially guaranteed by the integration of members of the informal and homeland security forces, the retention of pre-1994 personnel through the sunset clause and the retention of some apartheid-era security personnel due to their experience and expertise.[62] In the Western Cape, continuity has been particularly pronounced because the National Party remained in power well into the transition period. One result has been a very slow transformation in the makeup of the SAPS. In a province with an overwhelming black majority, the racial composition of influential police captains in 2002 remained wildly unrepresentative, with white captains making up 73 percent of the total.[63] Revealing tensions that exist within the SAPS, a provincial plan to promote 279 "previously disadvantaged" officers as inspectors and captains was opposed by the white-dominated South African Police Union (SAPU) as "reverse apartheid" and was eventually dropped, over the objections of the black-dominated

Police and Prison Civil Rights Union (POPCRU). The latter accused SAPU of wanting to "maintain racism" and cited a national agreement that required a promotion ratio of 70:30. Explaining the rationale behind the proposal, Rod Beer, the spokesperson for the provincial police commissioner, argued: "We deliberately excluded white police officers from these appointments to correct the severe imbalances of the past. . . . We have an oversupply of white captains in the police service in the province.[64] In the Western Cape, as in other provinces, white officers from the apartheid era often remain in key management and decision-making positions. This imbalance contributes to the reproduction of tensions between residents and police and puts into question the extent to which legislation, foreign training, and modern methods constitute either transformation or reform. At a forum on crime and law enforcement, held in Cape Town in 2000 and attended by many of the leading authorities on criminal justice reform in the country, the summary statement of the proceedings included the following statement on the first six years of police reform:

> There has been very little transformation in the police. . . . The old order is still in power at the top, and the information these officers feed to the Minister is very dangerous. Even Operation Recoil and Operation Crackdown are being planned by the same people who planned operations in the past. The police ran the country before . . . The way certain police handle some situations could be described as sabotage.[65]

One glaring and somewhat intriguing example of how deeply continuity runs surfaced in 2002, when accusations of corruption and sabotage of investigations were made against seventeen senior Western Cape police, mostly old-guard apartheid-era officers. What made the allegations even more sensational was that they were made by former ANC intelligence operative Andrè Lincoln, on trial for fraud linked to his undercover work, and Senior Superintendent Jeremy Vearey, commander of the Operation Slasher unit investigating Cape Flats' gangs until he was suspended for gross insubordination. Lawyers for the two claim both had been targeted because of their investigations into corruption on the force.[66]

In June of 2002 Vearey went public with allegations that senior apartheid-era police still on the force were obstructing his investigation into corruption and a related investigation by former ANC intelligence operatives into organized crime, corruption, links to gangs, and abuses of human rights by police.[67] According to *Cape Argus* reporter Doug Carew, after the allegations were made, Vearey was told to transfer away from Slasher's investigative unit by former provincial police commissioner Lennit Max. Vearey ignored the order, which led to his suspension for insubordination. The specific charges Vearey and Lincoln made, contained in a letter sent by their attorney to provincial premier Marthinus van Schalkwyk, along with substantiating evidence, are that:

- there had been widespread corruption in relation to gang-related offenses,
- this corruption had not been properly investigated and/or taken seriously, and
- corruption has included police officials arranging for the withdrawal of charges in serious offenses and representing in writing that the charges had been withdrawn at the instigation of complainants.

Citing the letter, *Cape Times* reporter Tony Weaver writes: "Vearey had also uncovered 'serious and widespread corruption involving the theft of exhibits, the deliberate losing of ballistic evidence and postmortem reports' and deliberate sabotaging of cases."[68] The letter continues:

It became abundantly clear that these police officials were largely drawn from the "old guard" apartheid policemen who in certain cases had been guilty of gross human rights violations under apartheid, and who maintain a conspiracy of silence in relation to their activities.

Adding to the intrigue, some of the evidence Vearey and Lincoln obtained came from interviews they conducted with Eugene de Kock, the imprisoned apartheid police operative who ran many of the major counterinsurgency operations conducted against the antiapartheid movement.

De Kock also figures in another interesting case of apartheid-era holdovers who were linked to recent anticrime and urban renewal efforts on the Cape Flats. In his testimony before the Truth and Reconciliation Commission, he detailed a long list of counterinsurgency operations in which he participated, including bombing the ANC's London offices in 1983 and the numerous assassinations of senior ANC cadres. One of the many higher-level apartheid functionaries he implicated for his involvement was then director of the National Intelligence Service (NIS), Niel Barnard.[69] Barnard is important here because for a time he sat squarely at the intersection of the old-guard and new efforts at crime reduction and urban renewal. For a number of years Barnard was involved with the Multi-Agency Delivery Action Mechanism (MADAM), a precursor of sorts to the CFRS in that it represented an attempt to address the acknowledged problems faced by previous efforts, namely the lack of cooperation and coordination among various role players. Established in 1998, MADAM sought to establish functioning partnerships by acting as a mechanism through which to bring together the SAPS, provincial departments, local councils, and the SANDF under director general Barnard in targeting crime and development in an integrated manner.[70] MADAM has since been involved with a number of anticrime initiatives throughout the province aimed at social crime prevention, including the establishment of community safety forums.[71]

The challenge posed by holdovers is twofold: On the one hand they affect the design and implementation of operations in ways that are further alienating communities, through the continued emphasis, with a new rationale, of intelligence-driven operations, to take one example. This is seen in the way police expect people to accept a relatively passive role as eyes and ears while the "real" work of crime reduction, including formulation of policy and strategy, is left almost exclusively to law enforcement. There continues to be a tendency on the part of the SAPS to take an instrumental view of residents' role in partnerships and community policing and a related reluctance to relinquish real power. On the other hand, the carryover of individual officers and of an unrepresentative force generally complicates the extent to which community members can trust police, a problem greatly exacerbated by corruption and incompetence, to some degree a function of these holdovers. The power of these tensions should not be underestimated, as the emergence of PAGAD vividly demonstrates. As the meeting in Mitchells Plain wore on, community members became more vocal and agitated while voicing the many problems they faced in dealing with the police. One gentleman stood up near the end and said that it is these kinds of problems that lead easily to vigilantism, a remark that appeared to resonate with many others present, who nodded and murmured their agreement.

Corruption, continuity of institutions and personnel, and complicity of police with the gangs contribute to the further destabilization of the

Cape Flats because of their direct impact on communities and on relations between the communities and police. As the two primary groups involved become more alienated and the police become more isolated, the "necessity" of a war on crime becomes more "self-evident." The outcome to which this antagonism contributes today is the divided neoliberal city, but clear echoes of the apartheid era remind us that the war on crime and its consequences cannot be explained away simply by reference to the new regime of market discipline. The deprioritization of crimes against black women and children, for example, is no more unique to neoliberalism than it was to apartheid. Therefore, we should understand the governance of security within the context of historical constraints and opportunities, now framed by and articulated through the city's embrace of neoliberalism as it forges a relationship with transnational flows of capital, consumers, and accepted forms of social control on the one hand, and navigates its own internal challenges on the other. However, while policing in the township is not determined by neoliberalism, it is at the same time clearly stamped with its imprint, and current approaches to crime are rationalized at the scale of urban governance, if not at the level of everyday practice, through reference to neoliberal categories of growth, development, and urban order.

In the final chapter, we move away from crime prevention and policing to examine the deeper foundations of insecurity and disorder as they manifest in the townships today. Behind the gangsters, the police, the all too frequent outbreaks of violence, and the stern pronouncements they provoke lies the reality of massive poverty and inequality. For youth in particular, there has been a strikingly smooth transition from the underdevelopment of apartheid to the underdevelopment of neoliberalism, both marked by an active production of sociospatial marginalization. Understanding the profound lack of transformation that defines much of township life and the state's response to it is crucial for understanding how it is that there still exists a population of "surplus" youth to fill the prisons.

5

The Production of Criminality on the Urban Periphery

Throughout the townships, the policing of crime and gangsterism contributes to multiple insecurities for residents, working against the very development agenda it is meant to anchor. The previous two chapters attempted to show exactly why this form of security governance has survived the transition from apartheid to neoliberalism, how it produces insecurity, and the consequences for communities and the broader urban renewal agenda. In this final chapter we turn to the other piece of the governance equation, the relationship of the local neoliberal state to underdevelopment. Here, too, security and the police often figure prominently, although the lack of development itself should not be reduced to the repressiveness of the state's response to crime alone. Instead, underlying the continued underdevelopment of the Cape Flats is the shift referred to in chapter 1, from township residents as victims to township residents as problems. The shift, driven in large part by the imposition of a market-driven accumulation economy on a city still struggling with powerful historical tensions and deep inequalities, has subsequently shaped and been shaped by the current urban governance regime. Within this regime, the state in the townships both transforms and retains core features of the apartheid era through the relationship that continues to hold between security and development. We have seen how development policy that centers the fight against crime has been securitized through policies such as the Cape Flats Renewal Strategy (CFRS) and aggressive policing practices. The war on crime, however, should be viewed as only one, albeit central, aspect of a broader securitization of governance rooted in efforts by city and provincial leaders to fortify the neoliberal core and simultaneously impose a form of neoliberal discipline in the townships. This securitization of development has subsequently generated urban renewal initiatives that produce criminality and reproduce insecurity.

We have examined the role of the state in relation to the policing of crime; in what follows we look more closely at its relationship to underdevelopment. Wherever it is found, underdevelopment represents a form of insecurity even as it produces secondary insecurities, but it is typically the latter, and only some of these, that concern hegemonic governance regimes. Neoliberal governance in Cape Town has two important consequences for the posture of the state toward the periphery, both of which link underdevelopment to criminality. First, the lack of progress on development has not been met with passivity on the part of township residents. On the contrary, postapartheid Cape Town has seen frequent and often violent clashes between residents and state authorities, or private sector proxies, over the implementation of neoliberal urban policies that reflect deeply undemocratic planning and policy processes, as well as a not so thinly veiled rearticulation of apartheid-era socioeconomic injustices. These are not the only recent conflicts that we can tie to underdevelopment—as evidenced by the spate of xenophobic violence that roiled the city in 2008 and the alleged link between local operatives allied with the African National Congress (ANC) and attacks on organized shack-dwellers from the Kennedy Road settlement in Durban the next year—but they are especially relevant here because they are between the formal governance structures responsible for urban renewal in their official capacity and township communities.[1] Mirroring the response to remobilized communities across the nation, the local state has not only been quick to deploy security forces to confront protestors, but has also explicitly framed many of these actions and those who carry them out as criminal.[2] In doing so, the state connects gangsters, other "real" criminals, and many community activists, perhaps the most visible township residents from the vantage point of the urban core, through a discourse of criminality, obscuring, or perhaps misrepresenting, the larger, more fundamental conflict between the city's neoliberal agenda, security, and the demands of communities for socioeconomic development. Considered alongside the troubling rise in complaints by residents against police, the choice by state actors to respond to protests in this way suggests that securitization, itself embedded in neoliberal governance, has generated a form of punitive containment aimed at entire communities.[3]

The second important consequence of neoliberal governance for the state's approach to the periphery is the absence of youth development. Youth unemployment figures and other indicators of underdevelopment have been discussed earlier, but the deeper story here is of a systematic neglect of the youth sector that can be tied directly to the insecurities of crime and gangsterism, which in turn do command state attention and intervention. As the unemployment figures suggest, the city's townships are filled with "surplus" youth, unlikely to ever find productive work from the perspective of the neoliberal economy. This surplus, however, does not simply reproduce itself; rather, it is reproduced through the combination of factors, many of which have been presented already. Central to this reproduction from the perspective of development generally, and South Africa development after apartheid in particular, is the absence of the state. In this absence, as we will see, is ample opportunity for gangs to provide counter-structures that may mirror and stand in opposition to formal, "legitimate" governance structures. The resulting growth of gangs precipitates a securitized state response that, among other things, swells the prisons with young black men, further marginalizing already peripheral youth.

What both of these consequences suggest is that township residents and surplus youth remain invisible from the perspective of the state so long as they are quiescent; when they are not, the state responds in particular ways that are shaped by the new governance regime. This mobilization has shown limited effectiveness in ridding communities of insecurity and crime, but from the vantage point of the governance of security, thus far it has had some success in containing the problems of the townships, and city officials can claim the notable achievement of downtown revitalization. What we will examine in detail in this chapter is the contradictory posture of the state in relation to underdevelopment—at times absent, at others very present. The state quickly and forcefully advances to deal with protestors, criminals, and gangsters but is just as severe in its retreat from development and youth.[4] These apparently contradictory movements begin to make sense when placed in the context of governing a divided city, and it is when viewed in this context that we can properly make out the shape of neoliberal governance in the townships.

Chaos and Community: Policing Underdevelopment

The contradictions between social development, fiscal austerity associated with municipal neoliberalism, and the central role of law enforcement in urban renewal came to a head in September 2001:

> They [police] went about shooting at women and children without an ounce of remorse, and then one of the policemen told us we got

our just desserts. . . . I have been trying all these years to play my role and bring peace to the crime-ridden community, but this is where I draw the line, because the police in Mitchells Plain have proven today that they are no better than the gangsters, where there is no appreciation for life.[5]

The above quote comes from Tafelsig Neighbourhood Watch manager Brian Shadrick after he was shot in the arm and leg with rubber bullets by police. The context was not an Operation Slasher action against gang members but a response to residents resisting water cutoffs to 1,800 families for nonpayment of fees, the so-called Tafelsig water war. Six months after the city had introduced the CFRS, the Mitchells Plain neighborhood, targeted as a national crime hot spot and urban renewal zone, erupted in violence as riot police and, eventually, the military stormed the area to protect municipal workers and enforce the cutoffs. The government moved in as part of an emergent emphasis on cost recovery and privatization of services that began to sweep the city in the wake of diminishing federal support to municipalities and the onset of the neoliberal mandate of GEAR (the Growth, Employment And Redistribution initiative) to seek out private capital and reduce public expenditures.[6] According to the city, residents in Tafelsig owed more than R220 million in water arrears, part of R2.2 billion due the city in rent, water, electricity, and rates of other utilities.[7] Malcolm Newham, a city official, said the disconnections were meant to encourage those who owed money to pay.[8] City officials also stated that the community had ample warning that the cutoffs were coming, a point disputed by many residents. In the end, when the money was not forthcoming from the neighborhood, where unemployment at the time stood at more than 60 percent, the city moved in and residents set up barricades and burning tires to protect their access to water. Police responded with rubber bullets, live ammunition, and stun grenades. Ishmael Abrahams of the Western Cape Anti-Eviction Campaign said of the shooting, "People started running. The police cocked their shotguns in our faces and then they fired on us. It was like reliving the 1985 riots, where police could fire at will."[9] In the end, between eight and fifteen people were shot and at least twelve people were arrested; the injured included passersby, a reporter for the *Cape Argus,* and a five-year-old child. Residents and members of the community-based Western Cape Anti-Eviction Campaign filed charges, including attempted murder, against the police and complaints with the Independent Complaints Directorate.

After the first day of clashes and cutoffs, resident and Anti-Evictions Campaign organizer Ashraf Cassiem described the scene in Tafelsig:

> There seemed to be a million police in the area. People are standing outside everywhere in the streets weeping openly. The private workers and protection services have succeeded in carrying out most of the 1,800 water cutoffs. The riot police were called in around lunchtime and succeeded in having a standoff with most of the community while the others went ahead cutting off water and removing the meters. People are desperately trying to reconnect their water with pieces of old hose-pipe, or any pipe, and string—it doesn't seem to be working out. There is a feeling of crisis as so many households have been cut off. Nobody knows now where they can go to get water.[10]

The clashes made headlines in the city and sparked a parallel war of words, with city officials and mainstream media referring to "rioters" who refused to pay their bills, whereas organized residents and their supporters pointed to the cutoffs as part of a larger pattern of the state squeezing the poor, demanding unreasonable utility and other rates as part of an income-generating scheme in a time of skyrocketing unemployment and failed economic reform. In their opinion the incident in Tafelsig was indicative of a dangerous trend in the new South Africa to criminalize those who were to benefit from the demise of the apartheid system when they organize to demand change and accountability. The Tafelsig water war underscores the extent to which urban renewal is an often bitterly contested ground over which the state and communities regularly conflict, sometimes violently. It also suggests that the issue of police/community relations is not limited by the issues of crime and gangsterism but, as the renewal strategies implicitly acknowledge, is in fact central to the entire urban renewal and development project. It is not difficult to believe that the frequent clashes between communities and security forces, whether public or private, around socioeconomic concerns will impact the city's future more profoundly than the success or failure of the war against crime. If development continues to stall, the people continue to resist the deterioration of their living standards, and the state remains committed to responding, in President Mbeki's words, "with the full force of the law," these clashes will likely intensify, and a deep rift will continue to divide the government and the ungovernable.[11]

Officials in city and provincial government were not blind as to what was clearly a growing problem. Almost two years after the incident in Tafelsig, in early 2003, the city initiated a "listening campaign" intended to gather the views of residents on priority areas as part of the Integrated Development Plan (IDP) planning process. The campaign received almost 5,000 responses, which were then divided into 19 key thematic areas and ranked according to the percentage of comments that each area received. With the exception of responses related to the campaign itself, including questions about how representative the sample is, the areas covered the whole range of urban renewal and development challenges and problems facing the city's residents. The four most common responses, in descending order of priority, were: availability and upgrading of existing housing, economic development (job creation), policing and traffic enforcement, and social development, including youth development. The IDP then redivided the responses according to the specific issues to which they relate within the thematic areas, and in the process issues of high crime rates/more policing edges out job creation by one fifth of a percentage point to become the key priority issue. Despite this relabelling of resident responses, by either measure social and economic development are far and away the greatest priorities in the views of city residents surveyed by the Listening Campaign. As with the survey by the Institute of Democracy in South Africa cited in chapter 1, the division of these into a number of subcategories, although useful for illustrating the range of concerns people have, can also dilute the overwhelming emphasis respondents place on socioeconomic concerns. In the IDP campaign, when combined, these account for more than 85 percent of responses if divided by thematic area and about 83 percent if divided by key priority issue.

The Listening Campaign was a clear, and ultimately feeble, effort to repair a major fault line running under the urban renewal process. One of the most consistent criticisms made of the CFRS and related campaigns is that communities have insufficient input and are not adequately consulted; as a result, the whole process is often seen as being imposed from above. This is to some extent a function of the role that policing plays in the entire renewal strategy, as residents have little impact on policing strategies developed at the national and provincial levels, but it is also a consequence of political problems in the province, with all political parties too far removed from the people.[12] Urban renewal initiatives in particular have no real representation from communities, a criticism that surfaces in the Western Cape Provincial Development Council's (WCPDC) analysis of the city's urban renewal plan. In its estimation, both the IDP and the CFRS had either nonexistent or very weak community participation.[13] Over time and across the youth development sectors, these criticisms surface repeatedly.

The absence of adequate communication between communities and government and between levels of government indicates a broken process that contributes to the continued outbreak of hostilities similar to those in Tafelsig in 2001 and many others of lesser intensity. There was some hope in the ensuing years that the ANC–New National Party pact in the province and an ANC mayor would mean a more pro-poor policy, as high-ranking ANC officials in the province were vocal in speaking out against the heavy-handed police response to the residents of Tafelsig, which occurred under Democratic Alliance (DA) rule.[14] Although there were some positive developments initially, such as Mayor Mfeketo's rejection of the blatantly antipoor municipal bylaws, the feeling among many community organizations and researchers is that state repression against communities and organizations resisting the government's socioeconomic reform agenda continued largely unabated throughout the middle of the decade. As a result, a number of township areas remain politically insecure for reasons largely independent of the crime problem, and, somewhat ironically, the National Urban Renewal Programme and CFRS areas continue to be some of the most unstable in this regard. Khayelitsha, for example, has been the site of numerous battles between residents and the state over basic housing issues. Compounding the challenges involved with crime reduction, in many cases the state or private sector has deployed security forces to restore order, adding to the blurring of lines between the three prongs of the urban renewal strategy; residents, for example, are asked to trust and cooperate with the same police who enforce evictions and the government that deploys them. At the same time, they are told that socioeconomic reform is in progress and that their priorities have been heard, despite the fact that in the face of high unemployment rates, they are expected to pay what they say are unreasonable rates for vital, basic services. Recent events concerning housing in Khayelitsha illustrate that the situation on the Flats has become quite messy, but, just as with Tafelsig, what is difficult to ignore is the centrality of the conflict between the neoliberal governance regime and township communities.

Figure 6. Housing supply has never kept pace with demand on the Cape Flats, leading to the proliferation of informal backyard dwellings, often built with poor-quality scrap material. Bishop Lavis, Cape Flats. Photograph by Shannon Wentz.

The scope of the housing challenge is broad, ranging from the ongoing removal of residents for nonpayment to complaints of poor construction of government units and the demolition of illegal shacks put up by the homeless and evicted. In all of these cases, however, the mounting tensions around living space are palpable, especially as migrants from other parts of the country and abroad continue to arrive. One neighborhood in particular experienced a series of clashes over housing evictions in the first half of the decade. Residents of Mandela Park, in Khayelitsha's Site B, the targeted CFRS area, repeatedly fought authorities over evictions from government houses of residents for nonpayment and what they claim is a repeated failure on the part of city officials to meet with them about the housing problems in the area. In 2002 residents on numerous occasions resisted government evictions and "rightsizings": the eviction of people from their homes and their relocation to smaller, more "financially appropriate" dwellings that some community members refer to as dog kennels.[15]

The newly formed Mandela Park Anti-Eviction Campaign organized residents to reinstate evicted tenants, especially pensioners and the elderly.

As with water arrears, the municipal government is concerned over late housing payments and in response has implemented a cost-recovery program for housing as well. In 1995 it established Servcon Housing Solutions, a joint venture between the government and the Banking Council, to whose members most of the payments are owed. Servcon's role is to

> address the problem of "properties in the low income market
> on which repayments had ceased" and [Servcon] housed some
> of the MIF's [Mortgage Indemnity Fund, a government owned
> company also established in 1995 to address redlining by provid-
> ing guarantees on loans made in "risky" areas] non-performing
> loans. Servcon was mandated to find ways to restart payments on
> these loans or sell houses the banks had unsuccessfully tried to
> repossess.[16]

Mandela Park residents first began complaining about the poor quality of houses they bought from the banks in the late 1980s, and the unsuccessful repossession efforts were the result of early community resistance to the banks and the authorities.[17] In 1999, however, Servcon began large-scale evictions in the area, primarily for failure to make mortgage repayments. According to the Mandela Park Anti-Eviction Campaign:

> These evictions left whole streets empty, and the inadequate
> "rightsizing" houses where evictees were resettled led to
> numerous health problems amongst the old and the weak, with
> at least 15 people from Khayelitsha having died since being
> rightsized to these houses.[18]

Violence flared in mid-2002. In late June, 44 members of the Anti-Eviction Campaign, after alleging that they had been assaulted, were arrested by police and private security during a large protest in the city center as they sought a meeting with the Member of the Executive Committee (MEC) for Housing Nomatyala Hangana and were charged with trespassing. The day after the arrests, the Anti-Eviction Campaign was served with an interdict by Servcon and a number of banks to prevent it from interfering with upcoming evictions in any way. According to the Anti-Eviction Campaign:

> The banks are arguing that they should be allowed to rightsize approximately 2000 housing bond defaulters living in Khayelitsha into tiny dog kennel style RDP [Reconstruction and Development Programme] houses. It is a dire day indeed for the "new South Africa" when a poor community who voted ANC are not only threatened with eviction from their homes, but are not allowed to peacefully protest against the pending eviction. . . . The Mandela Park houses are full of structural defects and are not worth anywhere near the high prices that the owners have already paid for them. Morally too, the poor community of Mandela Park, which includes many pensioners, has a right to decent housing and to not be evicted in mid-winter. The legal action of the banks amounts to an 18th century style attack on the poor.[19]

Just over a week later, residents of Mandela Park and authorities battled when a sheriff, accompanied by police, attempted to repossess a woman's furniture. According to the Anti-Eviction Campaign, community members erected burning barricades and stoned municipal vehicles. Later in the day crowds in the streets, marching and chanting, were dispersed with rubber bullets and tear gas. Several residents were injured, some were beaten, and seven were arrested.[20] Later that month, residents again confronted police when a sheriff came to evict five families on behalf of Servcon. The tensions between residents and authorities escalated over the next few months, and in November, MEC for Community Safety Leonard Ramatlakane called for police to crack down on the Anti-Eviction Campaign in Khayelitsha.[21]

The situation in Mandela Park is by no means isolated, and Cape media regularly contain reports of nonviolent protests, boycotts, marches, and clashes between residents and authorities over development issues. However, although the rift between communities and the state over service delivery constitutes the biggest fault line beneath the urban renewal process and the most intense expression of conflict generated by neoliberal governance, there are also a number of administrative and political problems in the actual implementation of urban renewal projects that contribute to the tensions. For example, in Tafelsig and Khayelitsha's Site B, although the CFRS laid out a range of social and economic renewal projects for many of the bigger projects such as job creation centers and facilities for youth, there was virtually no detailed planning as to how they would actually be realized as late as 2002. A major problem, long recognized but not yet overcome, is the effective coordination between the many role players within and outside of government. As Janine Rauch points out, the problems appear to be systemic, as the National Urban Renewal Programme (NURP) was not incorporated into the 2002–03 draft IDP, despite the obvious overlap in the two programs and the fact that the IDP would be taking responsibility for much of the urban renewal in the NURP areas through the CFRS.[22] The problem of coordination is also discussed in the WCPDC critique, which points to the difficulties these weak links pose for communities trying to understand the chains of command and accountability when, as in some cases, local authorities initiate their own projects and access funds independently. What this suggests, they argue, is that communication between municipal and provincial structures needs to be greatly improved if there is to be real meaning behind the emphasis on integrated and multi-agency approaches and the process is not to degenerate into what they refer to as "projectization," whereby "renewal" becomes simply a set of often uncoordinated and unrelated projects with no real mechanisms for evaluation, accountability, and determination of sustainability. Commenting on the Multi-Agency Delivery Action Mechansism (MADAM), the renewal and antigang strategy mentioned in the previous chapter, social worker Llewellyn Jordaan said:

> MADAM is rubbish. I was part of MADAM in terms of safety and security, the year 2000, when we had the provincial gang strategy. And I never heard of MADAM again. We attended the conference, we've given inputs, we've given them the necessary information, how do you deal effectively with the gangs, even within this area. We have played our part in terms of assisting.[23]

The challenge of cooperation and continuity is made more difficult because of the link between the urban renewal process and the electoral process. Especially in the wake of the power plays between the ANC, the DA, and the now defunct NNP throughout the past few years, there has been little of the kind of continuity in municipal or provincial government required by sustained development projects. This problem surfaces in the WCPDC critique and was also mentioned by many youth workers, who are frustrated by the often tenuous nature of government funding and support in the context of high turnover rates and political wrangling.

This area in particular is one that many hoped would improve when the ANC was in control of the municipality and province.

These compromised governance structures and processes link developmental and anticrime–oriented projects. Joy Watson's case study of city safety programs, for example, reveals many of the same challenges mentioned in relation to urban renewal on the Cape Flats, and her discussion of the Safer Cities Programme provides an important perspective on the dual tracks of current efforts. The Safer Cities Programme was established in Cape Town in 1999 under the auspices of the United Nations Habitat Safer Cities Programmes. As with the NURP and CFRS, Safer Cities is meant to be an integrated, multifaceted, and bottom-up approach to crime prevention, creating dynamic partnerships among government agencies, police, nongovernmental organizations (NGOs), and community organizations, and is housed within the City Police Directorate. Safer Cities includes a number of social crime prevention programs and projects targeting gender violence and youth empowerment. Although the projects themselves are valuable, Watson argues that the Safer Cities initiatives share a number of basic problems, including inadequate links to a meaningful analysis of the causes of crime and to social development more generally and programmatic isolation that separates programs from broader strategies that are "linked like pieces in a puzzle" and part of a long-term cumulative approach.[24] Although this is precisely what the various renewal strategies and the IDP are intended to provide, Watson finds that although as always there are exceptions, too often development remains top-down, piecemeal, underfunded, and poorly coordinated. Addressing the issue of government programs that are meant to involve youth and communities in crime prevention, Mike, the youth worker on the Cape Flats, bluntly stated:

The budget's approved, programme's approved, [but] part of [the] rollout is to consult with community. So in other words, you're not consulting, you're informing. You're informing, you're telling the community, "this is what we're going to be doing." There's no space for engaging the issue. It's about, "this is what we're going to do, this is what we can do. Are you on board or not?" And sooner or later, I mean, it's been going on for years, people get sick of that kind of shit.[25]

Inadequate and sometimes self-serving community participation, fragmented programs lacking sustained coordination, and the effective absence of political will across the major parties are driving a deepening disillusionment in many township communities. When combined with a perception that the city is demanding more from residents on the one hand while delivering too little on the other, the clashes that frequently erupt are not difficult to understand. The choice by officials to respond to these tensions in the way they do, through criminalizing protest and deploying police, is at the heart of a securitized, neoliberal governance strategy for the townships. The relative omnipresence of the state where cost recovery and other concerns over market discipline are at issue is matched by an absence in the realm of development. Although this is true across social sectors, black youth are of special interest because of the crucial role they play in bridging underdevelopment, governance, and the war on crime. It is to this relationship that we now turn.

Trapped in Transition: Youth Renewal on the Cape Flats

Despite the snail's pace of development in the Cape, the dismal state of the schools and the labor market, and the prevalence of gangs, the city's young people more often than not do not become involved in criminal activity. The tendency of law enforcement and criminologists to stress the overrepresentation of youth in crime is therefore counterproductive to the extent that crime is understood as a youth problem rather than as one of the many challenges with which youth are forced to contend. The distinction may appear semantic but it is a difference of emphasis that too often is absent in practice in anticrime and urban renewal strategies. An urban renewal strategy whose primary focus was comprehensive youth development rather than the arrest of gang leaders would not only cut the legs out from under gangsterism, but would also concentrate state resources on the majority of youth who are not involved with crime and whose futures will determine the fate of the city. The reality at this point, however, is that virtually all of the city's coloured and black African youth are impacted by crime in their communities in a variety of ways, and for many the prospects for a decent education, gainful employment, and stable, supportive social environments in which to grow up are, at best, a distant hope.

Understanding the absence of the developmental state from the lives of youth development and the presence of the criminal justice system requires a bit of historical context. During apartheid a "developmental" state of sorts was in fact heavily involved in coloured communities, as a means of "supporting" the "crisis-ridden" coloured family. As Steffen Jensen has shown, this crisis was used by the state to legitimate a variety of interventions in the lives of coloured people, from prisons aimed at "delinquent" coloured men to welfare offices for coloured mothers, portrayed as the "solutions" to the crisis of the family. These interventions, importantly, were distinct from interventions in black African communities, which generally were of a more overtly repressive nature.[26] In both cases, however, this approach to governance had but one overarching aim: to maintain the hierarchies of racial apartheid through the manipulation of black populations by state institutions. Signaling an important shift in the transition, however, Jensen argues that perhaps the most revealing change in the state's relationship to coloured communities post-1994 was the phasing out of the child welfare grant, marking a decidedly neoliberal shift in the social contract, so to speak, between the state and coloured communities. The meaning of this retreat of the developmental state is not straightforward precisely because of the role of state intervention in the underdevelopment of coloured communities under apartheid. At the same time, the abandonment of even a highly problematic support of coloured children and mothers occurred just as interventions by the penal state intensified, albeit under cover of a different governing rationale, for all black youth. To date the most visible result has been a "dramatic swelling of the local criminal justice system," resulting in "a large number of young Coloured people living on the Cape Flats [experiencing] time in prison or reformatories."[27] These changes form the backdrop of the situation that exists today, with black youth falling under the gaze of governance structures primarily when they come into conflict with the law. The following sections examine the situation of youth in the Cape in relation to the reproduction of marginality and, closely tied to this, of criminality, which enhances the ability of gangs to successfully recruit. In the absence of development, the criminal economy thrives and the great mass of youth not absorbed by the labor market or by meaningful, long-term community-based youth programs provide fodder not only for the gangs, but also for the persistent discourses of "failed socialization" and deviance that have swirled around young people of color for decades.

When I asked the older gangster from the Americans gang how things had changed for coloured youth in the communities of the Cape Flats since 1994, his response was that things are basically the same. He paused for a moment and then added that because there are still no alternatives to gangsterism, maybe the situation had actually gotten worse. This sentiment is supported by a number of observers and researchers, who remark that in the 1970s, 1980s, and early 1990s, the antiapartheid movement provided another route for youth from the townships—and it was the rise of the youth movement of the early 1970s in particular that is often credited with the decline in gang activity over the next decade.[28] Although that movement has for the most part been demobilized, the gangs are still here, fully mobilized. In the absence of the former, the latter are uniquely positioned to provide the status, identity, and sense of belonging that political organizations did in the past, in addition to providing income and material goods. The older gangster stated that there were just no jobs for young people, and if you could give them shoes, brand names like Nike in particular, you could get them to do almost anything for you. The severity of joblessness is difficult to overstate. A recent survey of Mitchells Plain and Khayelitsha found unemployment in these two townships to be 46 percent overall, but more than 60 percent for people between the ages of 16 and 30.[29] In some neighborhoods like Tafelsig, community members say the number is even higher. The application of police operations like Slasher to this problem (where the consensus among observers is that too little social and economic renewal is happening) forces us to ask whether urban renewal offers any meaningful alternatives or solutions to "ungovernable" areas and youth.[30]

When I asked gangsters from the Flats to talk about social development and its relationship to the situation of youth on the Cape Flats, they provided a long list of challenges with which youth have to contend, saying there has been little change overall. They talked about jobs and unemployment, the lack of activities, and the lack of programs to deal with the situation. As a result, they say, youth become involved in drug dealing and prostitution. Also, their schools are full of guns and often their parents are negligent, not providing food, so that their children end up stealing to eat. One of the gangsters added that there is little trust in the local government because it has no pro-poor agenda. The people feel powerless, and in some places social services are so degraded and the gangs so powerful that not even the churches will try to fill the gap. When I spoke with Irvin Kinnes in 2002, he brought up the same phenomenon, referring specifically to the collapse of health clinics and libraries in the coloured community of Manenberg, which left huge gaps in the support services that youth have been promised under the new dispensation. The emergence of the *tik* (methamphetamine) epidemic across the Cape Flats in 2004 has only deepened these already formidable challenges, and created a host of new ones.

To date, a critical mass of basic changes to address the many facets of youth involvement with gangsterism has yet to emerge. Tensions between the state and the communities around urban renewal, as discussed previously, are provoking conflict pitting residents against the state, and in key renewal communities, a number of these are specific to youth development. At the end of June 2002, as residents of Mandela Park were marching on Parliament to protest evictions, the community of Tafelsig launched a petition drive against the city over the future of a local daycare center. According to the Tafelsig Community Forum and the Tafelsig Anti-Eviction Campaign, the two organizations behind the petition, the city was planning to close down the Joy Day Care Centre due to a lack of funds. This marked the second attempt to close down the center, which provides food for poor children and services for HIV-positive and disabled children. A year earlier the community successfully mobilized to resist the conversion of the center into offices for a DA councillor. In their statement announcing the petition drive, the organizations specifically refer to the hypocrisy of closing down a valuable community center when the city, in their view, spends millions of rands on expense accounts for city officials.[31]

A year after community members and police fought over evictions and repossessions in Mandela Park, conflict broke out again, but this time over a school the community had established to accommodate pupils they claimed had been abandoned by the government. People's Power Secondary School began in early 2003, initiated by students, unemployed teachers, and parents. The school also started a community garden, clinic, and computer classes for students from the area and from nearby Tafelsig. After a campaign of public pressure, including marches to Parliament, the Department of Education registered the school. In August, however, school organizers claim police came and chased students and teachers out of their classes in an effort to shut it down. This, they say, was the second time police had come. Police came at night and allegedly broke doors and smashed windows. A spokesperson for the school said of the latest raid:

> The ANC is always talking about voluntarism but when qualified
> teachers, parents and pupils start their own school, garden
> and clinic in an existing community centre, they unlawfully send
> police to disrupt classes. We have it in writing that the school is
> registered and now this is being unlawfully reversed by the police
> and the ANC.[32]

These conflicts are troubling in their own right, but more so because they are occurring precisely in those areas where urban renewal efforts are meant to be focused and because they have to do with services for youth and children. The political unrest in the target renewal areas of Tafelsig and Mandela Park around the very issues urban renewal is meant to address suggests that efforts to break the links between youth, underdevelopment, and gangsterism through the creation of constructive alternatives have a long way to go. The organizations clustered around the Anti-Eviction Campaign and Community Forums have been relatively consistent in their claims that the underlying causes of gangsterism are not being addressed, a view that echoes what local gangsters and youth workers consistently told me. The role that a lack of alternatives for youth plays in swelling the ranks of the gangs is also recognized by adults in the community; and in those instances where residents are able to communicate their needs to city officials, the absence of youth centers, sports organizations, and other outlets for youth regularly tops the list. This evidence thus supports the contention made by youth workers on a national level that youth development has been abandoned, and it throws into question the extent to which the social and economic prongs of the CFRS were actually being implemented during the early years of the decade.

Whereas clashes between the government and residents around socioeconomic development occur all too frequently, gangs continue to provide youth with many of the services that urban renewal has yet to deliver, and in a sustained and multipronged manner. Although on the one hand conflicts between residents and the state over the provision of services for youth and children (part of a larger pattern of nondelivery) speak to the push factor for entry into gangs, the pull consists of the development that gangs provide. Underdevelopment of the Flats not only leads to the emergence of organized political formations, as is evident in the resistance to evictions and service cutoffs, but also strengthens the hand of the highly organized and well-resourced gangs. Llewellyn Jordaan comments that:

> These drug lords and gang leaders are offering recreational facilities. They have big yards, pool tables, game machines, and beer; they have soccer clubs. . . . We need to set alternatives that will be much more exciting than the drug dealers' yards.[33]

In areas where schools and recreational facilities are scarce and unemployment tops 50 percent, it is not surprising that the yards of drug dealers have a certain appeal for teenage boys. The offerings of gangsterism are not limited to sports facilities; rather, as Jordaan and others point out, these should be seen as part of a more holistic set of very tangible services that, over decades, gangs have come to deliver. Referring to the popularity of assassinated Hard Livings boss Rashaad Staggie among some township residents, former *Cape Times* editor Ryland Fisher has said:

> He often paid their rent, provided work for many unemployed (and probably unemployable) youth, and when these youths landed in trouble, he would dispatch his lawyers to keep them out of jail. The stories of him driving through the sub-economic townships in his luxury German car, throwing R10 notes out of the window, are legendary and mostly true.[34]

But the gangs provide not only material goods. Similar to the role that political organizations played a decade ago, gangs provide for some young men status and a sense of self-worth in areas where legitimate and legal avenues are few or nonexistent. Gangsters spoke of the status that came with being in a gang, which, in addition to the money it often involved, gave young men access to girls, and said that in their experiences girls often wanted to be with gangsters. Their comments open a window into the often neglected role that the gangs play in conferring a masculine identity on members, or in providing a space in which masculinity can be acquired. In an area where the legal means of being a provider, one of the key conventional markers of masculinity, are beyond the reach of more than half of all males, gangsterism represents a means to becoming a man. Gangsterism is therefore not simply a response to economic instability but can also serve as a source of empowerment and self-identity in the face of an historically rooted economic marginalization and racial devaluation that are destabilizing in other ways as well. Gary Kynoch, although referring to gangs in Soweto during apartheid, makes an observation that still has relevance for the present day Cape Flats: "Gangsters," he writes, "prospered in defiance of the white state, they enjoyed wealth, power, prestige and sexual prowess despite their blackness."[35]

Kynoch and others have often argued that explanations of gangsterism that focus on economic forces are too narrow and tend to ignore or downplay the extent to which the access it provides to a positive and relatively stable, if problematic, heterosexual masculine status identity for young black men is as important to its seductiveness as is wealth. In a place like South Africa, where apartheid's structures and spirit systematically worked to undermine black people's agency and personhood, gangs and political organizations alike, in ways both similar and dissimilar, were institutions through which young men could respond to and resist this process of "emasculation." Clive Glaser, also writing on Soweto's gangs of the 1970s, observed:

> The gangs were a young male peer group phenomenon. They emerged at the intersection of personal and territorial familiarity as teenage boys, with the social space to be independent and mobile, grew up together on the streets. Play networks gradually evolved into gangs as the sense of masculine competitiveness heightened in the congested neighborhoods of Soweto. . . . It was a culture in many respects defined in opposition to femininity, which subjected women to terrifying levels of coercion and sexual violence.[36]

Elaine Salo, who researches gangs and masculinity on the Cape Flats, and Manenberg in particular, points to the often underappreciated implications for today of "the extent to which struggle movements such as the Bonteheuwel Military Wing or MK often based their opposition upon the very militaristic masculinity that it resisted."[37] This culture of militarism that evolved under apartheid, and the gender identities that underlie it, she argues, still predominate in the townships of the Cape Flats today. Here it had its own unique characteristics due to the different locations of black Africans and coloureds within the apartheid system, national personhood under apartheid defining black Africans as infants and coloureds as dependent "women." Although coloureds received labor preferences under the system, the "feminine" textile industries of the Western Cape locked out coloured men as providers. As a result, she writes, "Alternative ideologies of masculinity in the local context had to be found." In an environment already saturated with the militaristic and masculinized violence of apartheid, the use of physical violence became for young men "an alternative means to assert their claim to heterosexual masculinity and to personhood."[38] During the struggle, the use of violence against the state provided one such alternative route to status and "manhood"; today, the gangs provide another. Salo's analysis contrasts with more simplistic explanations of and solutions to violence on the Flats today. The role of gun violence and the demand for guns, for example, cannot be reduced to law enforcement issues that can be solved through the paramilitary policing structures the gangs in many ways mimic. According to Salo, guns represent more than the literal power of the weapon itself. "Guns," she writes, "are widely acknowledged as the ubiquitous currency of power and patronage on the Cape Flats—a man with a gun may be the only individual who is respected."[39]

Another layer to this aspect of crime and violence is that aggressive militaristic responses, in the form of a war on crime, can in fact reinforce this version of masculinity. Just as the gang structures share some elementary similarities with the repressive structures of the state that marginalized young black men, and against which the gangs were a reaction, paramilitary policing fuels rather than breaks what Salo calls the culture of militarism. At one level the war between gangs and the police represents competing and overlapping masculinities and arenas for proving manhood, with violence and prison as rites of passage in the process.[40] To the extent that urban renewal is intended to speak to youth across a range of needs, the growth of the gangs and the increase in violent crime since 1994 on the Flats has to be seen to some extent as a sign of its failure as an intervention on this level and an indication that the end of apartheid cannot automatically be conflated with the end of young black men's socioeconomic and political marginalization, or with what Salo refers to as the gendered identities it fostered. One young person who is active in youth development initiatives in Mitchells Plain spoke of what she sees as the main challenge facing young men:

> I think in my area it's identity. Certain guys, if they are not part of this gang, they are not "that guy," you know what I'm saying? Especially in my area. If they don't do this drug, if they don't . . . there's certain things, if they don't do it, they won't have that specific identity, and that encourages certain aspects of substance abuse, of doing the wrong thing, just to fit in.[41]

With the exception of small-scale efforts by independent NGOs, however, youth workers have agreed that to date virtually nothing has happened on this front of the social development process.

"We Must Have the Necessary People to Heal Minds"

Marginalization has been widely recognized as one of the greatest challenges facing young people in South Africa, especially to the extent that it intersects with criminality, and it figured prominently in the early discussions about youth development.[42] However, although today it is widely understood as being the result of inequalities inherited from the apartheid system, occasional echoes of yesterday's "failed socialization" explanations do surface, as in the prominent question: What is wrong with youth today? More recently, in the wake of the abandonment of youth, although marginalization is still acknowledged, the more meaningful discussions about the "problem of youth" appear as discourses about crime, as with street children in the city center. With regard to coloured youth on the Flats, on the other hand, the preferred reference is gangsterism, owing to the very real challenges it poses, especially for young coloured people, but also because of a common sensibility that conflates gangs and coloured youth. One young woman from Athlone expressed her frustration, asking:

How are we expected to run this country or even just survive in it if we are not even given the chance to be heard? We don't know what is expected of us because nobody tells us anything. The people think that all Coloured kids are ignorant and belong to gangs.[43]

This young woman's insight into "the people's" perceptions, invoking the relationship between silencing and criminalizing youth, exposes a deep flaw in the urban renewal process on the Cape Flats: The voices of young people themselves are often drowned out by the rhetoric of a war on crime and gangsters, and ignored in the policies that accompany it. Mike, the youth worker cited earlier, stressed the extent to which "youth development" becomes wrapped up in politics in ways that contribute to the very marginalization that programs are meant to alleviate:

They're [government] allocating money left, right and centre and when it comes down to the crunch, now they need reports, and they need numbers and they need to look good. What is happening with youth is really not the issue. That youth could be dead for all they care, for all they know. Because they are not even engaging with the youth. When they do come and speak they're coming with political agendas. This is happening in my workshop presentations, where representatives from the Department [of Corrections] come and have their whole little hoo haa about how good the department is. And these kids know, "Don't talk shit, this is the first time we see you. We know Mikey." . . . And kids are simple in that way. "There's the person engaging with me, there's the person that's risking his life every day. We walk with him to the taxi rank so that we can be safe. Where were you, with your little government . . . ?"[44]

Although this dynamic alone does not explain the priority given to the law enforcement prong of urban renewal, it does support the argument that the development process lacks meaningful input from those who are most affected and in need. The social and economic aspects of urban renewal on the Cape Flats, which are meant to assist in the integration of youth into their communities, are too often noticeable by their absence. This absence stands in contrast to the very visible high-profile operations at the vanguard of urban renewal's focus on criminality. The imbalance reflects the transformation of the social problem of marginalized black youth into the criminal problem of gangsterism at the same time that it reproduces this marginalization.

The real import of this process can be seen in the moment when youth do become a concern to the state, as criminals or suspected criminals. Although the experience of youth in prison is somewhat outside the purview of urban renewal, it has bearing on the process because imprisonment figures prominently in the lives of many township youth and has direct implications for crime and youth marginalization in these areas. South African prisons, like virtually all modern prisons, are criminogenic rather than rehabilitative, with between 60 percent to 70 percent of prisoners likely to either have been in prison before or to have returned on a similar charge[45]; this despite the rhetoric of the many official documents on reform of the prison system and for juveniles in the system in particular. In the words of one young prisoner serving time for gang-related activity, "I've been in jail several times. That's where we promote crime. It's a school of crime. We discuss the best methods of doing crime and other things such as potential buyers and pricing."[46] The damage done in prison is not limited to making better criminals—prisons also contribute to the reproduction of violent masculine and patriarchal norms, as well as the normalization of gangsterism and of prison as a rite of passage. In this sense, the culture of the prison mirrors and reinforces the values and codes of masculinity that many young men inhabit outside the prison walls. The connection is very real, as youth in prison are exposed to the well-entrenched prison gangs, which are increasingly affiliated with street gangs on the outside, and who control virtually every aspect of prison life, from the prison economy to the policing of masculinity and heterosexual gender roles, making it much more likely that nongang youth will join, or be forced to join, a gang.[47]

The capacity to use violence and be abusive is a sign of masculinity in prison: the more violent the crime, the more masculine it is considered (the exception is rape, which is not seen as a violent, i.e., masculine, crime). For example, prisoners will assault warders (guards) often with the aim of being seen and caught, as a means of marking status.[48] The hierarchy that exists within the prison, tightly controlled by the gangs, in many ways revolves around violence and heterosexual norms, with rape and sexual assault common disciplinary tools. Younger prisoners are generally coded female, or "wyfes," while older prisoners, especially gang members, take on the male role. The highly proscribed rules around sex and relationships are strictly enforced, and again, violence is the typical form of punishment. Young prisoners, even if sentenced for only a short time or simply awaiting trial, are likely to experience some form of violence, and very likely sexual assault or rape. One experienced youth worker familiar with the local prisons told me that the highest incidence of prison rape is in the section housing juveniles awaiting trial.[49] In other words, sexual assault is most prevalent in the areas containing children who have yet to even go to court, and who will likely serve short terms. Virtually all of them will eventually be returned to their communities, where it is unlikely that their brush with the war on crime will contribute to neighborhood safety and their own "youth development."

Prison thus contributes to the marginalization of young people, by compounding the trauma they experience and by normalizing the violence and gangsterism many of them are exposed to in their communities. In areas where jobs are already scarce, prison only makes these youth less employable. The member of the Americans gang, for example, commented that it is very easy for youth to end up in prison, and once they are released, the work training certificates they may have earned inside brand them as convicts. The evidence here echoes what many criminologists in South Africa and elsewhere know about the effects of incarceration on youth, suggesting that prison in fact facilitates their criminalization: Far from being a deterrent for youth, prison acts as an obstacle to their integration into their communities. Upon release, it is more likely that young men who have been through prison will remain marginalized, meaning that the incentives to either join or return to the gangs only increase.

Diversion programs do exist but currently are unable to come close to meeting the needs of all the young people who go to prison, reflecting the overall pattern with regard to youth development. For all their success, they also occur late in the chain of youth criminalization, which many diversion service providers readily acknowledge. Eldred de Klerk, from the Municipal Services Project, added that many diversion programs do not address the core social skills that many youth lack, and youth often do not have a sense of their own agency. This, in turn, contributes to their vulnerability in the face of the gangsterism that surrounds them and is precisely the reason that many adult residents in the townships stress the need for more productive alternatives for young people to build self-esteem and confidence.[50] Although diversion programs are useful and necessary, they need to be one part of a support system for youth that begins in the communities, in the schools, and in the home, not after arrest. It is this recognition that informs the rhetorical commitment of urban renewal to a holistic approach to youth development, but is also proving to be the weak link in implementation.

According to a youth worker from Johannesburg, one of the big problems with diversion projects is that not all of the organizations are able or willing to actually go into the communities where the youth live. He pointed out that the big difference between these projects and the one he is involved with is that his is community based.[51] Locally based organizations operate from the communities in which they work rather than coming in; they can visit youth at school and at home and are able to employ local youth to work with the project. The same is true of the youth projects I observed on the Cape Flats: Many of the youth workers are from the Flats and are thus part of the network of community insiders. That kind of access is crucial in building the kinds of relationships often absent between communities and police. But it is these smaller community-based projects that often have difficulty finding consistent funding, having to compete against larger, more well-established, but in many cases, less organic organizations. Although this is precisely the kind of problem that urban renewal is supposed to address, it does not seem at this point that enough is currently being done to keep substantial numbers of youth out of trouble with the law and out of prison, or to address the more fundamental reality of massive youth marginalization. The targeted intervention at the point of lawbreaking is contributing to an increase in rates of youth going to prison, either as sentenced prisoners or awaiting trial. In terms of outcome, however, incarceration of youth is in effect an antidevelopment strategy contributing to a worsening of the very problem of crime and gangsterism that urban renewal is meant to combat.

At this point the reality is that gangsterism fills many of the gaps the state and its urban renewal strategies have thus far been unable to reach, and does so by integrating some youth in the townships. These youth, marginalized socially and economically, drawn from a "surplus" population, function as a "reserve army" of sorts upon whose existence the vibrancy of the gangs ultimately depends. As Irvin Kinnes points out, if government cannot find a way to replace the meaningful, if ultimately destructive, alternatives that gangs provide, the crime problem will not go away, regardless of the number of police that are hired and prisons that are built:

> If the social and economic needs of communities such as Manenberg, Bonteheuwel and Mitchell's Plain are not addressed by policy makers in the long term, gangs such as the Hard Livings, the Americans and most definitely The Firm will continue to be regarded as the providers by the community and will thus continue to grow.[52]

Despite warnings like this from people with extensive knowledge of the area and the positive language of many urban renewal and city planning documents discussed in the previous chapter, there is every indication at this point that criminal justice will remain the primary focus and policing the operational arm of urban renewal on the Cape Flats. As such, development in the city both reflects and reproduces false binaries, rooted in the country's violent past but also supported by international "best practice," between crime and development, communities and criminals. To the extent that many commitments have been made nationally and provincially to move away from apartheid's criminalization of social and political problems and the obsession with a narrowly defined security, the current trajectory of urban renewal represents a regression from the principles of documents like "Ready to Govern." In the townships of the Cape Flats, this is most evident in the steady morphing of counterterrorist operations into anticrime/urban renewal operations under the guise of democratic police reform as defined in large part internationally by the United States, and the complementary underdevelopment of sustained socioeconomic programs that also conforms to internationally accepted norms regarding sound economic policy. It is no surprise that unrest in the targeted

CFRS areas is endemic, but it is important to note that this unrest manifests most prominently as gangsterism and organized community resistance to poor service delivery.

With regard to crime and gangsterism, the well-worn assumption that there exists a clear delineation between gangs and communities lies at the heart of the problem with current approaches and acts as their evident, if generally unspoken, justification. Only if gangsters were not integrated into communities could a war on gangsterism be waged without at the same time waging a war on the community. At the same time the broken foundation of police/community relations only exacerbates the tendency of the police to treat gangsters as outsiders. The extent to which a war on gangsterism bleeds into a war on youth and often takes on the appearance of an occupation or counterinsurgency campaign is directly related to the inherent messiness of what are assumed to be self-evident demarcations. The readily acknowledged overrepresentation of black youth in gangs and the masses of marginalized youth are the organic link between crime and development, the communities and the gangsters. It is their uncomfortable presence that exposes the fallacy of neat boundaries that can be policed with U.S. gang laws and high-density paramilitary operations and the inadequacies of urban renewal theories and practices that seek to eradicate gangsterism as a precursor to bringing socioeconomic development. The fallacy, however, is necessary if hard policing is to remain at the core of urban renewal and anticrime campaigns.

At the meeting between Tafelsig residents and police in Mitchells Plain, a woman stood up at one point and said, "We love the gangsters but hate the things they do." Although not all township residents may feel this way—as the prevalence of vigilantism suggests—her comment is important because it exposes a depth to the problem of gangsterism, and of marginalized youth, absent in the CFRS. As unpopular a sentiment as it may be, and as awkward as it is in light of current urban renewal priorities on the Flats, gangsters are a part of the communities in which they operate, and not just as a discrete category but as embedded individuals. They are emotionally entangled in the community as much as they are economically entrenched. They are brothers, fathers, sons, husbands, nephews, uncles; some are still the communities' children, others are the communities' men. They exist in these communities in ways that are complex, ambiguous, and full of contradictions and not simply as the root of their problems. They are bound up, for example, in larger problems of masculinity, violence, and domestic abuse that are only marginally attributable to the existence of gangs. Attempts to deal with this part of the community primarily with police and prisons are bound to fail. What youth workers and community organizers make clear is that these problems require integrated, multifaceted solutions that speak to the broad range of causes, that young people in gangs have the same needs and require the same services and support all youth do, and youth not involved with gangsterism require just as much of the state's attention as those who are involved. Commenting on the situation in Manenberg, former member of the Jesters and the 26s prison gang Adiel van der Heever told Marianne Merton, "The people of this place are affected by a lot of problems. They are socially, psychologically and physically affected. . . . Sending in more police is not the issue. We must have job creation. We must have the necessary people to heal minds."[53]

To date, however, it is not armies of social workers, youth workers, drug counselors, and teachers who are deployed to the Flats, but the South African Police Service, the municipal police, the defense forces, and private security personnel. Police continue to be ubiquitous in the townships or, as some observe, at its boundaries. Although there are many stories of individual officers committed to real reform and, more specifically, to a development-driven urban renewal, for many residents the police are not deployed as friendly bobbies on the beat under a new dispensation of democratic community policing, but all too often as riot police, paramilitary police, intelligence gatherers, or accomplices of the gangs they are meant to fight.

Apartheid, Democracy, and the Urban Future

Policing and urban renewal in Cape Town today are part of a lineage of governance strategies bound up with unresolved social tensions that have evolved over decades. These tensions have produced the social and spatial terrain with which now confront us. They run beneath this divided city, holding it together while always threatening to tear it further apart. What I have attempted to show here are some of the mechanisms through which these tensions are reproduced. To do so, I have argued that neoliberalism plays a central and defining role in the organization of urban governance while trying to avoid making claims, directly or by implication, that somehow sociospatial divisions, the conflicts they reflect and regenerate, and the response to these by the political and economic elite are inherently or exclusively a function of market accumulation processes and the actions of those who so eagerly attempt to implement them in pursuit of world city status. It is important for the analysis to be clear that the new city is built on the foundations of the old, which have yet to be dismantled, and that in both of these sharp inequalities, repression, and sometimes violent conflict constitutes integral features of everyday life. At some point, however, we must let go of this conceptual abstraction that allows us to speak so easily of new and old; the challenges may be familiar, yet references to the past steadily lose their explanatory power.

This becomes troubling if the result is a reinterpretation of divided Cape Town in which the city is taken largely as a creation of 1994, its historical baggage simply swept away. But it can be an opportunity if we acknowledge that the contradictions and conflicts of the past persist not simply as an effect of inertia; rather, they are powerful forces with the creative capacity to mutate and survive what are otherwise quite transformative eras. Cape Town was once a colonial city, then it became an apartheid city. After 1994, the hope was that it would become a liberated city. From the vantage point of the present, however, this possible future appears as a receding horizon. Instead, quite a different city has emerged, one in which making distinctions between past and present inequalities is of questionable value because such distinctions imply a linearity that is unsupported by the reality with which we are confronted today. Indeed, it may be more useful to speak about what organizes inequalities today than to search for their origins, for it is through organizing processes that "make sense" of them or harmonize them with prevailing ideologies that these inequalities are positioned to survive. And whatever their nearest historical antecedents may be, their existence today is refracted through mutually reinforcing discourses of market rationality, liberal democracy, and security, gathered around, articulated through, and deployed by what I refer to as a regime of neoliberal urban governance. In the long history of South Africa, this regime is very new, and it may turn out to be short lived. For now, however, it is central to the governance of inequality in the city and, it follows, to the all-important project of representing social inequality within the context of a somewhat altered political and economic dispensation. In this conclusion, therefore, I return to the comparison of the city center and the townships and attempt to draw out the lessons it may hold for our understanding of neoliberal governance regimes in the city and beyond.

Cape Town's Central Business District (CBD) and the Cape Flats are shaped by parallel processes that form part of a broader governance strategy driven by local, national, and transnational discourses, actors, and institutions. The net effect of these processes is to organize and manage the distribution of people and resources in the city under the rubric of development or urban renewal. Although the success of these efforts is always partial, contingent, and unstable, this strategy has been central to the reproduction of the very sociospatial segregation it is meant to overcome. Urban renewal, including the campaign against crime, has been a resounding success in the city center, whereas efforts across the Cape Flats have thus far made little headway in reducing social and economic instability. Further, whereas urban renewal in the CBD is a coordinated, relatively well-planned process that has been sustained over years, on the Cape Flats it is too often piecemeal, derailed by changes in political parties, marked by poor communication among the many role players, and lacking in committed funding. Because of the vast differences in size and population and very different starting points, a direct comparison has its limitations. Even under ideal conditions, the CBD would most likely "turn around" before the Cape Flats. Still, the revitalization of the CBD while the Cape Flats struggles to make measurable progress belies the oft-heard slogan emanating from downtown: that Cape Town is a city for all in which no one is left out.[1] But Cape Town is more than a divided city; it is a city marked by heavily fortified spaces and specific patterns of spatial policing, a city governed by a distinct, if not unique, politics of security. Neoliberal governance here, through private, public, and hybrid mechanisms, is rapidly adapting to the preexisting sociospatial fragmentation that has given the city its form, leaving its own imprint in the process and generating a more contemporary discourse of inequality and a set of practices aimed at security. Commenting on this in relation to the growth of the private security industry after 1994, South African criminologist Elrena van der Spuy writes: "In the context of a booming 'crime control industry,' we are witnessing the construction of 'islands of security' and 'safe corridors' insulated from the surrounding 'dangerous territories.'"[2] Through a language that rearticulates the apartheid-era geography of inside/safety and outside/danger, and its social reference points, neoliberal governance effects a troubling naturalization of these inequalities and the closing of a historic opportunity made possible by earlier, critical perspectives. The threat or danger posed by these inequalities from the vantage point of the downtown core is portrayed as emanating from "outside," as external to the very social reality in which the CBD is embedded and that makes this existence possible. What this portends is yet another era of conflict rooted in familiar struggles over urban space and resources, animated by powerful new iterations of old characters and narratives. Although these struggles have been a constitutive feature of Cape Town history for generations, what distinguishes their current incarnation from previous cycles lies in a specific interpenetration of local and transnational governance networks and discourses that is mediated by the language of neoliberal democracy. Through this, local struggles are reframed, although not without substantial resistance at times, and rearticulated; taken for granted injustices of the "past" are imbued with new meanings through overlapping discourses of crime, urban renewal, and world class cities, which are then deployed to manage them in ways that acknowledge this past while ignoring it. Economic and political leaders continue to pursue successful urban development, but the meaning of success in this context contains within it a clear disciplinary logic that assumes not the integration of the city, but its continued fragmentation.

Specifically, the success of urban revitalization in the CBD, an "island of security," is intimately connected to the exclusion of street children and vagrants, but with little real attention to what happens to them once they are out of sight. Once CBD governance structures have removed these "undesirables," they fall under the purview of a distinct, yet related, governance structure tailored to the townships, the "outside," "dangerous territories." This spatial approach to security, with its distinct set of meanings linked to urban renewal and crime, is what marks neoliberal governance in the city and shapes how those who inhabit it are policed. The practices that result, as we have seen, are concentrated on young black men. This simple and recurring truth only reinforces how powerful certain articulations of race, youth, and masculinity can be when combined in contested, tense, urban spaces; it is at this intersection that the governance of security is most volatile but, perhaps, also most productive. The meaning of black youth, from this perspective, is not entirely uniform across city spaces; rather, it shifts with the setting. In the city center, street children figured prominently and, relative to their numbers, disproportionately as ideological markers of urban decay and danger during the early days of the Cape Town Partnership, portrayed by proponents of downtown revitalization as urban terrorists. Their demonization in the English-language media and by renewal officials reached such a pitch that street children, and the AIDS orphans increasingly blamed for swelling their ranks, were referred to as a looming threat not only to the city center, but to the entire urban social fabric. Through this warning, a powerful and highly organized urban elite stirred up deep, and reliable, racial anxieties by evoking age-old images of violent, out-of-control black youth in what amounts to a moral panic that serves to discipline those same youth and legitimate keeping them out of the public urban spaces from which they have been excluded or their presence has been tightly proscribed for generations. The leading edge of urban renewal in the CBD is therefore a process of disappearing through a sleight of hand that relies on a shifting view of the poor from victims to problems.

The politics of race, representation, and urban renewal on the Cape Flats differ in important ways from the moral panic and attempt at banishing street children from the city center. These differences have to do primarily with the substantial demographic, economic, and geographic differences between the two areas, as well as with the relationship between them. A similar process operates, however, in that certain meanings linked to social, political, and economic realities are imposed on township youth such that their identity as alleged criminals is—again—reinforced, while other aspects of their social presence in the city are obscured, rendering their presence in affluent spaces as invasive. The observation made by the Americans gang leader that committing crime in the CBD has become more difficult and the campaign against street children both speak to the success of urban renewal initiatives in operationalizing these politics and simultaneously naturalizing outcomes that are produced only through great effort and great neglect. The danger and anxiety that street children and *skollies* represent is rooted in the deeper, unresolved tensions that are concentrated along the city's social and spatial borders. To understand their power, it is less useful to dwell on the crimes and petty nuisances of a handful of street kids who make their way into the city from the townships or on the real but far removed crimes of young gangsters than it is to be aware of the ever-present disquiet over the millions behind them.

If the outcome of urban renewal in the city center is the displacement of crime and "criminal elements" back over the border separating the Flats from the city core, then what we see happening thus far on the Flats is a complementary policy of containment of the millions. No one denies that gangsterism is a serious challenge to the communities of the Cape Flats, but the approach taken by the city seems to be less about reducing the threat that gangs pose to residents and more about stemming the tide of crime and violence coming from the townships, and their impact on perceptions of the city as a whole. The evocation of gangsterism as the rationale behind waging a war/waging urban renewal serves as a theatrical flourish through which to locate the "crime problem" on the stage of the Flats, rather than in the relationships between the city's unevenly developed halves. In the meantime, the complex and generative power of the social relations that continue to define Cape Town are obscured yet again. The conflation of the Flats with gangsterism, and gangsterism with coloured youth, differs from the moral panic around street children, however, precisely because the threat posed by gangsterism is all too real, even if its primary victims are the residents of the communities from which the gangs come. The central issue here on the question of representation is not the use of stereotypes about race, youth, and criminality to keep people out of the downtown, but to keep them on the Flats. Whereas the danger of street children is exaggerated as part of an urban revitalization project, the danger of young coloured gang members is simply evoked as part of a discourse of urban renewal that empowers the police to get tough with the Cape Flats gangsters, because no one, certainly not affluent white Capetownians, has to be convinced of their danger. As easy targets, gangs and crime come to represent the urban poor as a whole in terms that allow elites to safely pass over the quicksand of race and class while still squarely confronting the threat of underdevelopment. On the Cape Flats, however, the understanding of gangsterism is tied more intimately to a familiarity with the boys and men who inhabit the reductionistic identity of the gangster, and criticisms aimed at the antigang campaigns should be read as part of an overall concern regarding the intentions of the police. When attempting to make sense of how gangsterism shapes state responses to crime and poverty in the city, it is therefore important to be attentive to which perceptions of gangsterism it is that inform antigangsterism strategies. Doing so makes it fairly clear that images of the "black menace" continue to set the parameters within which state responses are formed. Generally speaking, the efforts to eradicate gangsterism, despite all of the commendable rhetoric, are infused with misrepresentations that lie at the heart of the city's racial and class anxieties. Nowhere is this more apparent than in the status of genuine socioeconomic development for youth on the Flats, the endemic harassment of black youth by police, and the swelling of the prison system. The volatile mix of youth, race, and crime, rather than creating an operating consensus around the need for a massive rollout of resources for young people, instead informs the rationale for a war on crime. The old barriers are reinforced and the simmering tensions underlying the city are pushed back into well-worn channels.

Historically, when marginalized young people have appeared on South Africa's stage as social actors, they are contained discursively within the context of the threat they pose to a particular social order, often as a precursor to disciplining them through the exercise of repressive state power. The legacy of youth marginalization and the debt that is owed the generations of young people who fought apartheid are generally acknowledged, although increasingly as artifact or ritual whose original power and meaning have dissipated. There is also a recognition that the hardships youth today face contribute to youth involvement in crime and that responses to crime need to take this into consideration. The policies for crime fighting and the accumulated record of the implementation of social crime prevention measures, however, reveal a consistent failure to put this recognition into practice. There is a tension within government and the police, reflecting broader social tensions, between the stated commitment to social crime prevention and the substantial pressures from many sectors of South Africa society, often for different reasons, to get tough on crime by lengthening prison sentences, bringing back the death penalty, and practicing hard policing. Although clearly problematic, if not counterproductive, support for this approach speaks to the understandable frustration that many South Africans feel with regard to crime and their own safety. Frustration alone, however, does not explain the choices made to adopt this particular approach to the crime problem, as frustrations over housing, poverty, and other socioeconomic issues easily match frustration over crime but have not generated the same level of concerted and sustained action by government. Given the often bitter fights over the use of state resources and the choices around public spending, it is perhaps unsurprising that the most vulnerable segment of the population, whose members control few resources, are politically disorganized, and are in many cases too young to even vote, lose out. The war on crime, with no clearly organized opposition, is as much a function of disempowered youth as it is of empowered adults.

To the extent that youth are central to the war on crime (in sharp contrast to their more peripheral position in the anemic initiatives on development), they occupy simultaneous positions of visibility and invisibility. As the research on youth development and the political commitments made to youth after 1994 reveals, the promises have been hollowed out and young people abandoned. Although there still exists an official rhetoric of commitment in both the public and private sectors that gives young people a certain visibility, the lack of delivery and substantive positive change indicate an absence of actual, living youth from the social development components of the urban renewal process. In other words, despite the talk about youth, when measured against services for youth there is an obvious political invisibility. This decline is a consequence of their powerlessness as a political bloc since 1994 and of a reframing of the utility of their capacity for militancy and violence. However, as the attention showered on street children and young gangsters suggests, not all youth are equally invisible, nor are they all neglected by the state. When young people step out of the shadows of quiet deprivation and into a more public light, the state has shown its determination and capacity to respond ruthlessly. Although the numbers of unemployed black youth on the Flats far outweighs the numbers involved with gangsterism, the latter become visible in the sense of commanding "public" attention, most commonly through their actual or perceived involvement with crime and disorder. The visibility of these young people then becomes the lever through which they are maneuvered into further marginalization, either in the prisons, in the gangs, or on the streets. The long-term consequences of this abandonment, barring radical interventions, are likely to be disastrous not only for youth, whose situation is already dire, but also for society as a whole. Ironically, although they may be socially, economically, and politically marginalized, youth continue to sit, as they did in the wake of Soweto, at the very heart of South Africa's transition and its future.

This reality is evident in the shape that urban renewal has taken across the city: as a crime containment strategy, a strategy of policing underdevelopment. That security governance becomes so centered on young black men, explained in certain academic, policy, and law enforcement sectors as simply reflecting the reality of who commits crime, is more a reflection of an accommodation to youth marginalization, and underdevelopment more generally, at the same time as it contributes to the transformation of marginalization into (re)criminalization. What underpins this set of relationships is the approach to development we see across the city: socioeconomic development and integration depend upon economic growth, which in turn depends upon security. But citywide security is an impossibility given the very inequalities that make it necessary. The response by the network of public and private actors who constitute the neoliberal governance regime is a bifurcated security strategy that mirrors the divided city. From this context emerges security-driven governance that may have roots in the apartheid era but is very much a response to contemporary contests over space and resources within the contested framework of a neoliberal growth strategy. The practice of cordoning off "dangerous territories" from "islands of security" reemerged quickly on this side of the transition, facilitated by the continuity in the security forces themselves and in some of the basic features behind the pre-1994 conflicts. The Cape Flats war arose directly from forces already in motion at the outset of the transition and did not, as authorities often claim, ignite because of a rogue vigilante organization challenging state authority. Instead, it was due largely to building pressures in the relationships between communities, gangsters, and the provincial state, still under National Party control at the time, centered around the social, political, and economic conditions in which many city residents had to live. These tensions had erupted before PAGAD and will do so again, barring a fundamental reordering of these relations and of the city's overall development strategy.

The policing of underdevelopment has produced, in the eyes of proponents, a significant dip in serious crime and has demonstrated to concerned parties that the state is serious about hammering the criminals. But just as the success of the security forces in the Cape Flats war gave rise to future insecurity in the form of gang transformations and growth, the strategy of amassing critical force capacity to take down the gangs as a precursor to implementing real development threatens to entrench a securitized "development" policy in which township residents become not simply problems but enemies of "society." The full scope of the danger is stated with urgency in an open letter sent to the city government in 2002 by the Anti-Eviction Campaign in relation to evictions:

> Rather than treating the human suffering of these and other evicted families in a humanitarian way, by giving the people free basic life services (like water, electricity, housing, education, etc.), the Government has chosen to spend millions of rands on private security companies. They also deploy heavily armed SANDF forces and police with dogs to forcibly evict thousands of households [and] cut off water and electricity supplies, all of which has contributed to the further destabilisation of our communities. These destabilisation policies that the government has deployed has served to promote corruption [and] gangsterism, making any crime fighting strategies ineffective.[3]

The source of the danger is a consequence of the current trajectory of urban renewal in two ways. First, the lack of progress in job creation, economic growth, and social development ensures a certain level of instability that is already manifesting as continued crime, gangsterism, and organized resistance in the form of community and political organizations. This in turn serves as justification for continued police pressure that too often is applied beyond its intended targets, even as it expands the list of acceptable targets and provokes further instability. Routinized violence, already a recognized problem in the country, is now perpetuated by gangsters, private security, and the state, and in the process of "securing the city," marginalized youth continue to be trapped in the violence of gangsterism, police repression, and prison. Rather than breaking the cycle of violence and gangsterism, the war on crime facilitates and contributes to it and, in turn, to the further deterioration of social stability. To date, as evidenced in new posturing by officials at the national level with regard to the "shoot to kill" policy, this lesson has been ignored. The truth remains, however, that the security-first approach will provide no more security or development to the neoliberal city than it did to the apartheid city.

A central concern of this book has been how the sociospatial fragmentation of the apartheid era is reproduced under conditions of formal liberal democracy. Central to this process is neoliberal governance, which in Cape Town is organized around the production of certain forms of security that are tailored to the contours of a world city in the making. It is fitting, then, to close by revisiting the themes introduced at the outset and reflecting on the significance of this case study for our understanding of neoliberal urban governance. The first of the five themes is that neoliberalism has no single or essential form but is shaped by the many localities and contingencies it encounters as it moves through spaces and across scales while retaining a conceptual coherence. In Cape Town, we have seen how deeply apartheid's legacy has shaped neoliberalism as ideology, policy, and practice, particularly through the urban spatial forms, social inequalities, and security practices it bequeathed the present. Neoliberalism in Cape Town has both distanced itself from and absorbed key elements of apartheid; although the racial politics of the past are explicitly rejected by proponents, practices difficult to distinguish from the pre-1994 period persist, if in somewhat innovative new forms, with similar outcomes. This legacy represents a broad framework of constraints and opportunities through which local neoliberal governance has developed its distinct characteristics, methods, and rationales. Furthermore, a close look at what may be the world's most segregated city allows us to see clearly that even within a given locality, neoliberal governance shows significant variation across urban spaces: there is no single form even within a city at any given time. Finally, we have seen how neoliberal governance becomes a "natural" part of the landscape, distinct from iterations in other places, through its embrace by local actors, its articulation through local interests, and its implementation by local institutions.

At the same time, the research here lends support to the idea of a punitive nature of urban neoliberalism *in general,* even if Cape Town is viewed as an extreme case, while deepening the analysis of the securitization of development as a core tendency of neoliberal governance. A central task of neoliberal governance in this city is the governance of security, and the understanding of security by local elites is consistent with and derived from neoliberal approaches to development that operate on a variety of scales.[4] Cape Town thus shares with many cities a form of governance in which the protection of valuable urban spaces and affluent social groups and regulation of dangerous populations and territories play outsized roles. Crime has proven invaluable in this context because it is a very real problem that can harmonize, or appear to harmonize, what otherwise might be antagonistic interests around specific representations of social problems, and policies to confront them. In practice the governance of security as a "war on crime," however, translates into the containment of urban majorities and the policing of borders between their communities and the centers of the urban economy; this qualitative difference from most cities in the global North, even those where crime and disorder deeply shape urban politics, is a distinguishing and well-established feature of governance in the South. Therefore, although it is true that there are as many articulations of neoliberal urban governance as there are cities in which we find it, the empirical evidence is such that we can safely claim it has relatively consistent core features that can be identified across discrete city spaces.

Second, building on the previous theme, just as neoliberal governance in the city is locally rooted, so too is it an expression of transnational networks that traverse scales and spaces, creating new politics, discourses, and opportunities in the process. Increased interest in cities and the governance practices associated with them represent, in part, a shift in global governance wherein cities become more central to geopolitics than they had been previously relative to the national state, as sites of conflict and control of populations, as much as command of economies. Many cities in the global South, by virtue of their demographics and their position within global networks, have become important spaces of security governance as their importance as sites of capital accumulation has increased, and it is through this increased centrality that urban neoliberalism acquires some of its key general characteristics. Clear links have emerged between aspiring world class cities in particular, which, although geographically distant, face similar sets of challenges, helping to drive an expansion of the global market for "best practices" in the governance of security, and in urban security governance more specifically. In both the CBD and the Cape Flats, the influence of policies, practices, and even narratives from the global North, and the United States in particular, have been profound. The STEP antigang and RICO antiracketeering laws, "broken windows" policing and its attendant narrative of urban disorder, municipal nuisance bylaws, and the CID model, each of which has played an important role in the city's approach to security and development, arrived in Cape Town through formal and informal networks emanating primarily from the United States. The turn to neoliberalism in Cape Town is also closely tied to shifts at the national level, most importantly as GEAR replaced the RDP, and is supported by national policies concerning crime and development, both of which facilitated neoliberal restructuring on the urban scale. Taken together, these mutually reinforcing and converging forces provided an important opportunity for the local urban elite to reframe the city's security and development challenges and pursue "reforms" associated with the global North, most notably the revitalization of New York City, even as other cities were pursuing a similar path for similar reasons. Upon arrival in the urban South, however, these reforms become part of security strategies deployed on a much larger scale, in a different sociohistorical context than in their place of origin, and with a permanence that distinguishes neoliberal governance in the South from the North despite the fact that urban spaces in both regions are part of the same networks.

Third, neoliberalism is an adaptive process rather than an end state that we find in various degrees of completion in different locales. Efforts to capture it conceptually will always struggle against this reality, and although it is often accurate to speak of neoliberalism as a project that groups and coalitions seek to implement, and to that extent as something that can be "measured," my concern here has been to highlight how it insinuates itself into existing policies, social processes, and historical trajectories, and the consequences for underdeveloped communities and marginalized groups. In just over a decade alone, Cape Town and the Western Cape province have seen three ruling parties: the National Party, the ANC, and now the Democratic Alliance. Neoliberalism has survived these changes, attesting to its hold on the urban elite despite conflict between them on many issues of policy and ideology and often serious opposition from outside their exclusive networks. An important aspect of this ability to adapt and survive is the extent to which neoliberalism provides a flexible vocabulary of prosperity and development that allows proponents to frame conflicts in a language that resonates with broad public interests and values while pursuing specific political and economic interests. The fight against crime is one important example, but the extent to which neoliberal narratives have successfully absorbed developmental narratives is even more fundamental to its survival. The most important expressions of this in Cape Town are the Cape Flats Renewal Strategy and the campaign to revitalize the

CBD; as different as they are, both demonstrated an ability throughout the decade to represent aggressive spatial policing as central to development and urban integration, to creating a "city for all." There may be many who question this representation, and some who see it as a disguise for racial governance, but its power to shape the city attests to a level of success in surviving many challenges over the years, whether through bold defenses of market-driven growth strategies or a more subtle camouflaging of policing underdevelopment as social development.

The state remains an important force in neoliberal urban governance, but the role it plays is not uniform across the city. In the CBD the primary role of the city and provincial governments is supportive, through legislation enabling the formation of improvement districts as well as the implementation of "quality of life" bylaws, and in the form of SAPS backup for private security and legislation for the creation of the municipal police. Taken together, these examples highlight just how integral the state remains in the governance of the central city in a number of distinct, although closely related, capacities. The downtown security network of private police, national SAPS, and local municipal police is in fact a state/private hybrid under the immediate authority of the downtown property owners, organized through the Central City Improvement District and empowered through the municipal government. Rather than fading into the background, the state, or components of the state, is an essential node within CBD governance structures, even if its role is less prominent on a day-to-day decision-making basis than that of private actors and institutions. Social development in the city center has also moved in the direction of private/public networks, as in the efforts by the Cape Town Partnership in conjunction with government agencies to wrest control of service delivery from NGOs in 2002. In general, however, both state and private social development have been "rolled back" in the CBD, and the primary effect of downtown governance networks vis-à-vis the urban poor and the "problems" they represent is expulsion.

In the townships, private actors, including private security, often play important roles, but responsibility for the overall planning and execution of governance generally, and security governance in particular, rests with the state. The SAPS and, to a lesser extent, the municipal police play an especially important role because of the primacy authorities have given to crime and security in the urban renewal process. Their role takes on additional significance given their use in enforcing evictions, water cut-offs, and other measures linked to municipal neoliberalism in that security is broadened to include not simply crime and gangsterism, but resistance to the conditions of underdevelopment in which communities find themselves today more generally. Through the Cape Flats Renewal Strategy and similar approaches, which foreground aggressive crime reduction measures, the state in the townships tends to blur the distinction between development and security, complicating efforts to distinguish between different aspects of the state. Although the state is certainly absent in terms of youth development, it is not entirely accurate to speak of the penal or punitive state as omnipresent. The complaints by many residents that police largely patrol borders, and those often from the safety of their patrol cars, and enter communities in force for only specific operations suggest a general abandonment by the state with the exception of occasional, short-term, and often highly traumatic interventions. Rather than attempting to characterize the role of the state in terms of absence or presence, it is perhaps more useful to track the patterns of how it operates in each of the city's two major territories. Doing so reveals that in the central city, it supports the process of expelling the urban poor, while in the townships it plays a more prominent role in containing them. Its relationship to neoliberal governance in Cape Town therefore appears to be both active, as a driver of many processes, and facilitative of a broader sociospatial governance network of which it is but one actor. More specifically, the state and the private sector become functionally divided while still intertwined and bound by an overarching governing ideology, with the state responsible for the urban "surplus" on the periphery and private governance institutions managing the business of the city's core.

Finally, neoliberalism in cities has shown itself to be a powerful force in shaping the urban terrain. As a form of governance, it produces, fractures, and destroys cityscapes, either combining with or eliminating competing or parallel governance regimes, and it would be difficult to ignore its role in the making of the contemporary city. The preceding themes are meant, in part, to emphasize that neoliberalism is not predictable, nor does it often, if ever, constitute the only force through which city spaces are produced, but they are also intended to show just how significant neoliberalism is in shaping urban governance in Cape Town. It is therefore useful to think of neoliberalism as a political project as much as an economic ideology, in that it becomes a means through which social groups can exercise certain forms of power for certain ends. This power, and the ends to which it is applied, are evident in the successful renewal of the city's central business district and, more specifically, the nature of this renewal, how it was defined, by whom, how it was carried out, and how it is maintained today. The argument made here is that policing the CBD for a particular type of development and the policing of underdevelopment on the Cape Flats indicate how central security, or a certain version of security, is to neoliberal governance in Cape Town and hence to its power to shape the postapartheid city. Although crime and security have clearly played important roles in Northern cities as well, it is in cities like Cape Town, marked not only by severe inequality but also by densely populated peripheries that are unlikely to be integrated with the sociospatial world of the core, that the future of security governance is likely to play its most important role and from which neoliberalism will draw increasing power, although also facing increasing risk. This combination of power and vulnerability will be a defining feature of cities and their politics for some time.

Cape Town may be somewhat unique given the high levels of sociospatial segregation inherited from the apartheid period; the difficult work of carving a world class city out of a much larger Third World urban space was accomplished prior to the era of the free vote. As a result, the reproduction rather than production of the divided city is perhaps the primary labor of neoliberalism here relative to many other cities in the process of market-driven reconfiguration. Reproducing urban space in this context is essentially a political challenge, one that is shaped by the city's own painful history of segregation and the recent arrival of neoliberal democracy. At the heart of this political challenge is reconciliation of formal democracy with segregation, inclusion in principle with exclusion in practice. It is in successfully meeting this challenge that neoliberalism has made its greatest contribution to urban governance, allowing urban elites to rearticulate the formerly white apartheid space of downtown as a nominally democratic and public space, even as its character as a space of privilege is maintained through private governance networks. The local power of this construction both reflects and contributes to a broader naturalization of central city politics. Neoliberalism provides a compelling language, potent symbols, dynamic institutions, and highly effective policies through which to link Cape Town's central business district to similarly valued, and valuable, spaces across the urban world that practice similar forms of exclusionary governance. That it has been so successful in urban cores while generating surprisingly little controversy attests to its continued relevance as an object of inquiry for those concerned with the governance of inequality in politically modern, "advanced" societies.

This attempted act of legitimization, of washing away the original sin of racial violence and state-orchestrated theft by diluting it with international "best practices" did not exorcise the specter of the past, but it has, for now, managed to keep it at bay. Yet history provides far too many lessons in the futility of repression, and in the townships of the city the contradiction between democracy and marginalization generates conflict with startling regularity, and perhaps increasing frequency. The surfaces of neoliberalism may appear smooth and polished from the city center, but from the periphery the cracks are evident all around. World class Cape Town may be successfully containing its dangerous territories for now, but its ability to control what happens within them is always partial and temporary. Counterregimes of governance, in the form of gangs, for example, have shown their ability to thrive in spaces abandoned by the state. Others will surely follow and may unexpectedly overrun the already stretched defenses of the urban elite, just as they have before. Neoliberal governance in this sense represents not only the reproduction of repressive governance but also new opportunities for challenging it. Cape Town is only one of many possible urban futures, but the steady march toward increased inequality and segregation in so many cities is difficult to miss. It is at this time an open question as to how far these cities can be stretched before they rupture. Across marginal areas like the Cape Flats, new spatial politics and new political spaces are being created, and for better or worse, it is only a matter of time before they render the neoliberal city ungovernable.

Notes

Introduction

1. Zama Femi, "Gang Wars Take Heavy Toll on Cape Matrics," *Cape Argus*, December 29, 2006.

2. Matt Medved, "Cops to Fight Gangsterism in Primary Schools," *Cape Argus*, May 29, 2007.

3. Aeysah Kassiem, "Crime Wave Engulfing Schools," *Cape Times*, May 18, 2007.

4. Aziz Hartley, "Rasool Unveils Plan to Fight Gangs and Drugs," *Cape Times*, May 23, 2007; Candes Keating, "High-Risk Schools to Get Top Security Measures," *Cape Argus*, February 8, 2007.

5. Rafaella delle Donne, "City's Heart Is Hardening, Say Homeless," *Cape Argus*, July 15, 2007.

6. Tony Roshan Samara, "Development, Social Justice and Global Governance: Challenges to Implementing Restorative and Criminal Justice Reform in South Africa," *Acta Juridica* (2007): 113–33.

7. David McDonald, *World City Syndrome: Neoliberalism and Inequality in Cape Town* (London: Routledge Press, 2007).

8. James DeFilippis, *Unmaking Goliath: Community Control in the Face of Global Capital* (New York: Routledge, 2003); David Harvey, "From Managerialism to Entrepreneurialism: The Transformation in Urban Governance in Late Capitalism," *Geografiska Annaler* B. 71 (1989): 3–17.

9. Neil Smith, *The New Urban Frontier: Gentrification and the Revanchist City* (New York: Routledge, 1996); Gordon MacLeod, "From Urban Entrepreneurialism to a 'Revanchist City'? On the Spatial Injustices of Glasgow's Renaissance," *Antipode* 34, no. 3 (2002): 602–24 .

10. Throughout the book I will use the basic racial categories employed by the Census: black African, coloured, Asian, and white. However, in distinction from the Census terminology, I use the term *black* standing alone as distinct from *African* to refer to all nonwhites. In terms of the category of youth, definitions can vary between countries and between government departments and nongovernmental organizations. At times the term is used fairly loosely, even in government documents and official reports, and at other times quite specifically. The

United Nations defines youth as between the ages of 15 and 24, and this is the definition that I will use unless otherwise noted or unless referring to a different definition employed by another party.

11. While not absent from the study of cities and urban governance, these shifts generally receive more attention from researchers working in the disciplines of political science, international relations, and critical security studies than they do from urban scholars. See Sandra J. MacLean, David R. Black, and Timothy M. Shaw, eds., *A Decade of Human Security: Global Governance and New Multilateralisms* (Burlington, Vt: Ashgate Publishing Limited, 2006); Caroline Thomas and Peter Wilkins, eds., *Globalization, Human Security, and the African Experience* (Boulder, Colo: Lynne Rienner Publishing, 1998); Robert Cox, ed., *The New Realism: Perspectives on Multilateralism and World Order* (New York: St. Martin's Press, 1997). As always, there are exceptions to the general neglect of the geopolitical in urban studies. See, for example, Stephen Graham, ed., *Cities, War, and Terrorism: Towards an Urban Geopolitics* (Malden, Mass: Blackwell Publishing, 2004).

12. See United States of America, National Security Council, *Countering Piracy off the Horn of Africa: Partnership and Action Plan* (Washington, D.C., December 2008); http://www.marad.dot.gov/documents/Countering_ Piracy_Off_The_Horn_of_Africa_-_Partnership__Action_Plan.pdf (accessed November 11, 2010); Max Manwaring, *Street Gangs: The New Urban Insurgency* (Carlisle, Pa: Strategic Studies Institute, U.S. Army War College, 2005).

13. Commission on Human Security, "Human Security Now," *Final Report on the Commission on Human Security* (New York, 2003). http://www.humansecurity-chs. org/finalreport/index.html (accessed November 11, 2010); Mahnaz Afkhami, Kumi Naidoo, Jacqueline Pitanguy, and Aruna Rao, "Human Security: A Conversation," *Social Research* 69 (2002): 657–73; Anwarul Karim Chowdhury, "Human Security: A Broader Dimension," keynote address, Fourth United Nations Conference on Disarmament Issues (Kyoto, Japan, July 27, 1999).

14. United Nations Development Programme, "Human Development Report 1994: New Dimensions of Human Security" (New York: Author, 1994); Kenneth Booth, ed., *New Thinking about Strategy and International Security* (New York: Harper Collins, 1991); Barry Buzan, *People, States, and Fear: An Agenda for International Security Studies in the Post–Cold War Era* (Boulder, Colo: Lynne Reinner Publishers, 1991).

15. "Relieve African Poverty or Reap Terror, Warns Blair," *Cape Times,* February 7, 2002; "Ignore Poor at Your Own Peril, UN Head Tells World Business Leaders," *Cape Times,* February 5, 2002; Mzwandile Faniso, "Nepad Leads the Way, Says World Bank's Wolfensohn," *Business Report,* March 7, 2002.

16. Jeffry Sachs, "Keeping Their Word," *Nepali Times,* March 22–28, 2002: 11.

17. Robert Cox, interview by the Australian Broadcasting Corporation, Radio National, *After the Golden Age,* no. 2: "It's a Global World," Radio Eye (November 11, 2002). My emphasis.

18. Mark Duffield, *Global Governance and the New Wars* (London: Zed Books, 2001), 15–6.

19. Peter Wilkin, "Global Poverty and Orthodox Security," *Third World Quarterly* 23 (2002): 634. It is debatable whether or not this process of merging security and development, and politicizing development aid, is a unique feature of the post–Cold War era. The political aid given by Western powers during the Cold War, starting with U.S. president Truman's aid to the Greek dictatorship for its counterinsurgency war against domestic communists and later folded into the Marshall Plan, comes to mind as an early example of a similar process.

20. For a more detailed discussion, see Samara, "Development, Social Justice and Global Governance."

21. David Harvey, *A Brief History of Neoliberalism* (Oxford: Oxford University Press, 2005); Sarah Babb, *Managing Mexico: Economists from Nationalism to Neoliberalism* (Princeton, N.J.: Princeton University Press, 2004); Massimo De Angelis, "Neoliberal Governance, Reproduction and Accumulation," *The Commoner* 7 (Spring/Summer 2003); Colin Leys, *Market Driven Politics: Neoliberal Democracy and the Public Interest* (London: Verso, 2003); Richard L. Harris and Melinda J. Said, eds., *Critical Perspectives on Globalization and Neoliberalism in the Developing Countries* (Leiden, Netherlands: Brill LV, 2000); Walden Bello with Shea Cunningham and Bill Rau, *The United States and Global Poverty* (San Francisco: Food First, 1999).

22. Bello et al., *The United States and Global Poverty*; Harvey, *A Brief History of Neoliberalism.* For a discussion of the rise of urban neoliberalism in the United States, see Alice O'Conner, "The Privatized City: The Manhattan Institute, the Urban Crisis, and the Conservative Counterrevolution in New York," *Journal of Urban History* 34, no. 2 (January 2008): 333–53; Jamie Peck, "Liberating the City: Between New York and New Orleans, *Urban Geography* 27, no. 8 (2006): 681–713.

23. Walden Bello, *Deglobalization: Ideas for a New World Economy* (London: Zed Books, 2005).

24. Bryn Hughes, "The 'Fundamental' Threat of (Neo)Liberal Democracy: An Unlikely Source of Legitimation for Political Violence, *Dialogue* 3, no. 2 (2005): 43–85. http://www.polsis.uq.edu.au/dialogue/3-2-4.pdf (accessed November 11, 2010); Leys, *Market Driven Politics: Neoliberal Democracy and the Public Interest*; Robert W. McChesney, *Rich Media, Poor Democracy: Communication Politics in Dubious Times* (Champaign: University of Illinois Press, 1999).

25. Walden Bello, "The Post-Washington Consensus: The Unraveling of a Doctrine of Development" (Focus on the Global South, October 18, 2008). http://focusweb.org/the-post-washington-dissensus.html?Itemid=1 (accessed

November 11, 2010). See also Pedro-Palo Kuczynski and John Williamson, eds., *After the Washington Consensus: Restarting Growth and Reform in Latin America* (Washington, D.C.: Petersen Institute, 2003).

26. Mark Purcell, *Empowering Democracy: Neoliberalization and the Struggle for Alternative Urban Futures* (New York: Routledge, 2008); Mike Davis, *Planet of Slums* (New York: Verso, 2007); Jason Hackworth, *The Neoliberal City: Governance, Ideology and Development in American Urbanism* (Ithaca, N.Y.: Cornell University Press, 2007); McDonald, *World City Syndrome*; Helga Leinter, Jamie Peck, and Eric S. Sheppard, *Contesting Neoliberalism: Urban Frontiers* (New York: Guilford Press, 2006); Defilippis, *Unmasking Goliath*; Neil Brenner, *New State Spaces: Urban Governance and the Rescaling of Statehood* (Oxford: Oxford University Press, 2004); Saskia Sassen, *The Global City: New York, London, Tokyo* (Princeton, N.J.: Princeton University Press, 2001); Michael Peter Smith, *Transnational Urbanism: Locating Globalization* (Malden, Mass.: Blackwell Publishers, 2001); David A. Smith, *Third World Cities in Global Perspective: The Political Economy of Uneven Urbanization* (Boulder, Colo.: Westview Press, 1996); David Harvey, *The Urbanization of Capital: Studies in the History and Theory of Capitalist Urbanization* (Baltimore: The Johns Hopkins University Press, 1985).

27. Jamie Peck, "Geography and Public Policy: Constructions of Neoliberalism," *Progress in Human Geography* 28, no. 3 (2004): 392–405; David Wilson, "Toward a Contingent Neoliberalism," *Urban Geography* 25, no. 8 (2004): 771–83.

28. Brenner, *New State Spaces*; Peck, "Geography and Public Policy"; Gordon MacLead and Mark Goodwin, "Space, Scale, and State Strategy: Rethinking Urban and Regional Governance," *Progress in Human Geography* 23, no. 4 (1999): 503–27.

29. Neil Brenner and Nik Theodore, "Cities and the Geographies of 'Actually Existing Neoliberalism,'" *Antipode* 34, no. 3 (2002): 349–79; Jamie Peck and Adam Tickell, "Neoliberalizing Space," *Antipode* 34, no. 3 (2002): 380–404.

30. Purcell, *Empowering Democracy*; Peck, "Geography and Public Policy"; Peck and Tickell, "Neoliberalizing Space."

31. John G. Dale and Tony R. Samara, "Legal Pluralism within a Transnational Network of Governance: The Extraordinary Case of Rendition," *Law, Social Justice and Global Development* 2 (2008). http://www.go.warwick.ac.uk/elj/lgd/2008_2/daleandsamara (accessed November 11, 2010).

32. Brenner and Theodore, "Cities and the Geographies of 'Actually Existing Neoliberalism,'"; Peck and Tickell, "Neoliberalizing Space."

33. Davis, *Planet of Slums*. See also Loïc Wacquant, "The Rise of Advanced Marginality: Notes on Its Nature and Implications," *Acta Sociologica* 39, no. 2 (1996): 121–39.

34. Emma Graham-Harrison, "Spreading Slums May Boost Extremism—UN agency," Reuters Foundation (September 13, 2004), http://www.alertnet.org/thenews/newsdesk/L1312006.htm (accessed November 11, 2010).

35. Russell W. Glenn, Christopher Paul, Todd C. Helmus, and Paul Steinberg, "*People Make the City*," Executive Summary: *Joint Operations Observations and Insights from Afghanistan and Iraq* (Arlington, Va.: RAND National Defense Research Institute, 2007), http://www.rand.org/pubs/monographs/2007/RAND_MG428.2.pdf (accessed November 2, 2009). For critical views, see Stephen Graham, "Robo-War Dreams: Global South Urbanisation and the US Military's 'Revolution in Military Affairs,'" Working Papers Series No. 2 (London: Crisis States Research Centre, November 2007), http://www.crisisstates.com/download/wp/wpSeries2/WP20.2.pdf (accessed November 11, 2010); Raúl Zibechi, "The Militarization of the World's Urban Peripheries," trans. Maria Roof, *America's Program, Center for Interational Policy* (February 9, 2007), http://cipamericas.org/archives/835 (accessed November 2009); Mike Davis, "Tomgram: Mike Davis on the Pentagon's Urban War Planning," *TomDispatch* (April 19, 2004), http://www.tomdispatch.com/post/1386/mike_davis_on_the_pentagon_s_urban_war_planning (accessed November 11, 2010).

36. Tony Roshan Samara, "Policing Development: Urban Renewal as Neoliberal Security Strategy," *Urban Studies* 47 no. 1 (2010): 197–214; Samara, "Development, Social Justice and Global Governance"; Michel Foucault, "Governmentality," in *The Foucault Effect: Studies in Governmentality*, eds. Graham Burchell, Colin Gordon, and Peter Miller (Chicago: University of Chicago Press, 1991).

37. O'Conner, "The Privatized City"; Matt Clement, "Bristol: 'Civilising' the Inner City," *Race and Class*, 48, no. 4 (2007): 97–114; Randy Lippert, "Urban Revitalization, Security, and Knowledge Transfer: The Case of Broken Windows and Kidde Bars," *Canadian Journal of Law and Society* 22, no. 2 (2007): 29–54; Peck, "Liberating the City"; Kevin Ward, "Entrepreneurial Urbanism, State Restructuring, and Civilizing 'New' East Manchester," *Area* 35, no. 2 (2003): 116–27; Gordon MacLeod and Kevin Ward, "Spaces of Utopia and Dystopia: Landscaping the Contemporary City," *Geografiska Annaler* 84 B, 3–4 (2002): 153–70; Andrea McArdle and Tanya Erzen, eds., *Zero Tolerance: Quality of Life and the New Police Brutality in New York City* (New York: New York University Press, 2001); Dennis R. Judd and Susan S. Fainstein, *The Tourist City* (New Haven, Conn.: Yale University Press, 1999); John Hannigan, *Fantasy City: Pleasure and Profit in the Postmodern Metropolis* (New York: Routledge, 1998).

38. Peck, "Geography and Public Policy."

39. Daniel O'Connor, Randy Lippert, Dale Spencer, and Lisa Smylie, "Seeing Private Security Like a State," *Criminology and Criminal Justice* 8, no. 2 (2008): 203–26; Nik Theodore, Nina Martin, and Ryan Hollon, "Securing the City: Emerging Markets in the Private Provision of Security Services," *Social Justice* 33, no. 3 (2006): 85–100; Erick Volker, "Preventive Urban Discipline: Rent-a-Cops and Neoliberal Glocalization in Germany," *Social Justice* 33, no. 3 (2006): 66–84; David Bayley and Clifford Shearing, *The New Structure of Policing: Description,*

Conceptualization, and Research Agenda (Washington, D.C.: National Institute of Justice, 2001); Clifford D. Shearing and Philip C. Stenning, "Private Security: Implications for Social Control," *Social Problems* 30, no. 5 (1983): 493–506.

40. O'Connor et al., "Seeing Private Security Like a State,"; Jennifer Wood and Benoit Dupont, "Urban Security, from Nodes to Networks: On the Value of Connecting Disciplines," *Canadian Journal of Law and Society* 22, no. 2 (2007): 95–112.

41. Ted Leggett, "Crime as a Development Issue," paper presented to the conference *Crime and Policing in Transnational Societies* (Johannesburg: South African Institute for International Affairs, 2001); Christopher Stone, "Crime, Justice, and Growth in South Africa: Toward a Plausible Contribution from Criminal Justice to Economic Growth," *CID Working Paper* 131 (Cambridge, Mass.: Center for International Development, Harvard University, August 6, 2006).

42. Katherine Beckett and Steve Herbert, *Banished: The New Social Control in Urban America* (New York: Oxford University Press, 2009); Löic Wacquant, *Urban Outcasts: A Comparative Sociology of Advanced Marginality* (Malden, Mass.: Polity Press, 2007); Ruth Wilson Gilmore, *Golden Gulag: Surplus, Crisis, and Opposition in Globalizing California* (Berkeley and Los Angeles: University of California Press, 2007); Steve Herbert and Elizabeth Brown, "Conceptions of Space and Crime in the Punitive Neoliberal City," *Antipode* 38 (2006): 755–77; Dennis Rodgers, "Disembedding the City: Crime, Insecurity, and Spatial Organization in Managua, Nicaragua," *Working Paper Series* (London: Development Studies Institute, London School of Economics, 2004); Charlotte Lemanski, "A New Apartheid? The Spatial Implications of Fear of Crime in Cape Town, South Africa," *Environment and Planning* 16 (2004): 101–12; Les Johnson and Clifford Shearing, *Governing Security: Explorations in Policing and Security* (London: Routledge, 2003); Löic Wacquant, "The Penalization of Poverty and the Rise of Neo-Liberalism," *European Journal on Criminal Policy and Research* 9 (2001): 401–12; Teresa Caldeira, *City of Walls: Crime, Segregation, and Citizenship in Sao Paolo* (Berkeley and Los Angeles: University of California Press, 2000).

43. I use the term *police* to refer to agents of policing in general, and specify between public and private police when appropriate.

44. Tony Pfaff, *Development and Reform of the Iraqi Police Forces* (Carlisle, Pa.: Strategic Studies Institute, U.S. Army War College, 2008), http://www.strategicstudiesinstitute.army.mil/pdffiles/pub840.pdf (accessed November 11, 2010); Otto Marenin, *Policing Change, Changing Police: International Perspectives* (New York: Garland Publishing, 1996); David Bayley, "A Foreign Policy for Democratic Policing," *Policing and Society* 5 (1995): 79–93; United States Department of Justice, *Policing in Emerging Democracies: Workshop Papers and*

Highlights (Washington, D.C.: U.S. Departments of Justice and State, December 14–15, 1995).

45. In addition to much of the literature already cited in the discussion of urban security above, see Paul Amar, ed., *New Racial Missions of Policing: International Perspectives on Evolving Law-Enforcement Politics* (New York: Routledge, 2010).

46. Tony Roshan Samara, "Order and Security in the City: Producing Race and Policing Neoliberal Spaces in South Africa," *Ethnic and Racial Studies* 33 (2010): 637–55.

47. Theodore, Martin, and Hollon, "Securing the City"; David Bayley and Clifford Shearing, "The Future of Policing," *Law and Society Review* 30 (1996): 585–606; Trevor Jones and Tim Newburn, "The Transformation of Policing? Understanding Current Trends in Policing Systems," *British Journal of Criminology* 42 (2002): 129–46.

48. Jennifer Wood and Benoit Dupont, *Democracy, Society, and the Governance of Security* (Cambridge, UK: University Press, 2006); Herbert and Brown, "Conceptions of Space and Crime in the Punitive Neoliberal City."

49. Samara, "Order and Security in the City."

50. Daily Mail Reporter, "South Africa's Zuma Urges Police to Shoot to Kill amid Fears Crime Will Put Fans off Attending World Cup," *Daily Mail*, September 29, 2009, http://www.dailymail.co.uk/news/worldnews/article-1216952/South-Africas-Zuma-urges-police-shoot-kill-amid-fears-crime-fans-attending-World-Cup.html (accessed November 3, 2009).

51. BBC News, "SA Minister Defends Shoot-to-Kill," November 12, 2009. http://news.bbc.co.uk/2/hi/8357482.stm (accessed November 21, 2009).

52. Steffen Jensen, *Gangs, Politics, and Dignity in Cape Town* (Oxford: James Currey; Chicago: University of Chicago Press; Johannesburg: Wits University Press, 2008).

53. Nor is this association unique to South Africa. Marx, in his theorization of primitive accumulation, made note of the relationship between urban migration and the criminalization of poverty during the period of enclosure and the English Industrial Revolution, and similar dynamics emerged in both the postbellum and post–civil rights eras in the United States as well. See, for example, Jennifer S. Light, *From Warfare to Welfare: Defense Intellectuals and the Urban Problems in Cold War America* (Baltimore: The Johns Hopkins University Press, 2005); Angela Davis, "From the Prison of Slavery to the Slavery of Prison: Frederick Douglass and the Convict Lease System," in *The Angela Davis Reader*, Joy James (New York: Blackwell, 1999): 74–95; Karl Marx, *Capital, Volume One* (London: Encyclopedia Britannica, 1952): Part 8, chapter 26.

54. Gary Kynoch, "From the Ninevites to the Hard Livings Gang: Township Gangsters and Urban Violence in 20th Century South Africa" (Johannesburg: Institute for Advanced Social Research, Wits University, 1999); Jeremy Seekings, "Media Representations of Youth and the South African Transition, 1989–1994,"

South African Sociological Review 7, no. 2 (1995): 25–42; Allistar Sparks, *The Mind of South Africa: The Story of the Rise and Fall of Apartheid* (New York: Ballantine Books, 1991); Paul La Hausse, "The Cows of Nongoloza: Youth, Crime, and Amalaita Gangs in Durban, 1900–1936," *Journal of Southern African Studies* 16, no. 1 (March 1990): 79–111.

55. Martha K. Huggins, "Exclusion, Civic Invisibility and Marginality: The Murders of Street Youth in Brazil," in *Marginality, Power and Social Structure: Issues in Race, Class and Gender Research in Race and Ethnic Relations* 12, ed. Rutledge Dennis (Oxford: Elsevier Ltd., 2005): 71–92; Teresa P. R. Caldeira, "The Paradox of Police Violence in Brazil," *Ethnography* 3, no. 3 (2002): 235–63.

56. For recent critical views on this phenomenon, see John Hagedorn, *A World of Gangs: Armed Young Men and Gangsta Culture* (Minneapolis: University of Minnesota Press, 2008); Mustafa Dikeç, *Badlands of the Republic: Space, Politics, and Urban Policy* (Malden, Mass.: Blackwell Publishers, 2007); Wacquant, *Urban Outcasts: A Comparative Sociology of Advanced Marginality*; Luke Dowdney, *Neither War nor Peace: International Comparisons of Children and Youth in Organised Armed Violence* (Rio de Janeiro: Children and Youth in Organised Armed Violence, 2007). Although young men are represented disproportionately in the discourse and practice of criminal justice and the criminalization of poverty and marginality, women in many cases are gaining ground. See Julia Sudbury, *Global Lockdown: Race, Gender, and the Prison-Industrial Complex* (New York: Routledge, 2005).

57. Jensen, *Gangs, Politics, and Dignity in Cape Town*. See also Christiaan Beyers, "Identity and Forced Displacement: Community and Colouredness in District Six," in Mohamed Adhikari, *Burdened by Race: Coloured Identities in Southern Africa* (Cape Town: University of Cape Town Press, 2009): 79–103.

58. Jensen, *Gangs, Politics and Dignity in Cape Town*, 6.

59. South African Tourism, *Adding Colour to the Rainbow Nation: South African Coloured Heritage*. http://www.southafrica.net/sat/content/en/us/full-article?oid= 16856&pid=732&sn=Detail (accessed November 11, 2010).

60. Jean Redpath, *The Hydra Phenomenon, Rural Sitting Ducks, and other Recent Trends around Organised Crime in the Western Cape*, Second World Conference, Modern Criminal Investigation, Organised Crime, and Human Rights (Durban: Durban Institute for Human Rights and Criminal Justice Studies, 2001), 19. This perception, and the discourse on gangs generally, appears to be changing, but currently research on black African gangs in contemporary Cape Town is very limited.

61. Jean Redpath, *The Hydra Phenomenon, Rural Sitting Ducks, and other Recent Trends Around Organised Crime in the Western Cape*; H. F. Snyman and B. J. M. Wagener, "The Role of the Chinese Triads in South African Organised Crime," *Acta Criminologica* 10, no. 1 (1997): 107–11.

1. Security and Development in Postapartheid South Africa

1. Mike Nicol, *The Star*, July 3, 1996. Cited in Hein Marais, *South Africa: Limits to Change* (London: Zed Books, 2001), 195.

2. Wendell Roelf, "ANC Aims for 51% in Western Cape," South African Press Association, January 14, 2004.

3. Steffen Jensen, *Gangs, Politics, and Dignity in Cape Town* (Chicago: University Press; Johannesburg: Wits University Press, 2008), 116.

4. Ibid, chapter 4.

5. Patrick Bond, *Elite Transition: From Apartheid to Neoliberalism in South Africa* (London: Pluto Press, 2000). Bond's book, along with Hein Marais' *South Africa: Limits to Change*, offers the most comprehensive and informative accounts of how neoliberalism came to dominate post-apartheid South Africa.

6. Marais, *Limits to Change*. See especially chapter 6, "The Whiplash of History."

7. Donwald Pressly, "ANC MP Tells of Gear Battle," *I-Net Bridge*, October 23, 2003.

8. Marais, *Limits to Change*; Bond, *Elite Transition*; Patrick Bond and Peter McInnes, "Decommodifying Electricity in Postapartheid Johannesburg," in *Contesting Neoliberalism: Urban Frontiers*, eds. Helga Leitner, Jamie Peck, and Eric S. Sheppard, 157–78 (New York: Guilford Press, 2007).

9. Judith Christine Streak, "The GEAR Legacy: Did GEAR Fail or Move South Africa Forward in Development?" *Development Southern Africa* 21, no. 2 (2004): 271–88; Geoffrey E. Schneider, "Neoliberalism and Economic Justice in South Africa: Revisiting the Debate on Economic Apartheid," *Review of Social Economy* 61 (2003): 23–50; Zine Magubane, "Globalization and the South African Transformation: The Impact on Social Policy," *Africa Today* 49, no. 4 (2002): 89–110.

10. Statistics South Africa, "Labour Force Survey September 2001" (Pretoria: Author, 2002).

11. Yul D. Davis, Annie B. Chikwanha, and Robert Mattes, "The Changing Public Agenda? South Africans' Assessments of the Country's Most Pressing Problems," *Afrobarometer Media Briefing* (Pretoria: Institute for Democracy in South Africa, 2002); Afrobarometer Briefings, "The Public Agenda: Change and Stability in South Africans' Ratings of National Priorities" (Pretoria: Institute for Democracy in South Africa, June 2006).

12. Statistics South Africa, "Labour Force Survey" (Pretoria: Author, March 2007); Glenda Daniels, "New Survey Puts SA Jobless Rate at 45%," *Mail and Guardian*, March 1–7, 2002.

13. Statistics South Africa, "Labour Force Survey"; Eric Ntabazalila, "Unemployment Figures Rise, As Do Lotto Buys," *Cape Times*, May 13, 2002.

14. Donwald Pressly, "Asgisa's Scope Too Limited," *Business Day*, March 29, 2007; Terry Bell, "Critique of Asgisa Is Music to Cosatu's Economic Strategists,"

Business Day, September 29, 2006; Irene Louw, "Cosatu Blasts Asgisa Proposals," *City Press* (Johannesburg), February 19, 2006.

15. Brian Bunting, *The Rise of the South African Reich* (Middlesex, UK: Penguin African Library, 1964).

16. Truth and Reconciliation Commission, Final Report, vol. 2, chap. 1, sec. 33, 38 (1998).

17. Mathieu Deflem, "Law Enforcement in British Colonial Africa: A Comparative Analysis of Imperial Policing in Nyasaland, the Gold Coast, and Kenya," *Police Studies* 17 (1994): 45–68. Paramilitary policing is, of course, not limited to colonial contexts or to Africa. See, e.g., Martha K. Huggins, *Political Policing: The United States and Latin America* (Durham, N.C.: Duke University Press, 1998); Peter B. Kraska, *Militarizing the American Criminal Justice System: The Changing Roles of the Armed Forces and the Police* (Boston: Northeastern University Press, 2001).

18. Gavin Cawthra, *Securing South Africa's Democracy: Defence, Development and Security in Transition* (New York: St. Martin's Press, 1997).

19. Louise Ehlers and Sean Tait, "Finding the Right Balance: Immediate Safety versus Long-Term Social Change," *SA Crime Quarterly* 27 (March 2009), 23–30.

20. African National Congress, "Ready to Govern" (policy guidelines adopted at the National Conference, May 28–31, 1992). http://www.anc.org.za/227

21. Janine Rauch, *The 1996 National Crime Prevention Strategy* (Johannesburg: Centre for the Study of Violence and Reconciliation, 2001).

22. Bond, *Elite Transition,* 83.

23. Ted Leggett, *Rainbow Vice: The Drugs and Sex Industries in the New South Africa* (New York: Zed Books, 2001); Ted Leggett, "Crime as a Development Issue," paper presented to the conference *Crime and Policing in Transnational Societies* (Johannesburg: South African Institute for International Affairs, 2001); Christopher Stone, "Crime, Justice, and Growth in South Africa: Toward a Plausible Contribution from Criminal Justice to Economic Growth," *CID Working Paper* 131 (Cambridge, Mass.: Center for International Development, Harvard University, August 6, 2006).

24. Graeme Simpson and Janine Rauch, "Reflections on the First Year of the National Crime Prevention Strategy," in *Between Unity and Diversity: Essays on Nation Building in Post Apartheid South Africa,* ed. Gitanjali Maharaj, 295–314 (Pretoria: Idasa, 1999).

25. Mark Shaw, *Crime and Policing in Post-Apartheid South Africa: Transformation Under Fire* (Bloomington: Indiana University Press, 2002), 126; Dirk van zyl Smit and Elrena van der Spuy, "Importing Criminological Ideas in a New Democracy: Recent South African Experiences," in *Criminal Justice and Political Cultures: National and International Dimensions of Crime Control,* eds. Tim Newburn and Richard Sparks, 184–208 (London: Willan Publishing, 2004).

26. Ted Leggett, "Mr. Fix-it Tackles Crime: An Interview with Steve Tshwete," *Crime and Conflict* 17 (Spring 1999): 5–8.

27. Gavin Cawthra, "The Fragility of the Peace Dividends: Demilitarising South African Society," *Interfund* 3(1) (1999).

28. Louise Ehlers and Sean Tait, "Finding the Right Balance: Immediate safety versus long-term social change," *Crime Quarterly* 27 (March 2009): 23–30. http://www.iss.co.za/uploads/CQ27ELHERS.pdf (accessed November 2010).

29. Address by Minister of Safety and Security Charles Nqakula, MP, Budget Vote 25, Safety and Security, and Vote 23 Independent Complaints Directorate (June 22, 2004).

30. Ehlers and Tait, "Finding the Right Balance."

31. Republic of South Africa, "South African Police Service Amendment Act, 1998," *Government Gazette* (Pretoria), October 28, 1998. http://www.info.gov.za/view/DownloadFileAction?id=70741 (accessed January 2006).

32. Martin Schonteich, "Fighting Crime with Private Muscle: The Private Sector and Crime Prevention," *African Security Review* 8, no. 5 (1999): 65–75.

33. Shaw, *Crime and Policing,* 103; Ehlers and Tait, "Finding the Right Balance."

34. Kris Pillay, "Repositioning the Private Security Industry in South Africa in the 21st Century," *Acta Criminologica* 14, no. 3 (2001): 66–74.

35. Schonteich, "Fighting Crime with Private Muscle."

36. Eric Pelser, *Nedcor Institute for Security Studies Crime Index* 2, no. 4 (Pretoria, 2000): 7–10.

37. Ibid.

38. Bill Dixon, *The Globalisation of Democratic Policing: Sector Policing and Zero Tolerance in the new South Africa* (occasional paper series, Institute of Criminology, University of Cape Town, 2000); Christian Parenti, *Lockdown America: Police and Prisons in the Age of Crisis* (New York: Verso, 2000).

39. Pelser, *Nedcor Institute for Security Studies Crime Index.*

40. Samara, "Policing Development."

41. Gavin Cawthra, "The Fragility of the Peace Dividends: Demilitarising South African Society," *Interfund* 3, no. 1 (1999): 3.

42. J. Meyer and B. Frean, "Young Violent Criminals Shock SA Courts," *Independent Online,* January 17, 2003; Sarah Oppler, "Assessing the State of South Africa's Prisons," *African Security Review* 7, no. 4 (1998): 41–56; Republic of South Africa, Department of Corrections (2009). http://www.dcs.gov.za/WebStatistics (accessed November 1, 2010).

43. *Nedcor* 5, no. 5 (2001).

44. Republic of South Africa, Department of Correctional Services, *Basic Information* (2007) http://www.dcs.gov.za/WebStatistics (accessed November 1, 2010).

45. Budget Debate: Vote 21, Department of Correctional Services, Address by the Deputy Minister of Correctional Services, Ms. Cheryl Gillwald (MP), National Assembly, Cape Town, June 15, 2004.

46. Makubetse Sekhonyane, "Emergency Measures: Early Releases to Alleviate Prison Overcrowding," SA Crime Quarterly 1 (2002).

47. All crime statistics, unless otherwise noted, are taken from the Web site of the South African Police Services, at www.saps.gov.za.

48. The statistics for rape are certainly inaccurate, as the figure for 2006–07 covers only nine months, due to changes in the rape law. See "Violent Crime Rates Down, but Still High," South Africa, The Good News, July 2, 2008. http://www.sagoodnews.co.za/crime/violent_crime_rates_down_but_still_high_3.html (accessed November 1, 2010).

49. Ted Leggett, "Improved Crime Reporting: Is South Africa's Crime Wave a Statistical Illusion?" SA Crime Quarterly, July 1, 2002; Adrienne Louw, "Bad News? Crime Reporting," Crime and Conflict 8, no. 1 (1997).

50. Mark Shaw, "South Africa: Crime in Transition," Occasional Paper 17, Institute for Security Studies (March 1997). http://www.iss.co.za/uploads/Paper_17.pdf (accessed June 2005).

51. Lillian Artz, "Access to Justice for Rural Women: Special Focus On Violence Against Women," (Cape Town, Institute of Criminology, University of Cape Town, 1999).

52. Statistics South Africa, Census 2001: Census in Brief (Pretoria: Author, 2003). Socioeconomic data, unless otherwise noted, are taken from the Census brief.

53. Karen Small, Demographic and Socio-economic Trends for Cape Town: 1996 to 2007 (City of Cape Town, Strategic Development Information and GIS Department, December 2008). http://www.capetown.gov.za/en/stats/CityReports/Documents/2007%20Community%20Survey%20Summary.pdf (accessed November 1, 2010). According to these data, the coloured population has decreased as a percentage of the total since 1996, while the black African population is on the rise.

54. David McDonald, World City Syndrome: Neoliberalsim and Inequality in Cape Town (London: Routledge Press, 2007).

55. City of Cape Town, State of the City: Development Issues in Cape Town (2006).

56. Small, Demographic and Socio-economic Trends.

57. Karen Small, 2007 Community Survey Analysis for Cape Town (City of Cape Town, Strategic Development Information and GIS Department, October 2008). http://www.capetown.gov.za/en/stats/CityReports/Documents/2007%20Community%20Survey%20Report.pdf (accessed November 1, 2010).

58. Tim Mosdell and Amiena Bayat, Towards Pro-Poor Service Delivery—Perspectives on Affordability and Willingness-to-Pay in Cape Town, South African Cities Network (2002).

59. "The Cape of Poverty," South African Press Association, May 13, 2003.

60. Integrated Development Plan, 2003-4 (Cape Town, 2002), 31. *City of Cape Town.*

61. Small, *2007 Community Survey Analysis for Cape Town.*

62. City of Cape Town, *Seven Strategic Priorities for Cape Town, 1997.* Cited in Susan Parnell, Edgar Pieterse, and Mark Swilling, eds. *Democratising Local Government: The South African Experiment* (Cape Town: Juta Publishing, 2004), 256.

63. *Nedcor* 2, no. 2 (1998).

64. Institute for Security Studies, *Crime in Cape Town,* Monograph 23 (Pretoria, 1998). The report attributes the slightly higher age of victimization to the particularities of the antiapartheid struggle, and it is possible the situation has changed in the years since 1998.

65. *Nedcor* 5, no. 2 (2001), 6.

66. Sarah Duguid, "Child Abuse Study Shows Shocking Levels of Sexual Ignorance," *Mail and Guardian,* March 8–14, 2002.

67. Charlene Smith, "SA's Dead Speak: How We Died," *Mail and Guardian,* June 22–28, 2001: 3.

68. Institute for Security Studies, *Crime in Cape Town.*

69. *Nedcor* 3, no. 6 (1999).

70. *Nedcor* 3, no. 3 (1999).

71. Independent Complaints Directorate, Statistics 2003–04 (Pretoria, 2004). It should be noted that although all ICD reports from 1999 to 2009 are listed on the ICD Web site as of December 2009, many of the links themselves are inactive, and therefore much of the data are unavailable. For a discussion of all the available data from the ICD as of 2009, see Samara, "Policing Development."

72. Independent Complaints Directorate, Statistics 2004–05 (Pretoria, 2005).

73. David McDonald and Leila Smith, "*Privatizing Cape Town: Service Delivery and Policy Reforms Since 1996,*" Occasional Paper Series 7 (Municipal Services Project, February 2002).

74. Ashwin Desai, "Neoliberalism and Resistance in South Africa," *Monthly Review* 54, no. 8 (2003): http://www.monthlyreview.org/0103desai.htm

75. McDonald and Smith, "Privatising Cape Town."

76. Bryan Rostron, "The New Apartheid?" *Mail and Guardian,* February 15–21, 2002.

77. *Towards an Economic Development Strategy for the City of Cape Town: A Discussion Paper* (March 2001): http://info.worldbank.org/etools/docs/library/166856/UCMP/

78. Western Cape Investment and Trade Promotion Agency, "Western Cape Tourism Trend Card 2003," http://www.capegateway.gov.za/Text/2003/12/wctourismtrendscard.pdf/. All tourism data is from this report unless otherwise noted.

79. Gugulakhe Masango, "Tourism Expected to Provide R31 Billion to Economy," *Business Report,* August 2, 2001.

80. The 2002–03 IDP identifies tourism as the primary component of job creation under the priority of poverty alleviation, whereas the 2003–04 IDP is less emphatic about the ability of tourism to be a primary mechanism of job creation.

81. T. Ntuli and P. Potgieter, "Exploring the Impact of Crime on Tourism in St. Lucia," *Acta Criminologica* 14, no. 1 (2001): 58.

82. African National Congress, "A Development Oriented Growth Path for the Western Cape-Draft Document" (Athlone: ANC Western Cape Region, October, 1998) http://www.anc.org.za/290 (accessed January 2005).

83. Cited in *Western Cape Provincial Development Council WCPDC), Urban Renewal Strategy for the Cape Town Unicity: A Critical Assessment* (Cape Town: WCPDC, 2002), 4.

84. Desai, "Neoliberalism and Resistance."

85. City of Cape Town, Integrated Development Plan 2002/2003: One City One Plan (2002).

86. Mark Sangster, "Interventions and Initiatives" (Cape Town, 2001). The Chief's statement has been posted on the city's official webpage, located at http://www.capetown.gov.za/

87. Ashwin Desai, *We Are the Poor: Community Struggles in Postapartheid South Africa* (New York: Monthly Review Press, 2002; Patrick Bond, *Cities of Gold, Townships of Coal: Essays on South Africa's New Urban Crisis* (Asmara, Eritrea: Africa World Press, 2000). See also the Western Cape Anti-Eviction Campaign at www.antieviction.org.za.

88. Norman Joseph, "Technicoloured Attack on Crime," *Cape Argus,* January 17, 2002; M. Williams, "City Security: Safety or Overkill?" *Weekend Argus,* January 12, 2002; M. Merten, "ANC Pitches for W Cape," *Mail and Guardian,* October 12, 2001.

2. Children in the Streets

1. A more detailed discussion of policing and governance in the central city, their transnational aspects, and exclusionary character is provided in Samara, "Order and Security in the City: Producing Race and Policing Neoliberal Spaces in South Africa." The central improvement district model is discussed in more detail by Tony Roshan Samara, "Marginalized Youth and Urban Revitalization: Street Kids and Moral Panics in Cape Town," in *Moral Panics over Contemporary Children and Youth,* ed. Charles Krinsky (Surrey, UK: Ashgate Publishing, 2009), 187–202.

2. David Everatt, "From Urban Warrior to Market Segment? Youth in South Africa 1990–2000," *Quarterly Journal of the South African National NGO Coalition and Interfund* 3, no. 2 (2000), 12.

3. Ibid., 14.

4. Ibid., 21.

5. See also Wilfried Schärf, "Reintegrating Militarised Youth into the Mainstream in South Africa: From Hunters to Gamekeepers?" Paper presented at the Urban Childhood Conference, Trondheim, Norway, June 1997.

6. Graeme Simpson, "Shock Troops and Bandits: Youth, Crime and Politics," in *Crime Wave: The South African Underworld and Its Foes*, ed. Jonny Steinberg (Johannesburg: Witwatersrand University Press, 2001), 95–114.

7. Ibid., 124.

8. Schärf, "Reintegrating Militarised Youth," 7.

9. Jeremy Seekings, "Media Representations of 'Youth' and the South African Transition, 1989–1994," *South African Sociological Review* 7, no. 2 (April 1995): 25–42.

10. Everatt, "From Urban Warrior to Market Segment?"

11. For a more detailed discussion, see Tony Roshan Samara, "Youth, Crime and Urban Renewal in the Western Cape," *Journal of Southern African Studies* 31, no. 1 (March 2005): 209–37.

12. Seekings, "Media Representations of Youth," 26.

13. Samara, "Youth, Crime and Urban Renewal in the Western Cape."

14. S. Braehmer, Z. Kimmie, R. Greenstein, R. Morake, and K. Seutloadi, *Youth 2000: A Study of Youth in South Africa* (December 2000). http://www.case.org.za/~caseorg/images/docs/youth_2000.pdf

15. Martin Schonteich, "Age and AIDS: South Africa's Crime Time Bomb," *African Security Review* 8, no. 4 (Pretoria 1999): 34–44. The disproportionate involvement of youth with crime has been contested with regard to the United States. See Mike Males, "Forget the 'Youth Menace': Crime, It Turns Out, Is a Grown Up Business," *Los Angeles Times*, December 15, 2002. For a brief discussion of this topic in relation to South Africa, see Tony Samara, "State Security in Transition: The War on Crime in Post Apartheid South Africa," *Social Identities* 9, no. 2 (June 2003): 298.

16. David. J. Smith (1995) "Youth Crime and Conduct Disorders", in *Psychological Disorders in Young People: Time Trends and their Correlates*, eds. Michael Rutter and David J. Smith (Chichester), 395

17. For a more detailed discussion on this point, see Samara, "Development, Social Justice and Global Governance." Girls and young women do commit crimes, but the vast majority of street crime and the crimes associated with gangsterism in the Cape, particularly the violent crime that poses such a challenge for South Africa, are committed by males. Although marginalization affects both boys and girls, and in many cases girls more so, when I use "youth" or "young people" in relation to committing crime and the criminal justice system, I am referring to males, except where noted. Lisa Vetten is one of the few people writing about girls and gangs in South Africa: see her "Invisible Girls and Violent Boys: Gender

and Gangs in South Africa," *Quarterly Journal of the South African National NGO Coalition and Interfund* 3, no. 2 (2000): 39–49.

18. Dirk van Zyl Smit, "Criminological Ideas and the South African Transition" (Cape Town: Institute of Criminology, University of Cape Town, 1997).

19. Ann Skelton, "Juvenile Justice Reform: Children's Rights and Responsibilities versus Crime Control," in *Children's Rights in a Transitional Society,* ed. C. J. Davel (Pretoria: Protea Books, 1999), 100.

20. UNICEF, "UNICEF Welcomes Signing of Child Justice Bill into Law," *Press Centre News Note,* May 18, 2009. http://www.unicef.org/media/media_49695.html (accessed November 5, 2010).

21. Leandra Sylvester-Rose, *Youth Programme Concept Paper* (Western Cape: Department of Social Development, 2009).

22. Julia Sloth-Nielsen and L. M. Muntingh, "Juvenile Justice Review 1999–2000," *South African Journal of Criminal Justice* 14, no. 3 (2001): 394.

23. Martin Schonteich, "Age and AIDS."

24. Republic of South Africa, Department of Correctional Services, *Basic Information* (2010). http://www.dcs.gov.za/WebStatistics (accessed November 1, 2010).

25. Republic of South Africa, *National Offender Population Profile in the Department of Correctional Services* (Pretoria: Department of Correctional Services, 2009).

26. Ibid.

27. Deon Ruiters, *NICRO on Children, Crime, and Development: An Overview of Diversion in South Africa* (Cape Town: National Institute for Crime Prevention and the Reintegration of Offender, November 2003).

28. Louise Ehlers, "Children's Views on a New Child Justice System," Article 40, 2 (August 1999).

29. David Simon, "Crisis and Change in South Africa: Implications for the Apartheid City," *Transactions of the Institute of British Geographers* 12, no. 2 (1989): 189–206.

30. John Western, *Outcast Cape Town* (Berkeley and Los Angeles: University of California Press, 1996).

31. "Where Money Needs to Go: Business Nodes Key to City's Future Health," *Cape Times,* July 10, 2001.

32. Antje Nahnsen, "Discourses and Procedures of Desire and Fear in the Re-making of Cape Town's Central City: The Need for a Spatial Politics of Reconciliation," in *Ambiguous Restructuring of Post-Apartheid Cape Town: The Spatial Forms of Socio-Political Change,* eds. Christoph Haferburg and Jurgen Oßenbrügge (London: LitVerlag, 2003), 139.

33. Bill Dixon, "The Globalisation of Democratic Policing: Sector Policing and Zero Tolerance Policing in the New South Africa," (occasional paper series, Institute of Criminology, University of Cape Town, 2000), 42.

34. Ibid.

35. The Cape Town Partnership. http://www.capetownpartnership.co.za (accessed November 5, 2010).

36. Julie Berg, "Private Policing in Cape Town: The Cape Town City Improvement District—Pluralism in Practice," *Society in Transition* 35, no. 2 (2004): 228.

37. Sangster, "Interventions and Initiatives." Community Patrol Officers are police reservists employed by a local authority. See M. Memeza, *Assessing City Safety Developments in Cape Town: July 2000,* report prepared as part of the City Safety Project (Johannesburg: Centre for the Study of Violence and Reconciliation, 2000).

38. Anthony Minnaar, "The Implementation and Impact of Crime Prevention/ Crime Control Open Street Closed Circuit Television Surveillance in South African Central Business Districts," *Surveillance and Society* 4, no. 3 (2005): 174–207.

39. Sangster, "Interventions and Initiatives."

40. Dixon, "The Globalisation of Democratic Policing," *The Economist,* 340, no. 7978 (August 10, 1996): 30.

41. Bunty West, "Capetownians Fed up with Litter, Vagrants," *Cape Times,* February 22, 2000.

42. See introduction to this book, note 36.

43. N. David Miller, "Crime and Downtown Revitalization," *Urban Land* (September 1987): 18.

44. Nahnsen, "Discourses and Procedures of Desire and Fear," 39–40.

45. Gustav Thiel, "Cape's 'Private Army' in Strong-arm Row," *Cape Times,* January 9, 2003.

46. Tony Weaver, "Revamp 'Will Transform Cape Town Nightlife," *Cape Times,* May 13, 2003.

47. Elliot Sylvester, "It's Official—Cape Town Is Clean and Safe," *Cape Argus,* March 6, 2002.

48. J. le Roux and C. Smith, "Is the Street Child Phenomenon Synonymous with Deviant Behavior?" *Adolescence* 33, no. 132 (Winter 1998): 915–25.

49. South African Press Association, "Report Highlights Street People's Needs," May 16, 2000.

50. Helen Bamford, "Millions Spent on 'Solution'—But Kids Are Still on Streets," *Cape Argus,* March 18, 2002.

51. Interview with Renée Rossouw, June 2004.

52. This is the consensus of youth workers I spoke with over the course of the research.

53. Lindiz van Zilla, "Iron Fist Comes Down on 'Street Gangs,'" *Cape Times,* December 3, 2002.

54. Peter Dickson, "Municipal Police on the Cards for Cape Town," *Independent Online,* March 15, 2001.

55. Stanley Cohen, cited in Michael Welch, Eric A. Price, and Nana Yankey, "Moral Panic over Youth Violence," *Youth and Society* 34, no. 1 (September 2002): 3–30.

56. Samara, "Marginalized Youth and Urban Revitalization"; Samara, "Youth, Crime and Urban Renewal in the Western Cape."

57. Rachel Bray, *Predicting the Social Consequences of Orphanhood in South Africa*. CSSR working paper no. 29 (Cape Town: Centre for Social Science Research, University of Cape Town, 2003): 42.

58. Ibid., 5.

59. Ransford Danso and David A. McDonald, "Writing Xenophobia: Immigration and the Print Media in Post Apartheid South Africa," *Africa Today* 48, no. 3 (Fall 2001): 115–37.

60. The readership of the big three papers ranges from 37 percent white for the *Cape Argus,* double their proportion of the total population, to 42 percent for the *Weekend Argus* and 43 percent for the *Cape Times.* And in a province where the average monthly wage by household is R3,000 for black Africans, R6,200 for coloureds, and R14,000 for whites, half of the readers of the *Times* and *Argus* earn more than R7,000 monthly and one-fourth earn more than R12,000. Family income figures are from the Bureau of Market Research, University of South Africa, and reprinted in L. van Zilla, "Income Gap Becomes a Gulf," *Cape Times,* July 23, 2002. Readership information comes from the *Independent Online* site for South African papers at www.iol.co.za.

61. Bray, *Predicting the Social Consequences of Orphanhood in South Africa*, 39.

62. Le Roux and Smith, "Is the Street Child Phenomenon Synonymous with Deviant Behavior?"

63. M. Peters, "Homeless Children Holding City Centre in Grip of Crime," *Weekend Argus,* February 2, 2002.

64. Elizabeth Jahncke and Bunty West, "Cape Town Clean-up Depends on the Deter-gents," *Cape Times,* November 2, 2000.

65. Gustav Thiel, "Cape Town Soon to Be a City That Never Sleeps," *Cape Times,* December 19, 2001.

66. Le Roux and Smith, "Is the Street Child Phenomenon Synonymous with Deviant Behavior?" 916.

67. Charlotte (Lemanski) Spinks, "A New Apartheid? Urban Spatiality, (Fear of) Crime, and Segregation in Cape Town, South Africa" (working paper series, London School of Economics, Development Studies Institute 2001), 13. It is important to point out that perceived loss of control can be as anxiety producing as actual loss. South Africa is still highly stratified according to race and class, and the white and wealthy still exercise considerable control over space, as the direction of urban renewal suggests. Fear of loss can therefore be considered a motivating factor just as much, and perhaps more so, than actual loss.

68. Samara, "Order and Security in the City."

69. Western Cape Provincial Development Council, *Urban Renewal Strategy for the Cape Town Unicity*, 6

70. Samara, "Marginalized Youth and Urban Revitalization."

71. Ibid.

72. Norman Joseph, "Metro Cops Beat Us Up Daily, Street Children Claim," *Cape Argus*, May 15, 2002.

73. Samara, "Marginalized Youth and Urban Revitalization."

74. For a more detailed discussion, see ibid.

75. City of Cape Town, *By-law Relating to Streets, Public Places and the Prevention of Nuisances*, approved by the city council, May 24, 2007.

76. A. Smith, "Cape's Night Courts to Tackle Petty Crime," *Cape Times*, May 6, 2003.

77. N. Dreyer, "Mayor Rethinks Policy on Vagrancy," *Cape Times*, December 22, 2003.

78. Samara, "Marginalized Youth and Urban Revitalization."

79. M. Peters, "Zero Tolerance in Mother City Puts Kids in Pollsmoor," *Cape Argus*, March 9, 2002.

80. Gustav Thiel, "Cape's 'Private Army' in Strong-arm Row."

81. Samara, "Marginalized Youth and Urban Revitalization."

82. Farr is cited in *CCIDs Making a Significant Impact Across the City*, City Improvement District news brief (Cape Town, May 13, 2002).

83. Tony Roshan Samara, "Playing Cape Town: The Politics of Stadium Development for the 2010 World Cup," in *Urban Spaces: Planning and Struggling for Land and Community*, eds. James Jennings and Julia Jordan-Zachery (Lexington Books, 2009); interview with Clinton Osbourne, July 2008.

84. Interview with Clinton Osbourne, July 2008.

85. Bamford, "Millions Spent on 'Solution.'"

86. Ibid.

87. Interview with Clinton Osbourne, July 2008. For a more detailed discussion, see Samara, "Order and Security in the City."

88. Western Cape Provincial Development Council, *Urban Renewal Strategy for the Cape Town Unicity*, 29.

89. Seekings, "Media Representations of 'Youth' and the South African Transition, 1989–1994."

3. Gangsterism and the Policing of the Cape Flats

1. Norman Joseph and Lynett Johns, "Blitz Begins after 37 Die in Battles," *Cape Argus*, May 17, 2002.

2. Norman Joseph, "Army Moves in as Cape Flats Gang Wars Go Mad," *Cape Argus*, May 17, 2002.

3. South African Press Association, "Army to Help Fight CT Gang Wars," March 13, 2003.

4. Western Cape Department of Education, media statement by Minister André Gaum, March 14, 2003.

5. Kishor Harri, "Policing Gangsterism in the Next Millennium," *Cape Town* (1998): 2.

6. Marianne Merten, "Gangs: A Brotherhood Sealed in Blood," *Mail and Guardian*, August 2–7, 2002.

7. Harri, "Policing Gangsterism," 30.

8. African National Congress, Statement to the Truth and Reconciliation Commission (August 1996). http://www.anc.org.za/2639; Zenzile Khoisan, *Jakaranda Time: An Investigator's View of South Africa's Truth and Reconciliation Commission* (Cape Town: Garib Communications, 2001).

9. Benjamin White Haefele, "Gangsterism in the Western Cape: Who Are the Role Players?" *Crime and Conflict* no. 14 (Summer 1998): 19–22.

10. Ibid.

11. Irvin Kinnes, "Reclaiming the Cape Flats: A Community Challenge to Crime and Gangsterism," *Crime and Conflict* no. 2 (Winter 1995).

12. Janine Rauch and David Storey, *The Policing of Public Gatherings and Demonstrations in South Africa, 1960–1994*, paper commissioned by the Commission on Truth and Reconciliation, Research Department (May 1998); Gavin Cawthra, *South Africa's Police: From Police State to Democratic Policing?* (London: Catholic Institute for International Relations, 1992).

13. Mark Shaw, *Crime and Policing in Post-Apartheid South Africa* (Bloomington: Indiana University Press, 2002), 66–8.

14. For example, see Khehla Shubane, "A Question of Balance: Crime Fighting in a New Democracy," in *Crime Wave: The South African Underworld and Its Foe,* ed. Jonny Steinberg (Johannesburg: Witwatersrand University Press, 2001), 184–200; and Robert Gelbard (former United States Assistant Secretary of State–International Narcotics and Law Enforcement Affairs), "Drug Trafficking in Southern Africa," paper presented at conference *War and Peace in Southern Africa: Crime, Drugs, Armies and Trade* (Johannesburg: South African Institute of International Affairs, 1996).

15. Samara, "Development, Social Justice and Global Governance."

16. Andre Standing, "The Social Contradictions of Organised Crime on the Cape Flats," Occasional Paper 74 (Pretoria: Institute for Security Studies, June 2003).

17. Haefele, "Gangsterism in the Western Cape."

18. City of Cape Town, Executive Committee, Discussion of the Cape Flats Renewal Strategy, HO 31/4/1 (May 15, 2001): 7.2.

19. L. Camerer, A. Louw, M. Shaw, L. Artz, and W. Scharf, *Crime in Cape Town: Results of a City Victim Survey*, Monograph 23 (Pretoria, Institute for Security Studies, April 1998).

20. Marianne Merton, "Only Time Will Tell in Manenberg," *Mail and Guardian*, June 15, 2001.

21. Irvin Kinnes, *From Urban Street Gangs to Criminal Empires: The Changing Face of Gangs in the Western Cape*, Monograph 48 (Pretoria: Institute for Security Studies, June 2000): 5, 11.

22. *Cape Times*, "One Hundred Days on the Job—and Crime Has Dropped," December 3, 2003.

23. Interview with Eldred de Klerk, program manager, *Policing Programme*, University of Witswatersand Graduate School of Public and Development Management (June 2002).

24. Standing, "The Social Contradictions of Organised Crime on the Cape Flats."

25. Interview, March 2002.

26. Jean Redpath, "The Bigger Picture: The Gang Landscape in the Western Cape," *Indicator South Africa* 18, no. 1 (March 2001): 34–40.

27. Steve Kibble, *Drugs and Development in South Africa: How Europe Can Help* (London: Catholic Institute for International Relations, KKS Printing, 1998).

28. Interview with Irvin Kinnes, April 2002.

29. City of Cape Town, Executive Committee, Discussion of the Cape Flats Renewal Strategy.

30. *Integrated Development Plan 2003/2004* (Cape Town: City of Cape Town, 2003), 28.

31. Jean Redpath, *The Hydra Phenomenon, Rural Sitting Ducks and Other Recent Trends around Organised Crime in the Western Cape* (Cape Town: Institute for Human Rights and Criminal Justice Studies, 2001), 4.

32. Janine Rauch, *Thinking Big: The National Urban Renewal Programme and Crime Prevention in South Africa's Metropolitan Cities* (Johannesburg: Centre for the Study of Violence and Reconciliation, December 2002), 9, 12.

33. Western Cape Provincial Development Council, *Urban Renewal Strategy for the Cape Town Unicity*: 33.

34. Ibid., 35.

35. Clifford Shearing, "Toward Democratic Policing: Rethinking Strategies of Transformation," from the conference report *Policing in Emerging Democracies: Workshop Papers and Highlights* (Washington, D.C.: National Institute of Justice, Department of Justice, 1995), 29–38.

36. William Dixon, *The Globalisation of Democratic Policing: Sector Policing and the Zero Tolerance in the New South Africa, Cape Town* (occasional paper, Institute of Criminology, University of Cape Town), 30.

37. Ibid., p. 37

38. Kinnes, "Reclaiming the Cape Flats."

39. Randall G. Sheldon, "Assessing 'Broken Windows': A Brief Critique," Center on Juvenile and Criminal Justice" (2005), http://www.cjcj.org/files/broken.pdf; Jennifer R. Wynn, "Can Zero Tolerance Last? Voices from Inside the Precinct," in *Zero Tolerance: Quality of Life Policing and the New Police Brutality in New York City,* eds. Andrea McArdle and Tanya Erzen (New York: New York University Press, 2001): 107–27.

40. *Cape Argus,* "Police 'Go on Rampage' during Cape Gang War," January 8, 2003.

41. Martin Turner, "Cape Town Bomb Rocks Police Station," BBC News, January 30, 1999.

42. Anthony Minnaar, "The New Vigilantism in Post–April 1994 South Africa" (Institute for Human Rights and Criminal Justice Studies, May 2001).

43. South African Press Association, "Rein in PAGAD," *The Star,* December 18, 1996.

44. Bill Dixon and Lisa-Marie Johns, "Gangs, PAGAD and the State: Vigilantism and Revenge Violence in the Western Cape," *Violence in Transition* Series 2 (Johannesburg: Centre for the Study of Violence and Reconciliation, May 2001).

45. Wilfred Schärf, *Re-integrating Militarised Youths (Street Gangs and Self-Defence Units) into the Mainstream in South Africa: From Hunters to Game-keepers?,* paper presented at Urban Childhood Conference, Trondheim, Norway, 1997.

46. Benita van Eyssen, "Hope Rises for Cape Police in Gangster War," *The Standard,* January 21, 1999.

47. See Andy Duffy, "Police Linked to Cape War," *Mail and Guardian,* October 4, 1997, and Andy Duffy, "Baqua Slates Cape Cops for Shielding Gangsters," *Mail and Guardian,* March 6, 1998.

48. Henri Boshoff, Anneli Botha, and Martin Schonteich, *Fear in the City: Urban Terrorism in South Africa,* Monograph 63 (Pretoria: Institute for Security Studies, July 2001).

49. Tony Roshan Samara, "State Security in Transition: The War on Crime in Post-Apartheid South Africa" (doctoral dissertation, Santa Barbara, University of California, 2005). See especially chapter one.

50. Samara, "State Security in Transition."

51. Boshoff et al., *Fear in the City.*

52. Dixon, "The Globalisation of Democratic Policing," 46.

53. Samara, "State Security in Transition."

54. R. Davids, "'Operation Brutality': Reports about Police Violence Soar," *Cape Times,* February 22, 1999.

55. Eyssen, "Hope Rises for Cape Police in Gangster War."

56. Dixon and Johns, "Gangs, PAGAD and the State."

57. Minnaar, "The New Vigilantism in Post–April 1994 South Africa": 35–6.

58. H. Boshoff and M. Schonteich, "South Africa's Operational and Legislative Responses to Terrorism," in *Africa and Terrorism: Joining the Global Campaign,* eds. Jakkie Cilliers and Kathryn Sturman, Monograph 74 (Pretoria: Institute for Security Studies, July 2002).

59. South African Police Service, *Annual Report of the National Commissior of the South African Police Service* (Pretoria, 2001–2002).

60. Judy Damon, "Urban Terror Slashed, Now for Gangsters," *Cape Times,* March 29, 2001.

61. Harri, "Policing Gangsterism in the Next Millennium."

62. Norman Joseph, "Top Cops Lead Crime Blitz in Cape Town," *Cape Times,* July 2, 2001.

63. Samara, "Policing Development."

64. South Africa Press Association, "Gangsterism a Serious Security Threat— Nqakula," November 14, 2002.

4. The Weight of Policing on the Fragile Ground of Transformation

1. Judy Damon, "Urban Terror Slashed, Now for Gangsters," *Cape Times,* March 29, 2001.

2. Janine Rauch, *Thinking Big: The National Urban Renewal Programme and Crime Prevention in South Africa's Metropolitan Cities* (Johannesburg: Centre for the Study of Violence and Reconciliation, December 2002), 23. A skepticism toward soft approaches among some officials also emerged in Andre Standing's work on the Cape Flats and organized crime. See Standing, "The Social Contradictions of Organised Crime on the Cape Flats," Occasional Paper 74 (Pretoria: Institute for Security Studies, June 2003).

3. Sello S. Alcock, "Crime Stats Scam Exposed," *Mail and Guardian,* July 3–9, 2009; Lavern de Vries, "Crime Stats Scandal Hearing Set for Today," *Cape Argus,* July 1, 2009; Sharika Regchand, "Policeman Files Affidavit: Top Police Station 'Fiddled Crime Stats,'" *The Mercury,* June 11, 2009.

4. Glynnis Underhill, "Top Cops 'Knew Stats Were Cooked,'" *Mail and Guardian Online,* October 17, 2009. http://www.mg.co.za/article/2009-10-17-top-cops-knew-stats-were-cooked (accessed November 8, 2010).

5. Shanaaz Eggington, "Police in Crime Conspiracy," *Times Live,* December 12, 2009. http://www.timeslive.co.za/sundaytimes/article231137.ece (accessed November 8, 2010).

6. Independent Complaints Directorate (2004).

7. Independent Complaints Directorate (2005).

8. Interview, June 2006.

9. Interview, May 2004.

10. Interview, May 2004.

11. Interview, July 2006.

12. Irvin Kinnes, *From Urban Street Gangs to Criminal Empires: The Changing Face of Gangs in the Western Cape,* Monograph 48 (Pretoria: Institute for Security Studies, June 2000).

13. Bill Dixon and Lisa-Marie Johns, "Gangs, PAGAD and the State: Vigilantism and Revenge Violence in the Western Cape," *Violence in Transition* Series 2 (Johannesburg: Centre for the Study of Violence and Reconciliation, May 2001).

14. Jean Redpath, *The Hydra Phenomenon, Rural Sitting Ducks and Other Recent Trends around Organised Crime in the Western Cape* (Cape Town: Institute for Human Rights and Criminal Justice Studies, 2001), 18.

15. Deepak Gupta, "Republic of South Africa's Prevention of Organised Crime Act: A Comparative Bill of Rights Analysis," *Harvard Civil Rights–Civil Liberties Law Review* 37 (2002): 159–182; Jean Redpath, "Forfeiting Rights? Assessing South Africa's Asset Forfeiture Laws," *African Security Review* 9, nos. 5/6 (2000): 15–23.

16. Interview with Irvin Kinnes, June 2002.

17. "The Prevention of Organised Crime Act," *Government Gazette,* 402, no. 19553 (Republic of South Africa, December 4, 1998).

18. Brian van Wyk, "Are We Really Living in a Gangsta's Paradise?" *Medical Research Council News* 32, no. 3 (June 2001).

19. Ryan Pintado-Vertner and Jeff Chang, "The War on Youth," *AlterNet,* April 1, 2000. http://www.alternet.org/story/285/ (accessed November 8, 2010).

20. For one view on the need for harder policing, see Ted Leggett, "Editorial," *Crime and Conflict* 11 (Autumn 1998).

21. For one notable exception to the critique of current approaches to policing and criminal justice more generally, see Antony Altbeker, *A Country at War with Itself: South Africa's Crisis of Crime* (Jeppestown, South Africa: Jonathan Ball Publishers, 2007).

22. "Law Enforcement and the Criminal Justice System," (paper presented at Goedgedacht Forum for Social Reflection, Cape Town, June 2000).

23. Ibid.

24. Interview, August 2002.

25. Joy Watson, "Gender Planning in the City of Cape Town," (discussion paper, African Gender Institute, University of Cape Town, October 29, 2003). http://web.uct.ac.za/org/agi/

26. Interview, August 2002.

27. Interview, June 2006.

28. Interview, August 2002.

29. International Centre for the Prevention of Crime, *Crime Prevention Digest* (1997), cited in Ingrid Palmary, "Social Crime Prevention in South Africa's Major Cities," report prepared as part of the City Safety Project

(Johannesburg: Centre for the Study of Violence and Reconciliation, June 2001). http://www.csvr.org.za/docs/urbansafety/socialcrimeprevention.pdf (accessed November 8, 2010).

30. South African Department of Safety and Security, *In Service of Safety: White Paper on Safety and Security 1999–2004.* http://www.info.gov.za/whitepapers/1998/safety.htm#Section1 (accessed November 8, 2010).

31. Ibid.

32. Gareth Newham, "A Decade of Crime Prevention in South Africa: From a National Strategy to a Local Challenge" (Johannesburg: Centre for the Study of Violence and Reconciliation, 2005). Janine Rauch, "Changing Step: Crime Prevention Policy in South Africa," in *Crime Prevention Partnerships,* ed. Eric Pelser (Pretoria: Institute for Security Studies, 2002), 9–26.

33. Newham, "A Decade of Crime Prevention in South Africa."

34. The Safer Cities program is in many ways modeled after the UK Safer Cities initiative in the 1980s, which saw the first major introduction of CCTV systems in a city center. See Tim Newburn, "The Commodification of Policing: Security Networks in the Late Modern City," *Urban Studies* 38, nos. 5–6 (2001): 833.

35. Anthony Minnaar, "The Implementation and Impact of Crime Prevention/Crime Control Open Street Closed Circuit Television Surveillance in South African Central Business Districts," special issue of *Surveillance and Society*: "Surveillance and Criminal Justice," Part 1, 4, no. 3: 174–207. http://library.queensu.ca/ojs/index.php/surveillance-and-society/article/viewFile/2575/2624 (accessed November 8, 2010).

36. Wilfred Schärf, "Community Justice and Community Policing in Post-Apartheid South Africa: How Appropriate are the Justice Systems of Africa?" paper delivered at the International Workshop on the Rule of Law and Development, Institute for Development Studies, Sussex, UK, June 2000: 9.

37. Anna van der Hoven, "Domestic Violence in South Africa," *Acta Criminologica* 14, no. 3 (2001): 13–25; *Nedcor* 5, no. 3 (Institute for Security Studies, Praetoria, 2001).

38. Lillian Artz, "Access to Justice for Rural Women: Special Focus on Violence Against Women," report prepared for the Black Sash NGO (Cape Town: Institute of Criminology, 1999).

39. Gil Gifford, "Most Murderers Have a Friendly Face," *Cape Times,* December 18, 2001.

40. "Tshwete's Plan to Boost Force Wouldn't Impact on Violence," *Mail and Guardian,* February 15–21, 2002.

41. Redpath, *The Hydra Phenomenon,* 3.

42. Interview, July 2002.

43. Interview, June 2006.

44. Elrena van der Spuy, "Crime and Its Discontents: Recent South Africa Responses and Policies." Report at the proceedings of the conference Crime and

Policing in Transitional Societies, Johannesburg: South African Institute for International Affairs 2001, 171.

45. *Law Enforcement and the Criminal Justice System*, Goedgedacht Forum for Social Reflection.

46. Western Cape Provincial Development Council, *Urban Renewal Strategy for the Cape Town Unicity*, 43.

47. Interview, July 2002.

48. Ben Roberts, "Between Trust and Skepticism: Public Confidence in Institutions," *HSRC* [Human Sciences Research Council] *Review* 6, no. 1 (2008): 10–1.

49. W. Schärf, "Community Justice and Community Policing in Post-Apartheid South Africa."

50. Marianne Merten, "Gangs: A Brotherhood Sealed in Blood," *Mail and Guardian*, August 2, 2002.

51. Interview, August 2002.

52. Interview, August 2002.

53. Melanie Peters, "Police 'Rotten to the Core,'" *Cape Argus*, July 6, 2007. See also Julian Rademeyer, "SAPS 'Full of Criminals,'" *News24*, May 12, 2008. http://www.news24.com/SouthAfrica/News/SAPS-full-of-criminals-20080509 (accessed November 8, 2010).

54. Interview, August 2002.

55. Wilfred Schärf, "Bombs, Bungles and Police Transformation: When Is the SAPS Going to Get Smarter?" in *Crime Wave: The South African Underworld and Its Foes*, ed. Jonny Steinberg (Johannesburg: Witwatersrand University Press, 2001), 58.

56. Ethan A. Nadelmann, "The Americanization of Global Law Enforcement: The Diffusion of American Tactics and Personnel," in *Crime and Law Enforcement in the Global Village*, ed. W. F. McDonald (Cincinnati, OH: Anderson Publishing, 1997).

57. Andy Duffy, "Police Linked to Cape War," *Mail and Guardian*, October 4, 1997.

58. Interview, August 2002.

59. Ted Leggett, "The Sieve Effect," *SA Crime Quarterly* 5 (September 2003). Pretoria: Institute for Security Studies.

60. Redpath, "Forfeiting Rights?"

61. Boyane Tshehla, *Traditional Justice in Practice: A Limpopo Case Study*, ISS Monograph 115 (Pretoria: Institute for Security Studies, 2005).

62. Gareth Newham, *Tackling Police Corruption in South Africa* (Johannesburg: Centre for the Study of Violence and Reconciliation, June 2002) http://www.csvr.org.za/wits/papers/papoli14.htm (accessed November 8, 2010).

63. Eric Ntabazalila, "Union Vows to Fight Police Equity Plan in Court," *Cape Times*, January 11, 2002.

64. Ibid.

65. *Law Enforcement and the Criminal Justice System*, Goedgedacht Forum for Social Reflection.

66. Tony Weaver, "Apartheid Cold War Knocks on Kortbroek's Door," *Cape Times*, August 1, 2002.

67. Douglas Carew, "Veary to Remain Suspended," *Cape Argus*, September 14, 2002.

68. Weaver, "Apartheid Cold War Knocks on Kortbroek's Door."

69. V. Reddy, "Truth and Reconciliation Commission," South Africa Human Rights Yearbook 8 (Durban: Centre for Socio-Legal Studies, University of Natal 1997/98).

70. Marianne Merten, "Only Time Will Tell in Manenberg," *Mail and Guardian*, June 15, 2001.

71. Sean Tait and Dick Usher, "Co-ordinating Prevention: The Role of Community Safety Forums," in *Crime Prevention Partnerships*, ed. Eric Pelser (Pretoria: Institute for Security Studies, South Africa, 2002), 57–66.

5. The Production of Criminality on the Urban Periphery

1. S'bu Zikode, "The ANC Has Invaded Kennedy Road," *Pambazuka News* 450, October 1, 2009. http://www.pambazuka.org/en/category/features/59122 (accessed November 9, 2010); United Nations Integrated Regional Information Networks, "South Africa: Xenophobic Attacks Spreading," May 23, 2009. http://allafrica.com/stories/printable/200805231033.html (accessed November 9, 2010).

2. "Jo'burg's Water Wars," *Mail and Guardian*, September 1, 2003; Sechaba Ka'nkosi, "Radebe Vows to Fuse the Power Pirates," *Sunday Times*, December 2, 2001.

3. Löic Wacquant, "The Militarization of Urban Marginality: Lessons from the Brazilian Metropolis," *International Political Sociology* 1–2 (Winter 2008): 56–74.

4. Jamie Peck, "Geography and Public Policy: Constructions of Neoliberalism," *Progress in Human Geography* 28, no. 3 (2004): 392–405; Löic Wacquant, "The Penalization of Poverty and the Rise of Neoliberalism," *European Journal on Criminal Policy and Research* 9 (2001): 401–12.

5. Zain Cook, "Cape Town's Water War Rages On," *Cape Argus*, September 27, 2001.

6. David A. McDonald, *World City Syndrome: Neoliberalism and Inequality in Cape Town* (New York: Routledge, 2008).

7. T. Magazi, "Thousands Face Water Cuts," *Cape Times*, November 22, 2001.

8. Nazli Peer, "Eight Shot in Clashes over Water Cuts," *Independent Online*, September 27, 2001.

9. Cook, "Cape Town's Water War Rages On."

10. "Cape Town: Police Shoot into Community During the Attempt to Cut off Water to 1800 Homes," Western Cape Anti-Eviction Campaign statement, September 26, 2001.

11. Christelle Terreblanche, "Is a Storm Brewing in SA?" *Independent Online*, February 27, 2005.

12. Interview with Irvin Kinnes, 2002.

13. Western Cape Provincial Development Council, *Urban Renewal Strategy for the Cape Town Unicity*: 41.

14. South African Press Association, "Bullets Fly and Tyres Burn in Cape Water War," September 27, 2001.

15. Ashwin Desai, "Neoliberalism and Resistance in South Africa," *Monthly Review* 54, no. 8 (2003). http://www.monthlyreview.org/0103desai.htm (accessed November 9, 2010).

16. Ma Gebhardt, "Low Cost Housing Initiatives Stumble," *Business Report,* July 22, 2002.

17. Eric Ntabazalilia, "Frustration Fuels Anti-Eviction Campaign," *Cape Times,* November 11, 2002.

18. Mandela Park Anti-Eviction Campaign press release, February 25, 2003.

19. Western Cape Anti-Eviction Campaign press release, June 28, 2002.

20. Ibid., July 8, 2002.

21. Ntabazalilia, "Frustration Fuels Anti-Eviction Campaign."

22. Janine Rauch, *Thinking Big: The National Urban Renewal Programme and Crime Prevention in South Africa's Metropolitan Cities* (Johannesburg: Centre for the Study of Violence and Reconciliation, December 2002), 18.

23. Interview, June 2006.

24. Joy Watson, "Gender Planning in the City of Cape Town," (discussion paper, African Gender Institute, University of Cape Town, 2003).

25. Interview, July 2006.

26. Steffen Jensen, *Gangs, Politics and Dignity in Cape Town* (Chicago: Chicago University Press, 2008).

27. Andre Standing, "The Social Contradictions of Organised Crime on the Cape Flats" (occasional paper 74, Pretoria, Institute for Security Studies, June 2003).

28. Benjamin White Haefele, "Gangsterism in the Western Cape: Who Are the Role Players?" *Crime and Conflict* no. 14 (Summer 1998): 19–22.; Clive Glaser, *We Must Infiltrate the Tsotsis: School Politics and Youth Gangs in Soweto, 1968–1976* (Cape Town: African Studies Centre, University of Cape Town, 1996).

29. Standing, "The Social Contradictions of Organised Crime on the Cape Flats." These figures are using the expanded definition of unemployment, including those people not "actively" looking for work.

30. Ibid. Commenting on the turn to hard policing on the Flats, Standing writes: "While most acknowledge that these efforts have failed to significantly reduce crime in the area, some sense that the local authorities are increasingly turning to punitive measures to control areas deemed 'ungovernable.'"

31. Tafelsig Anti-Eviction Campaign press statement, June 24, 2002.

32. People's Power Secondary School press statement, August 4, 2003.

33. Marianne Merten, "Gangs: A Brotherhood Sealed in Blood," *Mail and Guardian,* August 2–7, 2002.

34. Ryland Fisher, "Section 205 Cry 'Halt'!" *Rhodes Journalism Review* 17 (March 1999).

35. Gary Kynoch, "From the Ninevites to the Hard Livings Gang," *African Studies* 58, no. 1 (July 1999): 55–85.

36. Glaser, *We Must Infiltrate the Tsotsis,* 3.

37. Elaine Salo, "'Amadla, Awethu, die Casspirs ga' nou Kerk toe!': Continuing the Culture of Militarism on the Cape Flats' Townships," *African Gender Institute Newsletter* (African Gender Institute, University of Cape Town, December 2001).

38. Elaine Salo, *Mans is ma soe: Ideologies of Masculinity and Ganging Practices in Manenberg, South Africa* (Africa Studies Centre, University of Cape Town, 2001): 19.

39. Salo, "Amadla, Awethu." The argument that gang formations are a response, in part, to the military hierarchies of white settler society is made by Haysom (1981) and C. van Olsen (1982), cited in Graeme Simpson, "Shock Troops and Bandits: Youth, Crime and Politics," in *Crime Wave: The South African Underworld and Its Foes,* ed. Jonny Steinberg (Johannesburg: Witwatersrand University Press, 2001), 118.

40. Don Pinnock, *Gangs, Rituals and Rites of Passage* (Cape Town: Sun Press and Institute of Criminology, 1997). For a discussion of this phenomenon in the U.S. context, see Elijah Anderson, *Code of the Street: Violence, Decency and the Moral Life of the Inner City* (New York: W. W. Norton, 2000).

41. Interview, July 2006.

42. Ingrid Palmary and Catherine Moat, *Preventing Criminality Among Young People: A Resource Book for Local Government* (Johannesburg: Centre for the Study of Violence and Reconciliation, 2002).

43. Diane Jefthas, "Youth Perceptions of Crime and Policing in Post-Apartheid South Africa" (unpublished honors dissertation, University of Cape Town, 1999).

44. Interview, July 2006.

45. Graeme Simpson and Janine Rauch, "Reflections on the First Year of the National Crime Prevention Strategy", in *Between Unity and Diversity: Essays on Nation Building in Post Apartheid South Africa,* ed. Gitanjali Maharaj (Pretoria: Idasa, 1999), 295–314.

46. Lauren Segal, Joy Pelo, and Pule Rampa, "Into the Heart of Darkness: Journeys of the *Amagents* in Crime, Violence, and Death," in *Crime Wave: The South African Underworld and Its Foes,* ed. Jonny Steinberg (Johannesburg: Witwatersrand University Press, 2001), 116.

47. Sasha Gear and Kindiza Ngubeni, *Daai Ding: Sex, Sexual Violence and Coercion in Men's Prisons* (Johannesburg: Centre for the Study of Violence and Reconciliation, 2002).

48. Ibid.

49. Interview, June 2004.

50. Interview, August 2002.

51. Interview, July 2002.

52. Irvin Kinnes, *From Urban Street Gangs to Criminal Empires: The Changing Face of Gangs in the Western Cape,* Institute for Security Studies monograph no. 48 (2000), 30.

53. Marianne Merten, "Only Time Will Tell in Manenberg," *Mail and Guardian,* June 15, 2001.

Conclusion

1. City of Cape Town, *Integrated Development Plan,* 2004–05: 14.

2. Elrena van der Spuy, "Crime and Punishment: A South African Saga", in *Between Unity and Diversity: Essays on Nation Building in Post Apartheid South Africa,* ed. G. Maharaj (Pretoria: Idasa, 1999), 350.

3. Western Cape Anti-Eviction Campaign press release, July 8, 2002.

4. Peter Wilkin, "Global Poverty and Orthodox Security," *Third World Quarterly* 23, no. 4 (2002): 633–45.

Index

police brutality: hard policing practices and, 46, 127–37; in Tafelsig water war, 156–65

policing. *See also* crime and criminalization: abuse patterns in, 46; budgetary increases for, 36–41; centrality in Cape Flats Renewal Strategy of, 106–11; community mistrust of, 143–52; corruption and, 143–52; gang activity and, 90–122; incompetence in, 147–52; in postapartheid era, 111–22; racial governance and, 18–21; racial tensions in ranks of, 148–49; social control through, 31–41; social crime prevention and, 137–43; tourism's impact on, 50–53; in township communities, 123–52; underdevelopment and focus on, 101–11, 153–79; United States models of, 66–69; urban security and governance and, 13–18, 210n.1, 224n.30

politics: crime and economic development and, 26–27; gang activity and role of, 94–97, 171–72; hard policing and role of, 135–37; neoliberal ideology and, 191–95; privatization initiatives and, 47–53; social crime prevention and, 143; urban renewal and, 157–65, 168–72, 183–95; youth marginalization from, 57–60, 186–95

poverty: criminalization of, 18–19, 153–79, 203n.53; gang activity and, 98–101

Prevention of Organised Crime Act (POCA), 117, 131–33

prison demographics: crime control campaigns and population increases in, 39–41; racial governance and, 32–34; youth

criminality and, 62–65, 166–72, 174–79

private sector: GEAR program and emphasis on, 27–30, 47–53; policing expenditure increases in, 37–41; private security forces in, 17–18, 77–78, 88–89, 159, 182, 192–93; township housing controlled by, 160–65

"projectization" phenomenon: urban renewal problems and, 163–65

"Promotion for a Safe and Secure Urban Environment," 82

Provincial Department of Community Safety, 145

public sector: policing expenditure increases in, 36–41; urban security and, 17–18, 88–89

public space: neoliberal governance and fragmentation of, 182–95; township conflicts over, 160–65; urban governance and control of, 84–89, 214n.67

quality of life bylaws: Cape Flats War and, 117; urban renewal and, 68, 80–89, 190–92

racial categories, 197n.10

racial governance: in Cape Town, 42–46; criminality and, 79–80; neoliberalism and, 18–21; organized crime prevention and institutionalization of, 132–37; social control through, 32–41, 86–89; tourism and, 49–53

Racketeer Influenced Corrupt Organizations (RICO) Act (U.S.), 131–32, 190

Ramatlakane, Leonard, 90–91, 162

TONY ROSHAN SAMARA is assistant professor of sociology at George Mason University.